PRAISE FOR

BROTHAS BE, YO LIKE GEORGE, AIN'T THAT FUNKIN' KINDA HARD ON YOU?

"George Clinton has one of the best memoir titles in recent history. Then you crack the book's spine and fall into the spell of his insanely gripping and outrageous stories."

—*Juicy* magazine

"This book (written with Ben Greenman) is an extended anecdotal jam . . . enthralling stuff."

—*Los Angeles Times*

"From the barbershop to the Mothership, from doo-wop to hip-hop, Dr. Funkenstein's tale is filled with honesty, insight, and a whole lot of rhythm goin' round. With this book, George Clinton gives up the funk and then some. The Bomb!"

—Alan Light, former editor-in-chief of *Vibe* and *Spin* magazines

"A perpetual conceptual moving target, George Clinton has always been more about the dogs than the dogma, and his ideas are always layered deep in the 24-track mix. In this insatiably readable memoir, he finally parks his Mothership and tells the tales that the funkateers have wanted to hear for years."

—Rickey Vincent, author of *Funk: The Music, the People, and the Rhythm of The One*

"People will come to this book looking for druggy tales and eccentric stories, and they will not be disappointed. However, they will also encounter a highly intelligent, visionary man who happens to have an encyclopedic knowledge of pop music, from doo-wop to hip-hop. P-Funk worked because George Clinton knew how to weave all the threads together."

—Nelson George

"Clinton's irrepressible spirit, eloquence, and musical acumen flow full-force through this candid, hilarious, outrageous, poignant, and resounding chronicle of perpetual creativity and hope."

—*Booklist*

BROTHAS BE, YO LIKE

AIN'T THAT FUNKIN'
KINDA HARD ON YOU?

MORE BOOKS BY BEN GREENMAN

FICTION

Superbad

Superworse

A Circle Is a Balloon and Compass Both: Stories about Human Love

Please Step Back

Correspondences

What He's Poised to Do

Celebrity Chekhov

The Slippage

NONFICTION

Mo' Meta Blues (with Ahmir "Questlove" Thompson)

BROTHAS BE, *YO* LIKE

GEORGE,

AIN'T THAT *FUNKIN'* KINDA *HARD* ON YOU?

A MEMOIR BY

George Clinton™

WITH **BEN GREENMAN**

ATRIA PAPERBACK

NEW YORK   LONDON   TORONTO   SYDNEY   NEW DELHI

ATRIA
PAPERBACK

An Imprint of Simon & Schuster, Inc.
1230 Avenue of the Americas
New York, NY 10020

Copyright © 2014 by Neutered LLC

First Atria Paperback edition September 2017

ATRIA PAPERBACK and colophon are trademarks of Simon & Schuster, Inc.

For information about special discounts for bulk purchases, please contact Simon & Schuster Special Sales at 1-866-506-1949 or business@simonandschuster.com.

The Simon & Schuster Speakers Bureau can bring authors to your live event. For more information or to book an event, contact the Simon & Schuster Speakers Bureau at 1-866-248-3049 or visit our website at www.simonspeakers.com.

Interior design by Paul Dippolito

Manufactured in the United States of America

10   9   8   7   6   5   4   3   2

Library of Congress Control Number: 2014021629

ISBN 978-1-4767-5108-5
ISBN 978-1-4767-5109-2 (ebook)

For Carlon

CONTENTS

INTRODUCTION: LET'S TAKE
IT TO THE STAGE (1978)

We were in Richmond, Virginia, waiting on the band. It looked like it might be a long wait; bad weather was whipping much of the United States, and violent storms had forced the FAA to cancel hundreds of flights. A few of us weren't flying. We had driven down from Detroit a few days earlier, stopping along the way for a fishing trip, and when we got to Richmond, we didn't go straight to the Coliseum, where we were headlining that night. Instead we met up with Bootsy Collins and his band and went into the studio to cut a track for his new album. The recording session was a ray of light in a dark afternoon. The storms weren't lifting, and the handful of musicians we had with us in Richmond weren't enough to carry the show. We needed everyone. And "everyone" was an understatement: we had ten players for the core of Parliament-Funkadelic, and another four on horns, and then the musicians for Parlet and the Brides of Funkenstein, the two female-fronted offshoot bands of the P-Funk empire. We were an orchestra and then some. And we were peaking—Parliament had hit the top of the charts with "Flash Light" the year before, and Bootsy was the biggest solo star in the funk world. But people had kept us at our peak, specific people, and many of them were trapped in other cities. Our road manager called around frantically, speaking to airlines and charter companies, until he finally found a pilot who flew private and was willing to bring the band in; the pilot was a Vietnam vet who had flown for the rock singer Alice Cooper, and after those two things, nothing scared him. In midafternoon, with only a few hours until showtime, the plane reached the band back in Detroit and they boarded for Richmond.

We were also waiting for costumes. During our tour the previous year, we had been outfitted by Larry LeGaspi, who had a store named Moonstone on Christopher Street in the West Village and made crazy sci-fi costumes for Labelle and other bands. Larry made us look wild and interstellar. In 1978, we simplified a bit and opted for silver Mylar costumes that were put together by a friend of the band. We loved the look, but the location was a problem. They were in Los Angeles, where planes were also stuck to the ground. We couldn't find another Vietnam pilot, so we waited and hoped the bad weather out West would lift. I hid out in the studio while Archie Ivy, my manager, held down the fort at the Coliseum, trying not to let the people over there catch wind of the fact that we were down a dozen people and about as many costumes.

Hours passed without a good word from the airports. Bootsy and I finished up at the studio and drove over to the Coliseum. Another hour passed. Still no band. Still no costumes. I wasn't the type to overreact or create a crisis where one didn't exist, but I also wasn't the type to cheat a crowd out of a show, and I wasn't sure how we were going to do what we needed to do with a skeleton crew dressed in jeans and T-shirts. I kept looking at the doors to the backstage area, one on the left side and one on the right side. Both were closed. They didn't move for so long that I didn't even think of them as doors anymore. They were walls.

It was two hours before showtime, and then it was an hour, and we still didn't have either the band or the costumes. Archie was starting to get nervous. He checked his watch too often, and more than once he left the room to make a phone call. I wasn't sweating so anyone could see, but I was sweating. Then there was a rattle on the other side of the wall that had once been a door, and Cordell "Boogie" Mosson, our bassist, came through, leading a trail of musicians. At the same time the other wall opened up to reveal the band's costumes. We quickly assembled ourselves, got instruments, got dressed. I'm not sure the promoters ever knew how close we were to disaster. When we walked out onto the stage, we saw thousands of flashlights out there in the crowd, fireflies in the darkness. People said we were geniuses for selling flashlights at our shows, but that didn't start until later in that tour—in Richmond, it was grassroots pure and simple, an idea that came from the people. We went up there in front of the darkness and the fireflies and started in with the drums, and the bass, and the guitars. The singers joined in, and as the lights above us surged, I went forward into the music, and the music went forward into the Coliseum crowd: P-Funk, Uncut Funk, the Bomb.

THE BOMB

The Bomb. That's the first thing I remember. It was the end of World War II, and I was four years old, living in Washington, D.C., where all the talk was about the atomic bombs the United States had just dropped on Japan: Little Boy on Hiroshima and Fat Man on Nagasaki. People hoped that they would bring an end to the war, because the country was getting worn-out, and not just the soldiers overseas. They were having blackout drills where you had to turn your lights off at seven o'clock at night, and the planes flying overhead couldn't even see the city. Other days there were military aircraft in the sky, rows and rows of them, and an overall sense of power, or threat, depending on your point of view. Nowadays people say they come from military families but back then every family was military: I had uncles who had been in the war and an aunt who was in the WACs. When the first bomb fell on Japan, people were happy, but they were also holding their breath: no one knew what was going to happen next. The only other thing I remember was potato chips. The Wise potato-chip factory was near us, and we could smell them in the air. Atom bombs, potato chips—you can't eat just one.

I hadn't been born in D.C. I was a proud product of the state of North Carolina, coming into the world in Kannapolis on July

22, 1941. I wasn't born in a hospital, and there are rumors that I wasn't even born in a house, that I emerged into the world in an outhouse. I can't confirm or deny that. I was brought to the city not long after. My parents, George and Julious, didn't live together for the most part, but for a little while they lived near each other. Both of them were government employees: my father worked at the U.S. Mint, disposing of money that had been taken out of circulation, and my mother cleaned up at the Pentagon. When the war ended, we moved again, this time to Chase City, Virginia, a small town about seventy-five miles from Richmond. I remember picking asparagus and running in fields. There were two white kids named Richard and Robert who used to take me and my brother Bobby Ray—a year younger than me—fishing and teach us about farming. They also told us how we should stay inside some nights because the Klan would come riding through on horses, wearing sheets. The way they described them to us, I imagined headless horsemen, holding their own heads like flaming pumpkins. I never actually saw them coming through town, but it's a vivid enough memory anyway. Other than that, racism was only an abstract concept to the younger kids in town. There was one movie in town and we all went to the movie, black folk upstairs and white people downstairs.

I was a pretty quiet kid. I watched the world because the world seemed so big. About thirty years later, in 1978, I went back to that house in Chase City, and I couldn't believe what I was seeing. There was a well outside that couldn't have been more than two feet deep that I had thought was six feet deep at least. There was a little creek that I thought was a river. I thought the backyard was a mile long and two miles wide. I would run around and not come back until dark. At that age, I didn't have a clear sense of being a musician or a songwriter or an entertainer or anything. I wanted to be whatever I was seeing in the movies: a cowboy, probably.

Around 1950, I said good-bye to Virginia, too. It was spring, I think. My father didn't show one day, and not very much was said about it. Some time later, a few weeks maybe, he reappeared, but something was different. He was driving a big black new Kaiser automobile, for starters, and the second he stepped out of the car he told us that we were leaving Virginia for New Jersey. I was excited to leave. It sounded like a fresh start, and not just because of the word *New*. We were going north. We were going in style, from the first moment we got on the highway all the way into New Jersey. From then on, to this day, I traveled the same routes and got familiar with all of the places, all of the road signs, the cigarette advertisements and so on. When we got into Philadelphia there were advertisements for Buttercup bread, Gillette razors. There were lots of Howard Johnsons lining the highway, and gas-station signs I had not seen before. That sparked my infatuation with being on the road and seeing the rest of the world. How could you not love it?

When my family pulled into New Jersey that first day, it was like a different world from Virginia. In Chase City, there had been only one movie house. In Jersey, there was one every four or five blocks, playing *King Solomon's Mines* or *Harvey*. There were more cars and kids and street peddlers and less sky and air. My mother moved north soon after my father did, and she ended up in East Orange, about ten minutes from where we lived in Newark. Now and then we'd head into New York City, and that was another thing altogether. There were buildings that blotted out the sky. There were more people than I ever knew existed.

Work brought my father to New Jersey, and work kept him there. He unloaded ships at the docks, and when he came home at night he had a wagon piled high with potatoes and apples and cabbage that he would sell. That strong work ethic of his was passed down to us, both by example and by constant lecture. All of us who made the move there—me, Bobby Ray, Tommy, and Shirley (we had three others, Brenda, Robbie, Marie, who moved there later, and Jimmy and Patsy were born in Jersey)—were working from pretty early on: not only did we do our chores at home, but he made sure that we got jobs at local stores, too, sweeping up at the end of the day. We did good clean work, not always fun, but that's what my father wanted. He was the boss, and all of us did what he said: get up in the morning, eat, wash up, clean up, keep things neat, don't get into trouble. He didn't play at all.

If I got my sense of hard work from my father, I got my love of music from my mother. My father was a churchgoing man and he liked singing gospel, but he worked all the time so it never really had a chance to take hold. He was part of little groups out of church, though, who organized living-room events where a few friends would get together and sing the hits of the day. He was a Sunday singer. My mother, on the other hand, had the music bug and had it bad. She played records around the house all the time and sang along with them. She liked blues, but not only the pure blues—she liked jump blues and rhythm and blues, too, everything from B.B. King and Muddy Waters to Louis Jordan and Wynonie Harris. It was the same kind of music that I would hear later on, in the sixties, coming back to me through British bands like Cream.

New Jersey in the fifties was a breeding ground for the next generation of American music—or, more specifically, African-American music, though it wasn't called that then. In East Orange, my mother lived right next door to Reverend Mancel Warwick's grocery store. He had been a Pullman porter and then a cook, and he had ended up as a promoter for gospel records. He was also Dionne Warwick's father. When we went to visit my mother, the Warwick kids were always out playing in the neighborhood, and I got to know them all: not just Dionne, but Cissy, Dee Dee, the whole family. I used to steal candy out of the reverend's store, and my friends and I played at the ballpark up the street, right there in East Orange. I wasn't any good at baseball. I couldn't even be on my own team. They called me Porky and Feet—I had huge feet, adult-size by the time I was twelve years old.

There was another branch of my family over in Passaic: my aunt and my cousin Ruth, who took me to the apartments in town where the Shirelles were working on "Mama Said." I was swept up right then and there. Ruth also took me to the Apollo, where I saw the Drifters, the Chantels, and dozens of other groups. I listened to them obsessively and loved them unconditionally. I loved the Flamingos, who had a huge hit with "I Only Have Eyes for You." I loved the Spaniels and especially their lead singer, Pookie Hudson, who became the model for almost every young singer within earshot. I loved the Bobbettes, who were from Spanish Harlem and had a hit with "Mr. Lee" in 1957, and the Blue Belles, who were from the Trenton-Philadelphia area and featured a girl named Patsy Holt. They had a hit with "Over the Rainbow," and she had a real powerful voice even then. Cindy Birdsong, who would later replace Florence Ballard in the Supremes, was also in that group. Years later, when Patsy was renamed Patti LaBelle and I was a hairdresser, I would end up doing her hair.

Even without the music, I loved living in Newark, in part because I was royalty. All you had to do was look at the signs. One of the main drags in Newark was called Clinton Avenue, and there was a whole area called Clinton Hills. They were all named after the early American politician George Clinton, who had been the governor of New York and the vice president under Thomas Jefferson and James Madison. Some days the world seemed to revolve around me, a George Clinton who could go walking down a street named for him in an area named for him. In the middle of this neighborhood where I was royalty, in 1956, they built a new junior high school, and if you can believe it, they called it Clinton Place. And if you can believe that, in that first graduating class, there were no kids whose last names ended in A or B, so I was the first graduate: George Clinton of Clinton Place. You can believe it all because it's all true.

As I got a little older, I moved out of the jobs my father got for me and into jobs of my own. I remember delivering milk, working on the Alderney Dairy trucks. I rode a route on Avon Avenue, and the driver of the truck would tell me about all the people who lived there. One of them, he said, was Sarah Vaughan. I knew of her from my parents, who had lots of her records, and a little later she had a big hit with "Broken-Hearted Melody." I never saw her, just dropped bottles at her door. Years later we met backstage somewhere and I told her about it. "I brought you milk," I said. She kind of squinted and frowned until she realized what I meant.

Maybe my most important early employment was on the street named for me, Clinton Avenue. There was a record store there called Essex Records, and I had an after-school job there sweeping up. They didn't do returns too much back then—

when records didn't sell, they didn't go back to the label, but into the trash bin behind the store—and so lots of records ended up there. Some of them I kept for myself, and some of them, especially the white doo-wop groups and the white rockers, I took to school to sell to the kids. I was the record king of Madison Junior High School for a little while. When *American Bandstand* started, there was suddenly a way of seeing the differences between the artists—some of them, much to my surprise, were white. But in the mid-fifties, no one knew and no one really cared. You moved to what moved you and you got your hands on anything that made you feel larger. Little Richard would have been one of the records I sold to the white kids. I got fifteen cents a record. Jerry Lee Lewis was another one of the artists that moved, especially "Whole Lotta Shakin' Goin' On." Jerry Lee was my favorite too. He had a band that was tight as a motherfucker. Elvis was made to be funky and he had a crew surrounding him, but Jerry Lee was funky for real, stupid funky. When he got going he tore shit up. I also loved bands like the Isley Brothers: they were doing it like motherfuckers since "Shout" in 1959, moving and singing like three Jackie Wilsons all rolled into one.

IF YOU HEAR ANY NOISE, IT'S
JUST ME AND THE BOYS

Frankie Lymon was Michael Jackson fifteen years before the real Michael Jackson, a wrinkle in time, a little kid with a voice and stage presence no one could forget. His parents had been in a gospel group called the Harlemaires, and Frankie and some of his brothers were in the Harlemaire Juniors. Around 1955 or so, he got a new group called the Teenagers and released a song, "Why Do Fools Fall in Love," that was like a wake-up call for my generation. Maybe, come to think of it, he was more than Michael Jackson. Maybe he was Elvis Presley and Michael Jackson all rolled into one. He and the Teenagers headlined at the London Palladium. They made such a splash it's hard to fully communicate. Frankie was a little younger than I was, but we were all more or less the same age, and we had been singing just like him ever since the sixth or seventh grade. When Frankie Lymon hit, though, we were fourteen, and we saw immediately where it all might lead—to being cool, to getting girls, to being at the center of the school's social life. That happened in every school up and down the East Coast; once the Teenagers hit it was inevitable. Everyone sang, and everyone only sang. The acts that really mattered were vocal acts: the Platters, Sam Cooke, those kinds of people. No one played in a band, really—jazz was too old, a kind of fogey music that we heard and appreciated but didn't exactly understand. I only really knew two people from the neighborhood who were trained musicians: Wayne Shorter and Larry Young Jr. They were jazz players, though Larry also had a singing group called the Four Most. Wayne, a saxophonist who went on to play with everyone from Miles Davis to Art Blakey before founding Weather Report, was a couple years older than us. His playing sounded so strange, even when everybody started talking about how famous he was getting, as if it was beamed in from another dimension. We would hear him practice and we didn't process it at all. The way that horn sounded, we all thought it was busted.

At first my group's lineup was me, Charles Davis, Herbie Jenkins, Robert Lambert, Gene Boykins, and Gene Carlos. That was the first group of singers who stood still long enough to have pictures taken. Back then, the first thing you did after you got a group together was to name it. There weren't endless options, really: vocal groups were, for the most part, named after birds, cars, and cigarettes. I picked cigarettes, even though I didn't smoke. He caught me smoking cigarettes once when I was about eight, and he made me smoke a whole pack of Camels, which cured my taste for them immediately. The same thing happened with alcohol: I tried it when I was ten or eleven and my father made me drink a pint of Wild Turkey to prove a point, which got me sick enough to require a hospital visit. Still, I thought cigarettes were cool as a symbol, a little dangerous, a little adult, and Parliament was a big brand, so we became the Parliaments. Personnel shifted around a bit in that first year or two—some guys went out, other guys came in—but pretty soon we had a more stable lineup: me, Calvin Simon, Grady Thomas, Fuzzy Haskins, and Ray Davis. Each of us had a distinctive style, sometimes in imitation of people who were famous then, sometimes in anticipation of people who would be famous later. I went for a Smokey Robinson thing, with maybe a little bit of Pookie Hudson thrown in there. Fuzzy, who was second lead, was a soulful tenor with all the bluesy inflections, like Wilson Pickett, real rough. Calvin was like David Ruffin. Grady held down the low-middle notes. And Ray had the deepest voice, the bass baritone.

We started singing more seriously in and around the area, and that attracted the attention of some of the more established groups nearby. One was the Monotones: they're most famous for "Book of Love," which would become a huge national hit in 1958. At first they were led by the Patrick brothers, Charles and James, though when James left the group early on, Charles became the leader. This was a few years before "Book of Love," but people in the neighborhood were already buzzing about them. In 1956, they were on the Ted Mack *Amateur Hour*, where they won first place singing one of the Cadillacs' songs. The Parliaments, my group, had enough local juice that we were invited to go over to the studio where they recorded and cut a single, with a song called "Poor Willie" on one side and "Party Boys" on the other. I cowrote them both, though by "writing" I only mean that we made them up. There wasn't any actual recording of songs with a paper and a pen. We didn't mark up sheet music or even really commit lyrics to paper. We weren't formally trained that way. It was mostly singing what you knew, making up songs about sex and girls and nonsense comedy chants modeled after bands like the Coasters. We had two-part harmonies because there was only one dude among us who really knew the technique of harmonizing: we were just a bass singer and a bunch of other guys crowding around the same note. But what we lacked in musical sophistication, we made up for in showmanship and enthusiasm. As time went on, we became one of the hot groups in the neighborhood.

Pretty quickly, that spelled an end to high school. I got a few months into twelfth grade, and that was that. Much of the problem was that I was obsessed with music: absolutely positive that I wanted to commit my life to it, and that didn't leave much room for making sense of schoolbooks and assignments. I could do the schoolwork, but the work wasn't doing anything for me. I had one teacher who saw that I was bright enough, but she also saw that my determination to be a singer was larger than my interest in anything else. She covered for me for a little while, but by twelfth grade that plan was starting to slip a little bit. Another factor was Carol—not the Chuck Berry song, but Carol Hall. My first day at Clinton Place, the Parliaments were asked to sing over the PA system. We got together in our matching blue sweaters, sang during announcements, and were immediately schoolwide celebrities. We had fans, and Carol Hall was one of those fans, a cute high school girl who thought I was cute, too. Soon enough, we were going together pretty seriously, and by the start of my senior year of high school, we had Donna, a daughter. By the end of that year, there would be a son, too, George III. I was a young man but suddenly an old man in some sense, too, starting my life as a father at the same time that I was starting my career in the music business.

Being a neighborhood hotshot was great, but it wasn't the only thing, at least not with New York City nearby. New York was the epicenter of the world music business: it had the Brill

Building sound. Not just the Brill Building itself—which was on Broadway and Forty-Ninth and housed more than 150 music-publishing companies—but the other buildings in midtown, one at Fiftieth and one at Fifty-Third. If a popular song came out, there was a good chance that it started along that stretch of Broadway. Don Kirshner came from that scene; he ran Aldon Music, which had some of the best songwriters in the country, from Carole King to Neil Sedaka to Neil Diamond. One of my other favorites was Leiber and Stoller, who had brought out so many singles with the Coasters. I started traveling into the city in the late fifties to work as a music writer for Colpix, which was the Columbia Pictures–Screen Gems record label—the *Col* came from Columbia, and the *pix* from Pictures. One of the groups I worked with was the Jewels, three girls who had been called the Impalas. Later on they were the Four Jewels, and they ended up singing backup for James Brown.

I paid attention to the songs I was writing, but I also paid attention to the songs other people were writing, and not just as melodies and lyrics. I was also fascinated by the way the songs were marketed. You can say that's a P. T. Barnum thing, that it's in the tradition of great showmen and promoters, but to me it was a music thing, also. Take Phil Spector, for instance. He did this trick where he would buy up full-page ads in the music magazines, *Billboard* and *Cashbox*. That was $2,000 a page, or something like that, which was big money then, so you knew that any record man who bought a full-page ad was serious about his records. But it was what he did with the pages that knocked me out. He left them blank, except for a tiny dot in the middle. That's all there was one week: the tiny dot and then his Philles Records logo at the bottom. Then the next week the dot would get bigger, and the week after that, bigger again: same time, same station, like the slowest cartoon in the world. Eventually it would reveal itself as the new record he was releasing. That took foresight and it took money and it took a huge amount of self-confidence, creativity, and balls. To me the marketing concept was as important as the music itself. Later on, I would hear things about him that cemented his legend, like how he would find ten drummers for one song, use them all, pay them all, and then go back and listen to the tapes and figure out who sounded the best that day. I was also a huge fan of Richard Barrett, who was one of the original black music impresarios. He started out as a singer, Richie Barrett, and his biggest hit, which he wrote with Leiber and Stoller, was "Some Other Guy." The song was a trailblazer, in a way, because he put electric piano on it about three years before anyone else did. The Beatles used to play it live. Barrett discovered everyone from Frankie Lymon to Little Anthony and the Imperials to the Valentines. In the late fifties, he went on to work with the Chantels. They were one of the first black girl groups—they did songs like "She's Gone" and "Maybe"—and as a producer, he got a certain sound with them that was unbelievable. My ears perked right up when I heard his records. I knew he was doing something unique.

Another big influence on me, at least in terms of understanding how people responded to music, was mambo, both the music and the dance. Back in the fifties, mambo was like our disco. Everybody got dressed up, really suited, for the mambo scene. Just like on the dance competitions they have on television now, ordinary people became celebrities by showing how they could move on the floor. Mambo was the universal language. Mambo would stop a gang fight. A hot girl who could dance could go across gang lines to get herself a dance partner. The gangs would call a temporary truce, letting this kind of thing happen, when they went to the gym to dance mambo. One of my unrealized ambitions, in fact, is to record Tito Puente's "Coco Seco," a great song by one of the giants of the genre. I wouldn't do anything strange or experimental with it. I'd do it in straightforward-cover style, just sing the hell out of it.

Watching the city, listening to everything, showing up at the Brill Building: that was my university education. At one point in the early sixties, there was a rumor that Elvis was coming in to pick a new song. He was back from the army and looking for a hit. Otis Blackwell was around the building. Already famous for "Fever," which Peggy Lee recorded, he had also written some huge songs for Elvis, "Don't Be Cruel" and "All Shook Up." By the time Elvis was coming back from the army, though, Otis Blackwell wasn't in the best shape. He was known to drink a bit. He was down and out and then some. Someone close to him, maybe Winfield Scott, his songwriting partner, got him all cleaned up, poured him into a new suit, and got him to the conference room where all the songwriting teams were lined up, waiting to present to Elvis. Otis went first, and he sang a little bit of the song he had brought: "I gave a letter to the postman, he put it in his sack / Bright and early next morning, he brought my letter back." That was "Return to Sender," and Elvis or Colonel Tom Parker nodded, and all the other songwriting teams just closed up their folders and went home.

I liked that idea, making songs that would make everyone else put their folders away. And I was watching with keen interest what was happening out at Motown in Detroit. That's when I made the switch in my mind from singer to songwriter. Through the late fifties and early sixties, I was still trying everything I could: writing for others, trying to put out singles myself, learning my craft. We had songs like "Lonely Island" and "Cry." At that time I was trying all kinds of stuff. I was singing bass and baritone. I thought "Poor Willie" might have been a hit, because it's the kind of thing the Coasters were doing so successfully at the time. And one of the sessions we did was with the Elegants, who recorded "Little Star," which ended up being a huge success. But as close as we came back then, we missed every time. I wonder sometimes what would have happened if we had recorded a song that really took off back in the early sixties. Would I have kept learning the things I did, staying at the edges of the music business, soaking up all I could and trying to subvert the formula? Or would I have just rested on those early laurels? It's hard to say. I was pretty persistent and stubborn about making my way through the music world. It might not have made a difference. But I know for certain that the way things went kept me focused on a goal that was always a little bit out of my reach.

Music may have been my passion then, but passion wasn't paying, especially since I had a young family to support. I already felt like it was make or break, and I was mostly broke. I had holes in the holes in my shoes. Then the hula-hoop factory came to town.

Sometime that year, two guys out in California, Richard Knerr and Arthur Melin, had an idea. Well, they weren't just two guys. They were the founders of the Wham-O company, which had launched back in the late forties making slingshots out of ash wood. The company got its name from the slingshots, from the sound of the shot hitting the target. Anyway, after about ten years, slingshots no longer paid the bills, and they began looking for a new product. One night, at a dinner party, a man from Australia told Knerr, or maybe Melin, about an Australian game where kids twirled bamboo hoops around their waists for exercise. That sounded to the Wham-O guys like something that might work well for American kids, also. The company had recently started using a new plastic called Marlex, and soon enough they had figured out a way to make these big, brightly colored hoops. Kids would stand inside the hoops and keep them up by swinging their hips. It doesn't sound like much, but it took off like a rocket. More than four million hoops were sold in four months. The toy became a bona fide phenomenon, a bigger deal, for a little while, than anything else, even rock and roll. Wham-O needed factories to make these hoops, and they needed them quick, and so in 1959, a manufacturing facility went up near me in Jersey almost overnight.

A little earlier I had been in a gang called the Outlaws—when I say "gang," I mean a group of guys to run with and not much more than that—and all of us went to the factory and got jobs. But the company was so far behind in meeting the demand for this craze, and so out of its depth, that it didn't organize the labor force to make new hoops. As luck would have it, the Outlaws discovered a way to make the hoops, and to make them fast. We figured out that the process of putting the hoops together would be great fun for kids who were six, eight years old, and we employed them. The hoops were fashioned from these long strips of plastic. You took one end and then the other, and then you made them meet in the middle, and voilà! A hoop! The kids had so much fun making the hoops that the Outlaws would just punch in for our shifts, leave the kids alone to do the work, and come back later. We had so many kids out at the factory that we started to overproduce hoops. We needed to rent a second warehouse just to capture what we were doing. At that point, the union caught wind of what we were doing and came around to shut down our Children's Crusade. We chased the union out, too. We weren't interested in being regulated. A few older union guys stayed behind to do the staples on the hoops, which they thought were unsafe for the kids, but otherwise the Outlaw children's hula-hoop factory worked like a charm.

Hula hoops saved me for a while, at least financially, but then they ran their course, like any other fad. Soon enough Wham-O shipped that shit off to Frankfurt, Germany, and then I needed work again. Someone from the factory found me another job unpacking tools, and I tried that for a minute, but that was about fifty-five seconds too long. That job wasn't going to work. I needed a new source of income quick, and so I started spending more of my time doing what I had been doing a little bit of already: barbershop work. And not the quartet-harmony version, either. This was the sweeping-the-floor, locking-up-for-the-boss, learning-a-little-of-the-trade version. The shop was called the Uptown Tonsorial Palace, which was a fancy name for a not-very-fancy place in Newark. I could make three or four hundred a week, which was more than you could make at most other kinds of jobs. I was good on a couple of hairstyles. The Quo Vadis was one of my specialties—close, high, and tight.

In 1960, I decided that I'd had enough of Newark. I was married at that point, with three kids, and I needed every bit of money I could get my hands on. There was more opportunity in Plainfield, about a half hour southwest, so that's where I went to work. The barbershop had a mix of older barbers who had lots of experience and younger barbers who were hungry to make the business work. About the only thing wrong with it was the owner, George White, who was dumb with money and made no sense in general. He used to chase younger girls and had several other nasty behaviors.

I was very industrious—I hit the ground in Plainfield running—and soon after I got there, Mr. White died. Since I had the most customers, I found a way to take over a share of the shop. The rest of the barbers paid me to use their chairs and I took twenty-five cents from every dollar they made. I renamed it the Silk Palace, made it a nice place with drapes and an elegant feel. We had a real running barbershop, chairs going all the time, shelves with product: Wildroot Cream Oil, Dixie Peach, all other kinds of hair grease. Later on, in a Parliament song called "New Doo Review," I mentioned Brylcreem, but that isn't something we would have had too much call for. That's a product that white kids would have used, not us.

Everybody who came to our barbershop wanted their hair straightened. We did a great deal of processing, which was the big thing for black hair in those days. Singers wanted processes, and also pimps and preachers. The older barbers tended to customers who wanted normal haircuts, while the younger barbers did pumps to get pumped up. Nobody around Plainfield kept their hair natural. I remember the first time I ever saw real natural hair. It was a little later, maybe 1960. My friend Ernie Harris and I were going to a meeting in New York City, and we were walking around midtown. On the sidewalk, we saw a woman with her hair all nappy and natural. We started laughing at her. Ernie probably said something. I don't know if we were coming from a barber's point of view or if that was just a natural reaction given the styles of the times. We had never seen anybody sporting hair like that, and certainly nobody doing so and feeling proud about it. And then damned if we didn't end up in the same office with that woman at CBS later that day, and damned if it wasn't Miriam Makeba, the South African singer, who had just had a hit with "The Click Song." Ernie almost never got embarrassed, but that time he did. She was real cool, though, real articulate about her choices, and clear about the differences between Africans and Americans, especially when it came to hairstyles.

Ernie was about the best singer in the neighborhood. If the record industry worked just by talent, he would have been one of the biggest stars around. He could sing like Wilson Pickett, rough and urgent. He could sing smooth. He could sing opera, both pretty and powerful. But he couldn't stand anyone telling him what to do, and he didn't really have the personality to move forward into the business. He didn't take risks and he didn't take shit. He was so good, and he knew it, but that meant that he didn't have the patience to get better. That's how you end up with these guys who are legendary neighborhood singers and don't go any further: it's like the best playground basketball player in your neighborhood who does things that no one can believe but never breaks through at a higher level. He came out with us on the road later, when the Parliaments started to have hits, and he cowrote a little in the Funkadelic years. The truth was that his style was different, too. He sounded much older than we did. The singing he did was for adults: it was supper-club singing, real smooth. We were doo-wopping, singing for teenyboppers.

I was cutting hair but sometimes cutting out early to work on records. That was the beginning of a pattern that would pop up over and over again during my life: I was doing real good with hair, making lots of money, but I was putting all that money directly back into records and music. We had other groups we considered our competition, healthy rivals like Sammy Campbell and the Del-Larks. Ray Davis was in that group, and later he came over and sang bass with me. Ronnie Taylor was also in that group: he was really close to me. They released records on Ea-Jay and other labels around the area. We went to play with them in Perth Amboy and New Brunswick and even in New York.

Not only were we writing songs like crazy, but we were trying to keep focused on music in other ways, too. By that time, there was an up-and-coming younger generation of musicians in Plainfield. At first, that scene was centered around the Boyce brothers. Their father, Clarence, had been in the Carnation Jubilee Singers, and their mother had a group, too, called the Plainfield Five. The group included Richard, Frankie, and Jo Jo—Frankie was the middle one, and a real fantastic guitar player. The Boyce brothers played with lots of other boys who later became part of P-Funk: Cordell "Boogie" Mosson, Garry Shider, Eddie Hazel, Bernie Worrell. They were all Plainfield kids, and lots of them came by the barbershop at one time or another. Years later, the Boyces were drafted, and Frankie went to Vietnam and died there. This wasn't until 1968 or so, but it was still a tremendous blow to everyone we knew.

The barbershop operated like a kind of community center—at the very least, it was a safe place where kids could come and hang out, less crazy and dangerous than other parts of the Plainfield streets. One of the first regulars was Billy Nelson, who lived right nearby. He came in early and came in often. Even at nine or ten years old he was the meanest little motherfucker you ever saw in your life. He fought with everyone, from little kids to grown men: two little boys might come around, four- or five-year-olds, on their tricycles, and Billy would slap them right off. He did everything he could to be tough. Sometimes he would go to Brooklyn and stay with friends in the projects, and he would come back thinking he was a gangster. He got on everyone's last nerve: old men would leap out of their chairs to have the chance to throw his ass out of the barbershop. Sometimes the story gets told that he worked there, but at least at first, that wasn't the case. He just showed up every day and didn't do a thing. Other boys actually worked, while Billy just popped up all the time running his mouth from eleven years on. Years passed before he even picked up an instrument.

Newark was rough, with all the poverty and violence. Plainfield, though, was more middle-class—higher employment rate, higher high school graduation rate, more stable and more learned—but there was still some bullshit going on. Kids in Plainfield were robbing parking meters and pay phones, tapping them for change. We heard stories of gangs of teenagers going through the streets at night trying to get into stores to get into their registers. There was one story of kids hitting a store while one guy stood lookout outside. He saw the cops down the street. "Come on out, guys," he called in a resigned voice before the police even reached the store. "They got us."

There were many overlapping populations in Plainfield: hardworking men, bums, prosperous businessmen, pimps. We had old prostitutes wearing fox furs that still had their heads on. They did snuff, and when they came to say hello to you, you could see residue on their faces. These self-styled sophisticated types clashed with a newer world of people who came up from the country.

My friend Ronnie Ford's family came up from Georgia. Fuzzy Haskins's family came up from West Virginia. They were so country they would shoot at you with a shotgun full of rice.

The men spent their time in barbershops and bars. We heard stories, saw stories, made new stories. Once a midget named Milton was making fun of another guy. Milton was only two and a half fucking feet tall, but his mouth was at least that big. "I was with your wife," he said. "Hot Dog Willie and I were wearing her out all night long. She was screaming my name." This guy looked at Milton for a long time, then took out a straight razor and sliced him straight across his belly. Milton went running out as another guy came in. "Hey, Milton," he said. "Pull yourself together." In the barbershop, you could make fun of everything, and did.

Hot Dog Willie's woman was a little bitty thing named Peggy, but you needed to keep track of her. One day one of the barbers saw her on the other side of the street. "Here she comes," he said. And then, in a blink, she was there. "Where he at?" she said. "I got my thirty-seven-cent pistol and I'm going to kill him." She waved the pistol around, and that was bad enough. But she had something even more dangerous than the gun—a can filled with potash lye and Pepsi-Cola. If you held that in your hand it was so hot you couldn't stand it. If you poured it on a car, the paint would peel right up. We told her to take her trouble right on out of our shop, but it was a while before she went.

The same thing, give or take, happened to my friend Ronnie. Ron was fifteen and he was going with a girl named Vi who was twenty-five. That girl, on finding out that he was running with other women, came in one night and sliced up all the barbershop chairs. When I came in the next morning and saw the chairs all cut, I thought my girlfriend had done it out of jealousy. I went to her house and started to scream at her. She turned state's evidence immediately. "It was Vi," she started screaming. "Vi!"

Ronnie's father eventually killed Hot Dog Willie. Willie, while drunk, went outside to lie under a truck. Ronnie's father didn't know that he was there and backed out right over him. I thought Ronnie's father might kill him one day, anyway, on general principle. He didn't seem to care for him too much.

And then there was Pete the Magician. He was a neighborhood drunk, too, but when they arrested him they didn't bother locking the jail door. He could walk right out of that place anyway. "Everything is an illusion," he said. Pete sometimes came around to the barbershop and did these amazing tricks. He put a straight razor in his mouth and chewed it with no damage to his mouth. He chewed glass. He would take a needle and thread, eat one and then the other, and then when he belched it all out, the needle would be hanging off the thread. Once he brought a deck of cards into the shop and had someone pick one. Then, without looking, he put that card in a paper bag, took a scissors, and stabbed the bag so the card had a hole in it. Then he dumped the rest of the cards in and threw the bag at the front window of the shop. The bag broke and the cards flew everywhere inside the shop, except for one card that was outside on the ground by itself. A guy walking by picked it up, or one of us went out to get it, and it was the card that was picked in the first place. Pete the Magician would hypnotize people and make them bark like dogs, or snatch the shirt right off them. Once he asked me for a twenty-dollar loan. "I ain't got no money," I said. He told me to open my wallet and look; there were twenties stacked deep in there. I gave him one, and we talked about it for a few minutes, and when I opened the wallet back up the money was gone and there were strips of newspaper. I didn't really believe it. But it was the first time that I started to think in an organized way about what the mind can do when you alter it and how the mind can be shifted away from what it thinks it knows. One day Pete just disappeared, the way a magician should, leaving no trace behind.

Drugs weren't big in the mid-fifties. I mean, reefer was around, always, but toward the end of the decade there was a substantial change, or a change of substance. It came after the downfall of the gangs, which followed a surge in street violence—there were beatings and worse, and one of my best friends got killed with a shotgun. When the gang phase waned, heroin stepped right in. All of a sudden there was heroin everywhere. My wife's two brothers who had been heavyweight boxers both went to jail for dope. It was especially prevalent among the younger kids. If you went into a diner, into a schoolyard, into a movie theater, you saw people on smack. The local track team, which was one of the fastest in the world, was a spectacle: two or three of the people on the relay were doing heroin, and they would nod out on their knees when they were getting ready to run. Someone had to holler to get them up. Old people in their seventies were doing it. Teenagers were doing it. There was a guy I knew who worked on Wall Street. Friends would go into the city and see him there, in a suit, looking sharp. Then he would come home and start using and nod out right in the middle of dinner, in the diner, his nose down into his coffee. It was so prevalent you wouldn't believe it. We used to get on people's nerves by asking them, "Who died last night?" That's how you said good morning.

Even the people who didn't do it would practice how to make the faces to look like they were doing it. We joked that we were going to make a movie called *My Favorite Nod*, all about how people looked when they were on dope. It was a cool thing to act like you were high. Everybody knew how to do it whether you did it or not. You had to pretend that you were awake when you were asleep. A guy named Jimmy Mack used to come in and wear his addiction like a badge. "I'm a junkie," he would say. "I'm a junkie." He was so corny it was hard to take him seriously. But if we doubted him for a second he would bring his works and open them up right on the barbershop floor for everyone to see.

One day, I was finishing up with a customer when two skinny white kids from Jersey City came into the shop. They were carrying a box, looking to one side and then to the other, like they were scared to death. One of them knew one of the barbers who worked with me, and the kid made some kind of expression that the barber recognized, and the barber signaled me to get rid of the customer. After a little bit of small talk that was just as nervous as their looks, they set their box down on the counter and showed us why they were so jumpy. The box was full of counterfeit twenty-dollar bills that added up to about a million two. They were terrified, staring, slapping each other like Abbott and Costello, because whoever they had taken the money from was bad news and then some. I say that they were kids but they were nineteen and we were twenty, maybe. We heard them out and then we bought all that funny money from them for $2,000. I remember running through the neighborhood, borrowing money from everybody on the block so that I could buy the stash. By the time I told the people who did know, we had it well stashed.

The bills were super crisp, with bright green ink. We had to put them in coffee to give them a used look: after that we'd flatten them out and stick them to the wall in the back of the shop. It was like we were hanging money out on the wash line. After a little while, the bills looked as good as not new, which meant that they could be put into circulation, and that's exactly what happened. We used it locally, or when we traveled. I furnished the shop with new $3,000 barber chairs. I paid for recording-studio time in New York. I told the musicians it was counterfeit but instead of $200 I would pay them $1,000. They didn't seem to mind. Belief in the federal green is strong, even when it's not real.

At around that time, the town was busted for dope. Even though heroin was still growing as a local plague, most of the barbers didn't use. We were in that age group that wasn't as affected: not as old as the jazz generation, not as young as the *My Favorite Nod* generation. But plenty of customers used. People nodded out in chairs. There was a local guy—I'll call him Sam—and he used to hang around the shop with everyone else. He was a regular kind of customer, maybe a little more interested in what we were doing. He even got with one of the mothers of one of the local kids. Nice enough guy. One morning, maybe five thirty, we were in the shop fixing up the money—soak, crumple, flatten, hang—and Sam showed up in a state trooper's uniform. A state trooper? It didn't make any sense except it made perfect sense. He had been working undercover. He stuck around that day and ran in maybe thirty people for using dope.

Afterward, he was standing there in the back room, talking to the few survivors of the bust. He had a soft spot for us because of what we were doing with the kids, letting them play music, giving them a safe place in the neighborhood. He glanced around at all the barbers, and didn't look up at the money on the wall, though the way he didn't look up was more intense than any stare. "Word to the wise," he said. "I heard there's some funny money around here. If I was a person who knew something about that money, I would do myself a favor and get rid of it." Then he tipped his hat and went out the door. Right then and there I started calling people and telling them to unload the money. "Don't bring it around here," I said. "We don't want it anymore." We still had plenty left, maybe around $200,000. We disposed of it through what you might call resale channels.

Maybe two or three years after that, I was reading the newspaper and saw an article about an older man who was in prison for counterfeiting. He was talking about how his grandkids had found printing plates and a huge stash of cash in Jersey City and made off with it. He didn't know what had happened to it, and the grandkids weren't talking. I had some idea. And about two or three years after that, I opened up a drawer and found a couple thousand dollars. It was almost like wallpaper at that point, an old pattern from a room I used to live in.

I'M INTO SOMETHING AND I CAN'T SHAKE IT LOOSE

By the end of the fifties, everyone who loved doo-wop could sense that it was winding down. We were sad to see it go, but also excited. We were perched on the edge of our seats for the next big thing. I was determined, though, not to pay much mind unless it was the next best thing, also. When "The Twist" came out in 1960, for instance, it hit the first mark but didn't come near the second, by a long stretch. I was already familiar with the song from the Hank Ballard and the Midnighters version, which had been released about a year before. The Chubby Checker hit, huge as it was, was kind of corny. But everybody did it, and they did it again a year later, when he released "Let's Twist Again."

Motown was something entirely different. You had Berry Gordy, who I knew because I had a habit of reading record labels obsessively. He had done some songs with Jackie Wilson, and you could hear that influence in the early Motown songs. I loved everything the label was doing: "Please Mr. Postman" by the Marvelettes, and then "My Guy" by Mary Wells. But then you had Smokey Robinson, and that was another rung up the ladder. "Shop Around" came out in 1960, and it had a weird long credit on the label: "The Miracles featuring Bill 'Smokey' Robinson." I knew the name a little bit from other label productions, but that song cemented my obsession with him. My feeling about Smokey was more than love: I studied him. He was a hell of a songwriter, the slickest one around. He had tons of hooks, puns up the ass, but somehow managed to resolve everything within the song. He could sing like a motherfucker. He had a hell of a group, too: the Miracles burned everyone up bad in the early days of Motown.

But to call him a triple threat undersold him by half. What really got me was the way he worked with different artists, how he could take a group that was already established and elevate them just by attaching them to the right song, or by developing their image in a certain direction. He was a shape-shifter, a magician. He could see what the other group needed, give them something, and then stand back and watch as his vision came true.

Take what he did with the Temptations. Even before they got to Smokey, they were already the best-looking and best-sounding group, doing songs like Curtis Mayfield's "Gypsy Woman." The only act that got near them was Junior Walker, who wasn't the coolest but was undeniable, an old professional who embarrassed some of the younger groups when he got onstage. But when Smokey got to the Temps, they went up a notch. He paired them with "My Girl," and everyone else in the game was suddenly in last place. They were the power pack. And then Smokey turned to Marvin Gaye and did just as well with him. He had this uncanny ability to take a measure of other people's artistry and focus it, strengthen it, make it more than it ever could have been without him. That was one of the most important lessons I learned: when you're writing songs, don't limit yourself to one emotion. Don't think that your only goal is to be confessional: this girl hurt you by leaving you, this world is getting you down. Don't think that your only goal is to be aggressive, or wounded, or jubilant. Instead, express everything that's in you, and then find multiple singers and musicians who can help you articulate those emotions in different contexts. There are any number of thoughts and feelings that are valid at any given time, and the goal is to get them all out into the world. Smokey Robinson taught me that.

And so, one day, the Parliaments packed into a 1956 Bonneville and went to Detroit. The car was a juiced-up specimen that belonged to a friend of ours, William "Stubbs" Pitt. That car was like a rocket. The cops would try to catch Stubbs racing around Plainfield, but they'd fail because all he had to do was drop the accelerator pedal. He was gone. The next day the cops would come to the barbershop and ask after him. "Where's Stubbs?" they'd say. "We couldn't catch him." Sometimes, though, illegal drag races took place at night where the cops would look the other way. Sometimes they would even place bets on the racers. They all bet on Stubbs. On the drive to Detroit, I stayed in the front as a passenger, mostly because I was good at staying awake. Stubbs drove the whole way. Something happened to the transmission right outside of Toledo, Ohio, and he jumped out and went up under the car and fixed it. He put his jumpsuit on over the top of his suit. We were all wearing suits. That's how you had to dress when you were going to make an impression at Motown. They were supercool, and we thought we were even supercooler.

We went from New Jersey to Michigan so fast it was like we were traveling by plane, and we came into Detroit just before daybreak and parked in front of the Motown offices on West Grand Boulevard. As the sun came up, we saw all the legendary acts coming to the front lawn: the Temptations, the Vandellas, Marvin Gaye. It was a dream parade, but also a nightmare. On the drive out we talked like we were the baddest shit around. We were sure we'd make it. But when you see the Contours and the Four Tops walking across a lawn, real as real life, your bravado evaporates quick.

They toured us through the building before our audition, past all these little rooms packed with the giants of soul music. The experience was like going into a museum and seeing the old masters painting on the canvases in the galleries. For part of the morning, we had to wait in the lobby because the Supremes were rehearsing in the room they wanted to use to see us. Finally, Martha Reeves herself came out. We were amazed to see her. All jaws dropped. She led us back into the building, opened a door, and there was Mickey Stevenson, another Motown giant. He wrote and produced and was more or less in charge of the house band, who would become known as the Funk Brothers. We sang a couple of our own songs along with a few Motown hits, "My Girl" and "Do You Love Me." We had choreographed our routines beforehand and had good movement and good energy. When we finished, I had a sudden vision of what would happen when Motown signed us—we'd be in the company of all these other acts I idolized, learning from them, eventually working among them.

We had to wait again for much of the afternoon. Maybe the Supremes had a second rehearsal. Then Martha came back out to give us the news. They really liked us, she said, but they were going to pass. We sounded like a mix of two groups they already had on the label, the Contours and the Temps, and they didn't really know what to do with us. Then there was the problem of appearance. I was about five foot nine and stocky, as was Grady.

Calvin was much taller, and Fuzzy was even shorter. That unevenness fucked up the sense of visual perfection, and that kind of thing mattered then to Motown, because all kinds of perfection did. The Temptations were all six feet tall and thin and moved together like they were parts of a watch. Motown was a machine and we had a more obvious humanity. We were disappointed, but it wasn't like the ride back to Jersey was a funeral. I kept my spirits up, more or less, and the rest of the guys took their cues from me. They went along when opportunity knocked, and they hung back when it stopped knocking. They weren't as pushy as I was. For that matter, nobody we knew had cracked Motown coming in from outside of Detroit. We wanted to be the first, but it wasn't as if we were passed over for someone we thought was worse.

Motown must have heard something in the originals we sang for them, because they offered me a writing job through Berry's sister, Lucy Wakefield. At that time, I had a partnership with a cat named Sidney Barnes. Sidney looked like Little Anthony from the Imperials, right down to (or up to) his pompadour. He sang in a group called the Serenaders—they had recorded with MGM and Rae Cox and Gemini and would even be on Motown a little later for a minute and a half—and he used to come around the barbershop to get his hair did. He was going with Gloria Gaynor at the time, long before she became the reigning disco queen with "I Will Survive." Sidney and I had similar ideas about songwriting, and we became a team, working with people like Gene Redd and Cecil Holmes, experienced producers who would surface later in our career. Soon enough, we were working under Raynoma, who was Berry Gordy's wife at the time. She was his partner from even before Motown, when they started Rayber publishing, and she was one of the main people encouraging him to start Motown. They got married, had a son, Kerry, and almost immediately Berry started running around with Margaret Norton, which brought the marriage to an end quick. Berry and Margaret had a son, too, Kennedy, who became better known as the musician Rockwell, who had a hit in the eighties with "Somebody's Watching Me." Even though the marriage fell apart, Ray and Berry stayed business partners, and in their hasty settlement, he took the record company and convinced her to move to New York to run the East Coast office for Jobete, their publishing company. What he didn't realize at the time was that the real growth industry was in publishing. A record company could only press and sell records. A publishing company had a portable asset, and it could place songs with all kinds of crossover artists, from Frank Sinatra to Ray Charles. If you could get Tony Bennett to cover "For Once in My Life"—which, as it turned out, you could—you were making money through an entirely different channel. Ray Gordy was hanging with a man named Eddie Singleton, who she later married, and there was a small staff that included Sidney Barnes, George Kerr, and myself. As it turned out, Ray was a publishing shark—very good at the business, very sharp, earned respect from everybody around. Screen Gems was the biggest in the business, but Jobete came in so hard and fast that soon you couldn't keep up with them.

Despite the fact that Jobete was making money, they weren't current with basic funds for the company's operation. They couldn't keep the lights on. The Jobete office was about to go under until Ray decided to press up some of her own copies of "My Guy," the Mary Wells song, to raise funds. We were making extra records and selling them off the books. We used to do it out of the trunk of the car. One day, I was walking on one side of the street when I saw them on the other side, with their "My Guy" car, and then a few guys in dark suits crossing over to meet them. I stayed on my side of the street. It was the FBI, or maybe some fake FBI guys that Berry had hired to put a scare in them. He was none too happy about Eddie Singleton—even though he and Ray were split up, he didn't like the idea of her hanging out with this fast-talking dude—and the game that was being run on him. At that point, she had a profitable company, so he had to settle with her. He gave her a healthy amount of cash, reabsorbed Jobete, and that was the end of Ray Gordy's publishing career at Motown.

That was the end of mine fairly soon, too. Motown was looking for a new wave of talent after Mary Wells and Martha Reeves, and one of the groups they had their eye on was the Velvelettes, a trio of girls who went to college at Western Michigan University with Berry's nephew. We tried to sell them songs but failed, and they went on to work with Mickey Stevenson (who recorded "There He Goes" with them) and then Norman Whitfield (who steered them into some big hits, "Needle in a Haystack" and "He Was Really Saying Something"). My time as a Motown writer didn't bear much fruit, but like everything else, it put more branches on the tree. Years later, when they tore down the Graystone Ballroom building in Detroit, someone found some of the original paperwork for my contracts with Motown and sold them on eBay. A pair of twins from Holland bought the papers and sent them back to my daughter.

Gene Redd was a producer at King Records, which had started as a country-music label specializing in hillbilly records and evolved into an important R&B label: they released music by James Brown, and Roy Brown, and Otis Williams, and lots of other people. Somehow Gene got himself a deal out in Detroit, where Sidney and I were traveling regularly as a result of the Jobete work. One of the weekends we were out there, we met Ed Wingate. Mr. Wingate was in his early forties then, and he was one of the richest men in Detroit. In addition to being the main man for running numbers in town, Mr. Wingate had lots of legitimate business interests: all the cabs in town, all the motels, real estate that stretched from Woodward to Dexter. He also owned Golden World Records, a small label whose office was about ten blocks down from Motown. Detroit was filled with music men, but Mr. Wingate was a unique case. He wasn't a natural, really. He was a sweet guy, a man with money who was trying to find a way to be popular. And it worked: everybody loved him, because he knew enough to know that he didn't know enough, and that encouraged him to put people into place to help him. Golden World was a small label, but it made some waves along the way— his biggest successes came in the mid-sixties, with Edwin Starr, who sang "Double O-Soul" and wrote "Oh, How Happy" for Shades of Blue. And he had an instrumental called "Hungry for Love" that was credited to Barbara Mercer, though really it was the Funk Brothers moonlighting as an anonymous backing band.

Early on, Mr. Wingate used to fly me out to Detroit and let me stay at his house, a huge place on Edison. A little while later, we phased over to one of his motels. We were charged with a fairly simple task. Make music. Mr. Wingate wanted me and Sidney to be his go-to writing and production team, and he had visions of us leading him to heights the same way that the Motown production teams had elevated that label. I remember once I was sleeping in one of his motels, and I came awake to the sight of Mr. Wingate standing over my bed like a big black ghost. He had a gleam in his eyes that made it look like he was going to kiss me. "I have an idea," he said. There was a woman on the radio in Detroit, on WJLB, who called herself Martha Jean the Queen. She had a hook phrase she used to say on the air all the time: "I'm into something, I can't shake it loose, and I'll bet you." Mr. Wingate wanted us to make that into a song. He had a singer all picked out, a woman named Theresa Lindsey who had been at another label called Correc-Tone. "Make a song for her," he said. I was still in bed, but when I got out of it I told him I was pretty sure that there were two songs in Martha Jean the Queen's catchphrase. "I'm into something and I can't shake it loose" sounded like one, and "I'll bet you" sounded like another. He laughed. "Y'all gonna be my Holland-Dozier-Holland," he said. To make sure we were, he went out and bought us a piano for the motel. It was a big-ass Steinway, and he had to break the walls down to get it into the room. It was a small group then—me and Sidney and Mike Terry and a woman named Pat Lewis, who had been in the Adorables and would later be a backup singer for Isaac Hayes and Aretha Franklin. We were in that room coming up with lyrics and melody lines for hours. Eventually, we had both songs: "Can't Shake It Loose" for Pat and "I'll Bet You" for Theresa Lindsey. Later on, with Funkadelic, we repossessed and remade both of them, and they were also covered by Motown groups: "Can't Shake It Loose" by the Supremes and "I'll Bet You" by the Jackson 5.

Did Motown notice us? Not at first, maybe, but they started to come around when they had to share access to radio stations. And Golden World was only one constellation in a sky that was beginning to fill with independent record labels. Mr. Wingate and his partner, Joanne Bratton, also had Ric-Tic Records. Ollie McLaughlin, who started as a DJ up in Ann Arbor, came down and started Ruth Records. LeBaron Taylor had his Revilot label, which was just his middle name, Toliver, in reverse. Those years with Golden World were wall-to-wall work, mostly for other artists. I learned every aspect of the business, from writing and arranging to how to oversee recording sessions to getting the records out to local radio stations. If I had gone to work at Motown, that would have been one kind of education, where I was sitting at the knee of these industry giants. Golden World was another kind of education, where I was sitting at my own knee, and skinning it often. It was hectic and stressful and exhilarating, and since I was only in Detroit for weekends, mostly, there wasn't much time for anything else, really: no parties and no women. Besides, Mr. Wingate didn't play that. I used to like Pat Lewis, but he stopped that cold. "George," he said, "you can't have my girl Pat." She was his artist. He wanted us to respect work limits. And Mr. Wingate also saw that I was, in some way, a family man; I was always a favorite of his because I always sent whatever money I did have home to New Jersey.

I loved working for Mr. Wingate, and working with Sidney and Mike and Pat. I was starting to get a handle on Detroit, which was becoming my second home after New Jersey. That's not to say there wasn't a culture clash, and a fairly major one at that. Out there in the Midwest, I started running into a pimp element. I had always seen those kinds of guys back East, but this was different. In New Jersey, the word was never spoken. Pimps had a certain life that they lived with style and even a certain dignity—much later, when we invented the character of Sir Nose, we'd find out how New Yorkers felt about pimp culture. In Detroit, though, it was straight raw. Girls were choosing their pimps at twelve years old, or having pimps chosen for them. There was a farm system and not very much chance of escaping it. The shit was commercial and it was nasty. Detroit was a strange mix, country but also real slick, with Motown and the car companies. The result was a style that was about a half step back. Out in Detroit, they had their hair processed but didn't get it combed out. You might see a dude rolling down Hastings Street behind the wheel of a deuce and a quarter—that was the Buick Electra 225, which was named for the overall length of the car in inches. That was considered a top-flight ride there, but it would have been laughable in New York, where the minimum requirement would have been a Cadillac Eldorado. The clothes were the final thing. Detroit pimps wore store-bought suits. In New York, you couldn't be pimping and buy no goddamn store-bought suit. We had our clothes made from grade school, and we handed them down to younger kids. But Detroit was off the rack. Even Motown artists bought their clothes that way.

That didn't mean the Motown groups didn't have it going on. The best looking and the best dressed were the Four Tops, who were a conspicuous exception to the off-the-rack way of living. Part of it came from the fact that they had been around the block a number of times. Even though they were from Detroit—Levi Stubbs and Duke Fakir had gone to Pershing High, and Obie Benson and Lawrence Payton had gone to Northern High—they had gone away, first to Chess Records in the mid-fifties, then to Riverside, then to Columbia. They hadn't found their way back to Motown until 1963, but when they got there, they got there in style. They were the kind of dudes who came to the show in a suit clean as hell and wouldn't leave afterward until they put on a fresh suit.

There could be girls six deep waiting outside the stage door. They didn't give a fuck. They would take their time to look fine. They got that kind of respect for the look from a Las Vegas tour they had done with Dinah Washington before coming to Motown.

When I first went out to Detroit, I used to see the Tops all the time around town, along with other Motown acts. We'd all go to a club, and somebody would be playing there. Dennis Edwards, before he got in the Temps, might be singing. Or maybe it was the Contours, or a young group trying to break into the big time. The 20 Grand was the hottest place around; it was at Fourteenth and Warren, and there was a main stage and a jazz lounge and a bowling alley and even a big hall where they could serve banquets or host conventions. The main performance space was called the Driftwood Lounge, and everyone played there, from Maxine Brown to Chuck Jackson to the Flamingos to Brook Benton to Bill Doggett. Everyone. I can remember seeing Diana Ross there, and Berry Gordy's sisters. There's a rumor that Mick Jagger saw B.B. King for the first time there in the early sixties. P-Funk played there later on. Mr. Wingate owned the 20 Grand Motel, which was right next door to the club, and that did quite a productive business as a result of the club. If you had a late night and couldn't quite find your way home, whether as a result of alcohol or newly acquired company, you might end up sleeping off your evening at the motel.

★

At that time, Motown dominated the scene. I was still in awe of the label, but running parallel to them—and running parallel means you're on a different track. That difference between us, that distance, would become even clearer in the years ahead. But

I had another life, too, back in Jersey, at the Silk Palace. Things were humming along there. Heads were being cut. Ernie, Wolfgang, Grimes, and the rest of them were holding down the fort. For my part, I was away as often as I was there, leaving regularly to work on music: maybe with the Boyce brothers in town, maybe with Vivian Lewis in Perth Amboy. I was always doing something with somebody, though even when I was in the shop I tried to keep the focus on music. We had a jukebox in the shop. It wasn't the first time. In Newark, at the Uptown Tonsorial Palace, there had been a machine, too, but someone had to come and service the machine—by someone, I mean the gangsters who had those concessions, pinball and jukeboxes and other entertainments. In Plainfield, though, we owned the box, and I put the records on it and changed them whenever I wanted, and though this was technically a violation, nobody ever gave us any trouble. The jukebox gave us access to all the regional R&B and soul scenes that were cropping up across the country. There was the Philly sound, with the Orlons and Lee Andrews and the Hearts. Chicago had the Orioles, the Dells, and the Dukays. If you listened closely enough and read the labels for writer and producer credits, you could start to sort them by subtle differences and figure out which groups were from St. Louis and which ones were from Cleveland.

Even when I was on the move, I was immersed in music. I still technically lived in Newark, even though the shop was in Plainfield, and I had to take a bus to work every day. Sometimes there was radio on the bus, sometimes not, but there were always radios you could hear as you went through town, blasting out of the front windows of houses or from stores. Every day I listened to the urban network, with songs changing as I went crosstown. One song would be hanging on and I'd drift into the next block and another song would surge to replace it. It was a real-life cross-fade. And then when I got to work, it was wall-to-wall. The jukebox took care of it inside the shop, and whenever I was outside, I was in somebody's car. It was hard to get away from music, which was good, because it was nothing I wanted to get away from.

In movies sometimes you'll see young R&B groups making their bones, and in the scenes leading up to their breakthrough all they do is listen to other R&B groups. We weren't like that at all. Every kind of music flowed down to us, and because of that, every kind of music flowed through us. Our tastes were still rooted in soul, of course, but soul meant many things all at once. We knew all about Burt Bacharach, who was the king at that time, because of his work with Dionne Warwick, who was a local girl. It was heartwarming to see somebody you knew become that big all of a sudden. We knew all about Curtis Mayfield, who was like a one-man Motown—he had that amazingly spiritual Impressions sound and an incredibly strong sense of his own songwriting. "For Your Precious Love" had come out when I was in high school, and then when Jerry Butler left the group and it looked like Curtis might falter without a lead singer, he just turned around and released "Gypsy Woman," which became their biggest single. Around 1960 or 1961, everyone wanted to be Curtis almost as much as everyone wanted to be Smokey. But the biggest of them all, at least for a little while, was Sam Cooke. He came to the barbershop once or twice, and he was like a cool pimp when you met him, so smooth, with a quiet confidence. Ladies loved him, of course, because he was handsome, and he seemed to always be on top of his game. I admired him for his business sense. Sam was every kind of pioneer: with crossover success, with songwriting, with the way he set up his own label, SAR, where he signed and promoted other groups like the Valentinos and the Simms Twins. Sam was going strong through 1964 with songs like "Good Times" and "That's Where It's At," and then, suddenly, in December 1964, he was dead, shot in a motel office in Los Angeles. He was naked except for his sport jacket. The woman at the motel said that he had pushed his way in and accosted her, asking about a girl he had come with, asking about his clothes, getting more and more belligerent until finally she had to shoot him in self-defense. It didn't add up to me then and it still doesn't. It seemed like he was on the brink of something major as an artist and a businessman. Maybe there were people who didn't want to see that happen. All I know for sure is how it affected us in the barbershop and, for that matter, music fans everywhere. We were numb all day long. It was like John Kennedy's assassination a year earlier. In both cases, I was on the bus when I heard the news, and I just kind of dropped down beneath it. I blanked out. You can spend your time obsessing about the particulars of a situation, inventing conspiracies, questioning the official version—and I've done plenty of that—but in the end you come back to something more fundamental, which is that that kind of sadness, that kind of subtraction, doesn't really belong in the world.

★

As the world changed, as we heard it changing, we started to hear the new generation of white rock and rollers, though they weren't rock and rollers in the sense they had been back in the fifties, where they were updating hillbilly music into rockabilly. In the sixties, they were coming from a number of different directions: from folk, from British blues rock, from more classically trained

musicians. Take Bob Dylan, for example. I didn't like his singing voice very much at first, but I liked his voice in the sense that
I saw immediately that he was creating a character for himself,
and that he meant to do something with his freedom. That was a
liberating idea for a young artist, that you could start at point A
and go somewhere other than point B. If you had a passport, you
could travel. And travel, mentally and creatively speaking, also
meant going beyond the shores of America to the British Invasion
groups. They were coming and we had to take notice. I remember just before the first Beatles record came out, and how Murray
the K kept teasing it, saying that he was going to play it later that
week, then the next day, then that night. Finally he did—it was
"I Want to Hold Your Hand"—and I just sat there looking at the
radio. I didn't know what to think about it. I couldn't tell if it was
going to be a big thing or a nothing. It wasn't that I was unsure
of their talent. They had a couple of other records already out on
Vee-Jay, and from a songwriter's perspective you could tell they
had a real feel for melody and lyrics. They were like the Beach
Boys, in a way, making the Chuck Berry sound more mainstream,
but they had these songwriting skills that were unquestionable.
What I liked most about them wasn't the fashion, or the screaming kids. It was the fact that they had a great respect for American
rhythm and blues. To me that's what gave most of the English
groups their legitimacy. But when something was hyped the way
that was hyped, there was always the danger that it would fall
short, that people would close ranks, and that it wouldn't have
another chance to break through. As it turned out, I didn't have
to worry on their behalf. They did fine.

The other big band, obviously, was the Rolling Stones, and
though they had a great love for American blues, I didn't see

that at first. What I saw was a skinny English kid trying to do a James Brown impression. Later on, of course, that changed. I came around. I started to see that these groups across the ocean were absolutely sincere in their love for black American music, and that they were treating it both reverently and irreverently, and in the process making something new. A few years after that, I was listening to the radio and I heard Eric Clapton talking about Robert Johnson, and I was ashamed to admit that though I knew most of those songs—"Crossroads Blues," "Sweet Home Chicago"—I didn't know Johnson's name or anything about his life. How's that going to happen to a black man in America, to learn about blues music from a white man thousands of miles away? But that's the way it was. There was productive interpenetration—they took our music, remade it, brought it back to us, and we did the same thing to theirs. One of the people who was heavily involved in the early days of British rock, in fact, was a living example of that principle. His name was Jimmy Miller, and he was a Brooklyn kid who had briefly been a writing partner of mine in the early days in New York. Jimmy and I produced a record together in 1959, but the label that released it took credit away from both of us, so there's no official trace of that. I absorbed the blow and went on, but Jimmy was so hurt that he went to London, where he ended up doing some of the earliest Spencer Davis records, songs like "Gimme Some Lovin'" and "I'm a Man." He moved along with Steve Winwood to Traffic, where he produced their first two albums. I kept track of his career, and in the late sixties was amazed to find that he was working with the Rolling Stones. He ended up overseeing what many people think of as their golden period: he did everything from *Beggars Banquet* to *Goats Head Soup*, a stretch that includes *Let It Bleed, Sticky*

Fingers, and *Exile on Main Street*. When I knew him, he had been a drummer, and he contributed percussion to the Stones records, too—that's him doing the cowbell at the beginning of "Honky Tonk Women." I was happy to see that Jimmy was working with them, but it also changed my perception of the Stones. It proved to me, as much as anything else, that they were serious about rooting their music in American sounds.

In those early days, music was anything but simple entertainment. I loved it, but in the complicated way you might love another person. I was trying to strike a balance between being a fan who heard his favorite music on the radio, an aspiring songwriter who wanted to hear his own work on those same stations, and a group leader who was trying to keep those same aspirations alive in others. Maybe it was temperament and maybe it was delusion, but I always thought that we were going to take over the world. I always convinced myself that things were going somewhere good, and as a result, I kept moving all the time. You had to believe in the ultimate destination. Not everyone around me agreed. Billy "Billy Bass" Nelson, for example, got very down on things quick. When they didn't happen right away, he went slack and you could see the disappointment in his expression. Again, temperament was a factor, and also drugs. For some musicians, heroin had a way of making people depressed and pitiful, and making the idea of giving up romantic, somehow. But many of the other singers in the group, who were closer to my age, took the same stance I did.

The barbershop was a big help in maintaining perspective. The other barbers were a little older even than the Parliaments singers—Grimes was in his early thirties, and Wolfgang was in his mid-forties. That doesn't seem old now, of course, but back then it seemed ancient, and the shit they used to say made me see the world in focus. You'd be in there complaining, acting the brat, and they wouldn't even look at you. They would look at each other through the mirror, as if to say, "Why should we be happy?" It made you almost embarrassed. When they weren't cutting you with that look, they were telling you to your face that you were making too much of your own problems. Then they had a way of just cutting through all the nonsense and the bullshit. Once I went in there to worry about Ernie and the distance that was opening up between us. I knew that I wanted to keep going to New York to get more interviews and auditions, but I wasn't sure that Ernie was willing to do what was needed. Wolfgang looked at me levelly for a little while. Then he opened his mouth a little bit and said, "Let me put it like this. Some people will and some people won't." He didn't have to elaborate, to explain that Ernie, despite his talent, didn't have the temperament to suffer through the lower levels of the business, learn his way to the middle, and then find his way to the top. He didn't have to prop me up by telling me too much about myself. Some people will and some people won't. Later on in the sixties, there was lots of wordy philosophy about getting in touch with your feelings, hippie decoration on top of Eastern religion, but the barbershop was a purer version of it, and the sense of the world that it instilled in me colored most of the decisions I made, even in the darkest of times.

I didn't cat around in Detroit, exactly—like I said, Mr. Wingate frowned on that kind of thing—but that doesn't mean that I was an ideal husband. When I was back in New Jersey, I couldn't concentrate on home, and I was starting to go with other girls. Vivian Lewis, who was my singing and writing partner at Jobete, was just a teenager when I met her, but we got together after that, and she and I had a son named Tracey. Then there was Gwendolyn, who wasn't in the business at all. She was just a cute little girl, and I was just a horny little young boy. She got pregnant and had a boy named Stefon. I don't know if they ever told him that I was his father. For that matter, I don't think they told him that Gwenny was his mother—he was played off as a much younger brother in the family, like they sometimes did back then.

Being with other women was kind of like trying to break into the music business: a labor of love that took a whole lot of hustle to pull off. I don't know how the hell I did it sometimes, going from one house to another in the middle of the night, but that's the life I made for myself. I remember one night in particular when I came back to the house after spending a few hours with one girl and a few with another. When I got home, my wife had a dress laid out on the bed like she was heading out to dinner. I started yelling at her: "Where are you going? What do you think you're doing?" For a second, blinded by rage, I left the room. Out in the kitchen, I caught a glimpse of myself reflected on the inside of a window, and it all seemed ridiculous. What the fuck was my problem, yelling at her when my life was the way it was? Who was I to deny her a little freedom, or any at all? I think it was maybe a little of the wisdom of the barbershop leaking through. You can't make a young man less jealous but you can make him into a slightly older man who sees things more clearly. Live and learn, they say, but if you do it right, one is the same as the other.

FRIENDS, INQUISITIVE FRIENDS, ARE ASKING WHAT'S COME OVER ME

Where does an idea come from? In my experience, it comes from an afternoon in the barbershop with the other guys, shooting the shit, and Billy Bass Nelson banging on the guitar. He was still a kid, and he didn't know a thing about the fucking thing. He couldn't even change strings. So he was just strumming simple chords, and I was singing a lyric that had been stuck in my head for a while: "I just want to testify what your love has done for me." Billy and I sang that and let the words settle around us. That's how it is sometimes for hooks. You have to make sure that you hear them the way an audience might hear them if they're hits, over and over again, and whether they bear up under scrutiny.

The more we played this new song, the more I knew it would work, not only on the radio but also live. It was so infectious, and even there in the barbershop I could tell that there were so many turnarounds you could do once you got to vamping. Remember, this was all happening at a time in music before people understood the idea of a jam band. We came out of a Motown tradition that was strictly melodic, with tight hooks, but when that intersected with rock and roll we started to see there was the possibility of stretching out that feel to great length, not diluting the song but extending it. You could play it for five minutes or you could play it for a half hour, and it would have the same appeal. That was funk, in an early form. To me, Ray Charles was one of the funkiest people I knew, because he could take any song and make it work, for as long as he pleased, without any reduction in power.

The next day I wrote lyrics to go along with the chorus. "Friends, inquisitive friends / are asking me what's come over me / A change, there's been a change / And it's oh so plain to see." The lyrics were guided by the same principles as the music. I was trying to build on top of Motown, or rather what Motown had become. My main influence in writing the verses was the Four Tops, songs like "Standing in the Shadows" or "Reach Out," which themselves were a kind of soul imitation of Bob Dylan— verses that drew the vocals out, in a kind of monotone, until they bloomed into a big chorus.

Over the next few days, we worked it out: me, Grady, Fuzzy, Calvin, Ray, and Billy. The song got tighter and tighter. We were calling it "Testify," or "(I Wanna) Testify," and there was something glowing in it. You can't always tell when a song is going to be a hit, but you can tell when it makes the grade, and this one did. I decided to cut the record in Detroit, which meant that I'd have to go without the rest of the guys. They had to stay and work. Broke don't travel. It was hard for me to make the trip, even: I got a friend of mine named Deron Taylor to pay for my ticket out there, and I gave him half the songwriting credit in return. So I went out West—or Midwest—to cut the track, where I recorded it with Ron Banks from the Dramatics, who was about fifteen years old at the time. Pat Lewis did the backup vocals.

Even though I had imagined the song as progressing slightly beyond the Motown sound—even though I could hear the louder, longer, liver version in my head—what we recorded was still very much part of that rigorous pop-soul world. It's something that James Jamerson and the Funk Brothers would have done. The B-side was a song called "I Can Feel the Ice Melting."

Around that same time, Mr. Wingate got out of the record business. Music had been a toy for him to start with, and he wasn't interested anymore. He couldn't get soulfully into it, not in the way he would have had to if he wanted to continue. Plus, the landscape was getting a little crowded. Motown was starting to feel pressure from the other Detroit artists and was eager to eliminate the competition. The result was that they bought most of Golden World from him. The Motown agreement didn't include my team, which included Sidney Barnes and Mike Terry—the group that Mr. Wingate said he wanted to become his version of Holland-Dozier-Holland. Sidney, Mike, and I had just done a record by Darrell Banks, "Open the Door to Your Heart," that had as its B-side "Our Love Is in the Pocket." LeBaron Taylor, who was the program director at a local radio station and also had a label called Revilot, was in business with Darrell, and Mr. Wingate let me and Pat Lewis—and with us our Parliament record—go with LeBaron over to Revilot. It's a good thing he did. Pat would have been lost in the shuffle over at Motown, and Parliament would have been crushed by the politics and the internal competition.

So there we were, perched on the precipice of something either major or minor, standing on the verge of either success or obscurity. I went back to New Jersey, and Revilot put the song out, at which point it became an instant smash. LeBaron's connections helped the song get onto CKLW, which was a fifty-thousand-watt station based in Windsor, Ontario, that held sway over much of the upper Midwest. Many stations cut off at night, and the big stations that were broadcasting with that kind of power got heard anywhere and everywhere. Once a song got onto CKLW, it pretty much guaranteed that it was going to move up the ladder, market followed by bigger market, until it reached stations like WABC in New York. It was also number one on WWRL, which was an R&B station, and it hit the first week that Frankie Crocker was at the station. He presented us at a big block party in Harlem, which further cemented the idea that we had something hot on our hands.

All of a sudden, everything was different. We weren't a long-time doo-wop band struggling to make it in a climate where Motown was entering middle age and soul had replaced R&B. We were America's newest hit makers. The song took off so fast that we didn't have time to do anything in the way of understanding or processing. In fact, almost immediately we were on the road. If you were a band with one hit, you got invited to play in these radio-sponsored showcases, where you'd go out and play a song or two, and then you'd get off the stage and another band with one hit would come out and do the same thing. In those days, we didn't really even have a band yet. We had singers and we had songs and we had Billy Bass Nelson, who was thrust into the position of musical director. One of the first shows on that first tour was at the Apollo Theater, and it was disorienting in the extreme. For starters, we were headlining over the O'Jays, which made no sense except that we were the band riding a recent wave. The Peps, who later became the Undisputed Truth, were also on the bill. We knew we had to play "Testify," and for our second song, we planned to play "7-Rooms of Gloom," which was the current Four Tops hit, because that was still how we thought of ourselves—the band that Motown should have signed but didn't. "7-Rooms of Gloom" was a towering Holland-Dozier-Holland production with a painful howl of a lyric: "I see a house, a house of stone / A lonely house, 'cause now you're gone." It would have been nice to go out there and just tear the roof off of the song, send a message to the world that we were the equal of the Tops. But we didn't take into account how unprepared we were. We didn't realize that the Apollo was a union house, and that we would have to use the union musicians. As a result, we didn't get our charts written until late. And you couldn't travel that way with Motown material: that shit was sophisticated, with complicated time signatures and tight turns. The result was legendarily bad. It sounded like a bunch of drunk bagpipe players. People thought we were joking. At the end, we rolled into "Testify," stormed through that, and that righted the ship. We never tried to do that again.

The shows out on the road were less disastrous. We played ski lodges and teenage fairs and those kinds of venues, *American Bandstand* stuff, mostly in the Midwest. The record company made sure that we had a few thousand dollars to get us from one gig to the next, and that was the extent of the tour support. Mitch Ryder was on one bill with us. Ted Nugent was on another, with the Amboy Dukes. When we did those teen shows, we mostly just played the hit. When we had a second song, we knew better than to try for "7-Rooms of Gloom." We moved on to Eddie Floyd's "Knock on Wood," which had the same kind of pocket as "Testify." Stax was moving into a pop area that coincided with a new European brand of R&B. It was another shift in the landscape, but one where we could stand where we wanted without losing our balance.

★

After six hard months of package tours with a motley combination of backing players, I realized it was time to put together a real touring band. Luckily, we had the beginnings of one right in the barbershop.

Billy was the nucleus, but only in the sense that he was central to the overall project. He wasn't much of a musician back then. He could play "Testify" and he could play "Knock on Wood" and nothing much else: he wasn't a guitar player, really, and he hadn't started playing bass at all. But he started to have ideas about who we might add to the band. He had a friend who he mentioned with some regularity; as it turned out, one of the older barbers also knew him, because he was a boarder in the boy's mother's house. "Yeah," the barber said. "Eddie Hazel." Both of them kept telling me that Eddie was something on guitar, and that I needed to check him out, but I was always traveling, or in town and too busy. Finally, after "Testify," the demand was there, and so I supplied the time. One afternoon a shy teenager came by the barbershop and took his guitar out of the case carefully. We asked him to play, because it seemed like that's what he wanted to do. And he played. Man, did he ever play. When he was done, Ernie Harris flicked his glance over to me and said, "This is the guy." For rhythm guitar, we got another local teenager, Lucius Ross, who everyone called Tawl. We passed through a series of drummers before settling on Tiki Fulwood, the pride of Philadelphia, who also came in through Billy and Eddie.

Revilot wanted a follow-up to "Testify" almost immediately, and so we started kicking around ideas. We used to clown popular sayings, things from advertisements, and there was a big campaign then by Hertz, the rental car company: Let Hertz put you in the driver's seat. We were driving once, and we heard that ad on the radio, and Fuzzy turned to me and said, "Let hurt put you in the loser's seat." He said it offhandedly, but it sank in, and the next day I went and wrote out lyrics. I had the Smokey role, playing on words until the play was the thing. And so that was the next song, "All Your Goodies Are Gone (The Loser's Seat)." We cut it in Detroit, in United Sound, and again it split the difference between the Motown sound and Dylanesque vocals. Billy played on that, along with Eddie, who made the trip out, and there were session musicians, too. I wrote a B-side with Pat Lewis and Grady Thomas called "Don't Be Sore at Me," a song that years later became a Northern Soul favorite. Revilot rushed out the "Goodies" single and waited for the charts to embrace us once again.

We waited, and waited some more. Regionally, "Goodies" did fine. But the thrill was, if not gone, muted. CKLW didn't add the song as quickly—LeBaron had lost some of his juice with the station—and nothing else came as easily, either. Part of the problem, maybe, was the song itself. It had a little more R&B flavor in it than "Testify," which had appealed to black and white audiences equally. The racial neutrality of "Testify" was in the tradition of Motown: if you don't pick a side, you can go anywhere. "Goodies" traveled less easily. But part of it was just the cosmic comedy of it all. When you first get a hit record, you think that it's going to happen all the time. You never think in any deep way about the chemistry—or the chaos theory—of what makes a record move. "Testify" combined certain things that had never

been combined before, in perfect proportions. Everyone was in
the right place to get it played. A spark appeared and caught fire.
It happened because it happened. "Goodies," while not a failure,
didn't repeat the performance. On the other hand, it got added
into the set list for our concerts immediately. We had two songs,
which was at least twice as good as one. I was watching us make
a name for ourselves. I was hearing our songs on the radio. But I
was still listening to the Parliament in my head, and still realizing
that the radio version of the band was stuck in a slightly different
place, that it sounded like the past rather than the future.

Around that time, after one of our New York shows, a woman
we knew named Judy came backstage to talk to us. Judy was the
girlfriend and future wife of Bernie Worrell, and she wanted us
to know that she had decided that our band was the best place
for him. Bernie was from Plainfield, like the rest of us, and in
his youth we had heard about him constantly, from almost everyone: how he was a local Mozart who wrote his first symphony
before he was in junior high school, how he could do anything
from Ray Charles to classical music. Once, he had played a show
with us over at the Washington Street School. We sang doo-wop
and he sat in. He was amazing, but my memory of his participation in that show is overshadowed a little bit by my memory of
how Ron Ford, one of my best friends, started throwing change
at the stage, priming the pump, and then everyone started pitch-
ing dimes and quarters. We must have made an extra ten dollars
in change.

Soon after the Washington Street School show, Bernie came
in to the shop to get his hair done. It's a good thing he did, be-

cause he needed something for it, bad. You know how a baby elephant has a little tuft on the top of his head? Bernie was like that, and that's what we called him: Baby Elephant. We straightened his hair for him, with extreme effort, and he went off happy. It wasn't but a day before his mama whipped his ass, though, and it wasn't but another day that she came down to the shop to whip mine. She was sixty years old at the absolute very least, and she couldn't walk too good, but she got up on those old pins of hers and tried to beat me down for fucking with her son's hair. I think there was an issue, too, of pulling him away from the music that she wanted for him. Bernie was a musical genius. Everyone could tell that within seconds. And since his mama had spent all that money on formal training, she was going to be damned before she would let her beautiful talented boy end up with us: lowlifes, ne'er-do-wells, no-accounts. Also, she didn't like me because her husband's name was George and he wasn't a person for whom she had the fondest feeling. In fact, it was Bernie's name, too: he was George Bernard, but he only ever went by Bernie. Years after his mama tried to beat me, Bernie left Plainfield for advanced education, including at the Berklee School of Music in Boston, and as soon as he graduated from there he went out on the road with the R&B singer Maxine Brown and also with a band called Chubby and the Turnpikes. They went on to be the soul and disco band Tavares, though their drummer, Joey Kramer, went on to play in Aerosmith.

At the Apollo, Bernie expressed interest in joining up, which was enough of an audition for me. His arrival changed the whole mix, musically. Though his mother may have been unhappy to see him squander his talents, his piano teacher, a German lady, was thrilled that he was playing with us. She saw clear to a way where he could incorporate his formal training into something more contemporary—it was already a vibrant idea in Europe, to reintroduce elements of classical and jazz music into rock and roll. Our first rehearsals with Bernie confirmed her suspicions, and mine. We were the funkiest thing around, in ways that no one had ever really heard before.

We took the band around the country, playing our handful of originals along with some covers. With Bernie we could paint with more colors, mix together soul and rock and even a little bit of gospel. And we were starting to develop a stage presence that reflected that eclectic, edge-of-the-world sound. We used to laugh at Calvin, who wouldn't do anything but stand in the corner—he had been to Vietnam and was a little shell-shocked, though even without that he wasn't the kind of person to court attention—but even that became part of the act.

We were in Kansas City, in St. Louis, in Cleveland, in Chicago, in Toronto. The label bought us two Cadillac Eldorados and we tried to cram into them. At one point, we let Hertz put us in the driver's seat, and we rented a station wagon that we never exactly returned. We just kept it for six months until it stopped working. There were no credit cards, no deposits. What were they going to do? The second time around the circuit, we saw new faces along with the old, a sure mark of success. You're either adding audience or you're losing audience.

In movies about music groups on the rise, they're always held together by a common objective, brothers united against the impersonal world. We had that, but we had the other scenes, too, the ones of petty annoyances and road squabbling. Mostly they were because of Billy, who was a huge pain in the ass in the car. I never drove—I still don't have a license—so most of the time I was in charge of reading the map and planning the route. I'd do that down to the last little state highway, and then I'd go to sleep and wake up on a road that I was damn sure had not been part of my original schematic. Slowly I'd become aware of Billy lecturing the driver about this shortcut or that one. He always thought he had found a quicker way, never mind if it was a road that had been shut down for construction or a dirt road that ran through the property of Pentecostal snake handlers. Once we were in Pennsylvania and he thought he had a shortcut through to Ohio. We ran a roadblock, went about a mile along the road, and came out into a small town where we saw all these fucking creatures walking around, zombies or mummies, hands up in the air and dead looks on their faces. We were scared out of our fucking minds until we saw the movie lights. We didn't know what movie until about a year later, when *Night of the Living Dead* showed up in theaters. Not every shortcut was that memorable. Sometimes we'd just get lost. Billy was brilliant, always brilliant, but he had a hell of a time learning to use his brains responsibly: he had short-man attitude plus a big fucking mouth to go along with his big brain. Fuzzy and Grady just couldn't take it. They were about ready to kick his ass at any time of day or night.

If Billy occupied one end of the pain-in-the-ass spectrum, Eddie was at the other extreme. He had been sheltered by his mother, and he was real sensitive and shy. You could misuse him so easily, but he could misuse you as well. He would try to play you with his sweetness, usually to pull your girls away from you on the road—if you were bringing a girl from a show back to the hotel, you couldn't go near his room, or he'd steal them right out from under you. He was only sixteen when he started, but girls of all ages would just fall out the windows for him. They loved him, and once he picked up the guitar, guys did, too. My mother used to call him Old Crying Eddie; when he put his hands on his instrument, he was able to produce a deeply sad and introspective tone. He had learned that from his grandmother, who played an acoustic with three or four strings but could still make it sound like it had six. Those early touring days were like high school on the road. I took it upon myself to expose the band to all the new records that were changing the way that I thought about things. That was the first flowering of psychedelic rock, from the pop of the Beatles up to the molten lava of Cream, and though we weren't there quite yet as a band, I knew that was the direction we were heading.

★

We were doing fine, in the sense that we could get on stages and people would yell for our songs, or more specifically, our song, but I knew that we were in a narrow window of success, and that it was only a matter of time before it shut. It had taken us ten years to get our first record out, a full decade to get a hit, and the music world was evolving faster than anyone knew. At one show, I was outside the club, waiting for the rest of the band to arrive, and I heard an older woman talking to her husband. "There ain't nothing but a guitarist, a drummer, and an old fool," she said, "but they're pretty good." An old fool? We needed an infusion of new energy, a reinvention, and soon.

Part of the new blood came from north of the border. CKLW, the radio station that initially broke "Testify," was in Canada, and so we had a pretty strong following up there. We played clubs like the Hawk's Nest, which was co-owned by Ronnie Hawkins, the rockabilly singer who had been the original front man for the Hawks, who backed Bob Dylan on his first electric tour and went on to become the Band. Ronnie's partner in the place was a guy named Ron Scribner, who ran a local agency that managed the Guess Who, the Stoned Soul Children, and various session players who would become part of the Detroit rock scene, whether with the MC5 or Alice Cooper. We met Ron one of the first times we played up in Canada and developed a strong relationship with him.

At that time, there was a second wave of Plainfield musicians, Garry Shider and Cordell Mosson, that I wanted to launch as a spinoff band. We called them United Soul, which was a play on United Sound, the studio in Detroit where we did some of our recording. Garry was a great guitarist and singer, one of the most solidly spectacular figures in the whole organization, and Cordell, whose nickname was Boogie, was a hell of a bassist. We cut some tracks with them, but we needed a fertile place for them to play and evolve—and, just as important, a safe place for them to escape a drug and crime scene in Plainfield that was getting worse by the minute. So during one of those early tours, we took Garry and Boogie up there and set them up as United Soul. We got them the same gigs we had. They looked just like us, sounded just like us. It was like a franchise. And Toronto was right on it. They were one of the first cities to buy into the idea entirely. It was a whole other world up there, and one that I really liked. The racial relationship was cooler. They were more relaxed, not just in terms of black and white issues, but in general. There were lots of hippies, lots of open thinking. In fact, the draw was so strong that within a few years I decided to move up there myself.

★

That first stretch with the band was exhilarating, but it was difficult, and the difficulty was compounded by the fact that some of them were on smack. The older guys never touched the stuff. We associated it with jazz music and the writer Nelson Algren, with that period in Plainfield's history when the track team nodded off at the starting blocks. To us, it was corny shit. We smoked weed and if anyone had the money we might do a line of coke. But the young musicians had a different context for it. They saw soldiers coming back from Vietnam with needles in their arms. It was part of their generation and they participated fully.

Though the older guys weren't doing junk, they took advantage of younger thinking in other ways. When we toured, we took full advantage of the blossoming of free love, and some of the drugs that went along with it. The intensity of the experience varied from place to place, but Boston was one of my favorites in those days. It turned us out. We always had girls riding with us, and they always brought along every class of freak. We called those shows "Pimps, hos, and hippies," because that's what they were, and the groups converged in these wild after-show parties, orgies up the yin-yang. The girls took us out to Cape Cod, where people fucked on the beach and got high. But Boston wasn't all debauchery. Another time, we did a kids' performance on a flatbed truck: little kids, three years old and younger, watching Parliament in all its glory.

Boston was also our introduction to three important letters: L-S-D. At the time Timothy Leary was big on the scene, preaching his tune-in, turn-on, drop-out gospel, and at first acid was just a spectator sport for us. Then, once in Boston, I saw Billy Bass drop acid. He was always a mean little ass, severely severe in every way possible. So when I saw him with a tab of acid and then, a few minutes later, smiling and having fun, I couldn't believe it. Fuzzy was beaming also, which was almost as rare—he was a clown but he never let himself relax. Acid seemed like a miracle mood modifier, easy travel to other regions of your personality. The next day we went over to Harvard Square and all of us took some. That was a Noah's Ark day, rain so hard you couldn't even see your hand in front of your face, and the gutters were filling up with water, making little rivers in the street. We dropped acid and stood looking at the rain: sometimes it seemed to slow down, sometimes each individual drop came into perfect, sharp focus. And then, all of a sudden, everyone started taking off their clothes and wading in the rivers the streets had become. There were students, but there were faculty members, too. There were couples and there were single girls. There were fat people and skinny people and every other kind: older white women naked there in the water, with polka-dot freckles on their titties, and dozens of cute little girls getting bare-ass naked. Everyone was in the water, flopping around like fish, just feeling it.

Back in Newark, things were less cool. They heated up all through 1967. In fact, we were in New Jersey for the Irvington riots. Traffic was snarled and we had to walk despite the heat. We had just bought these new suits, and when we ran into the police blockade, the officers made us put our jackets on the ground, where they stomped on them to see if we had weapons. We canceled our show that night, which was a double bill with the Four Tops. Our next show was scheduled for Detroit, and by the time we got there they had started some riots of their own. We didn't really know about them before we went onstage. Even during our show, when people started coming onstage, yelling and flapping their arms, we didn't think much of it. That kind of thing happened not infrequently at our shows. But outside there were so many people in the street, running around tornado-style like they had been back in New Jersey, that we realized what was happening. That night, we were scheduled to drive down to our next show, in Chicago, but first we had to drop my friend Ron Ford at his house. We ran into a barricade, and the cops wouldn't let us pass. We pulled off to the side and Ronnie slipped out of the wagon and went home through the alleyways.

Changes in politics, changes in music, changes in drugs, changes upon changes. In the context of this new world, our old ways were fading fast. LeBaron wasn't flourishing; Revilot was going under. He had lost his connections and was getting squeezed tight by Motown. We recorded more songs and released more singles, some of which were very good, others of which were holding patterns, and still others of which were experiments that gestured toward the future. We had "Little Man." We had "The Goose (That Laid the Golden Egg)." We had "Look at What I Almost Missed." We had "What You Been Growing." We had "A New Day Begins." If there was an overall plot, it was that we were moving slightly toward rock and slightly away from conventional R&B. But the sound I had imagined when I first wrote "Testify" still wasn't quite crystallizing.

At some point, LeBaron decided he had to get out of Detroit while the getting was good. His exit was inauspicious at best. He went around to clubs where we had booked gigs, picked up some of our money from the club owners, and then skipped town. We didn't see him again for years, until he was well into his next career as a radio man in Philadelphia. Just as he vanished, we had our creative breakthrough in the form of a record called "Good Old Music." We had cut it with the entire band and released it with a B-side called "Time," which was a lean, midtempo, Motown-style track about a man who loses everything and has only time left. "Time" was very much in the spirit of the other Parliaments records. "Good Old Music," though, was entirely different. It opened with a hard drum part and then an organ line, and the first words I sang were about the music I was singing.

> *Everybody's getting funky*
> *In the days when the funk was gone*
> *I recall not long ago*
> *When the funk was going strong*

"Good Old Music" was a manifesto, a legitimate new beginning, and the record became a smash in stores almost immediately. But LeBaron had put it out just as he was leaving town, and there was nobody around to work it with the radio stations. We were in the strange position of having a hit on our hands—a revolutionary hit—but also standing in a cul-de-sac. Our identity as Parliament was evolving, but it was also evaporating.

Much of our inspiration came from our further absorption of rock and roll, and especially the black acts who were changing the face of the genre. The biggest one, of course, was Jimi Hendrix. He was a huge influence on me and on Eddie, and later on Bootsy. Shit, he was a huge influence on everyone. I had heard him first when he played with Curtis Knight and worked with King Curtis—he had been on a Ray Sharpe single called "Help

Me" that had caught my ear—but when he went off to Europe, I lost track of him. Most people did. Then he reappeared and I saw that he had changed, that he had absorbed everything that he had seen, some of which I had seen, too. The Who had these Marshall stacks, towers of amps, and Jimi came back playing with a rig like that. I knew that if he had figured that one out, it was only the tip of the iceberg; and when I bought his first album, it was titanic. That shit was all the way over. There was a visionary quality to it that's hard to fully process even now, forty-seven years later. It just seemed like a transmission being beamed in from outer space. Though we never got a chance to play with Jimi, I met him once a little later. Buddy Miles had invited our band up to the Chambers Brothers' place in New York. Jimi was just there at the party, minding his own business, mostly, getting high like everyone else was. Still, we were in awe. He was shy and soulful, very compelling in an understated way.

If Jimi was the first thunderclap, the second was Sly Stone. Dave Kapralik, who was the president of Epic Records, had worked with Ernie Harris, my old friend from the barbershop, and one afternoon Dave invited us into New York to a listening session. The record he played for us was the very first Sly and the Family Stone record, and as he put the album on, he explained that he was quitting his job at Epic to manage Sly. It seemed crazy to be leaving a comfortable record-business job to be a manager. Crazy, that is, until I heard the record. Sly did so many things so well that he turned my head all the way around. He could create polished R&B that sounded like it came from an act that had gigged at clubs for years, and then in the next breath he could be as psychedelic as the heaviest rock band. While Hendrix discovered his new sound in London, Sly was doing it in San Francisco, which had the most adventurous music scene around, with the Jefferson Airplane, the Grateful Dead, the Charlatans, and a thousand other bands who were playing around in the space between folk, blues, psychedelia, and hard rock. There was so much to absorb, and he was capable of absorbing it all. He was the only other act who could do what the Beatles were doing. But there were four of them—there was only one of him. In those early years, Sly was a massive influence on me. He stayed that way for years and then, later, became a collaborator and a partner in crime.

Those were the leading lights, but there was a constellation around them. To be alive and paying attention in 1967 was to get a crash course in all this and more. The first Jimi Hendrix record came out in May. *Sgt. Pepper's* followed in June. Cream's *Disraeli Gears* came along in November. And then there were major records from Tim Buckley, Aretha Franklin, the Kinks, Buffalo Springfield. One of the most interesting groups working the seam between soul and hard rock was Vanilla Fudge, a group of Long Island musicians who played covers of popular songs at a glacial pace. Shadow Morton, who was best known for his work with girl groups like the Shangri-Las, produced them with heavy guitars and slowed-down vibrato. On their debut record, which came out right in the middle of that glory period, they did great Beatles covers, "Ticket to Ride" and "Eleanor Rigby," but the stuff I liked the best was the R&B material, Curtis Mayfield and the Impressions' "People Get Ready" and the Supremes' "You Keep Me Hanging On." I could really get into that. Most rock and roll was loud and fast. That's how we played at first. Turn everything up as a surefire way to get attention. But when you brought the pace way down, that required more discipline. If you could hold a song at that slower tempo without getting monotonous, the result was amazing.

All of these bands were cracking open something new, and we were receptive to it. We had gone through "Testify," moved on to "Goodies" and "Goose," and ended up with "Good Old Funky Music." We had covered quite a bit of ground, from doo-wop through Motown to the brink of this unexplored land. But we also knew that if you're going to call on something to change, then you're going to have to change what you call that thing.

SOUND A LITTLE SOMETHING
LIKE RAW FUNK TO ME

Armen Boladian had been big on the Detroit scene since the early sixties. He and his partner Bernie Mendelson handled promotion and distribution for many of the smaller labels: not just Revilot, but Ric-Tic, Thelma, and others. Armen liked me, especially the way I interacted with radio stations, and he liked taking me around for promotional purposes. We would meet with jocks, help with charity events, and so on: there was a big annual show for St. Jude's Children's Research Hospital in Memphis, for example, which was associated with the comedian Danny Thomas and his daughter Marlo. As the Parliaments ran their course with LeBaron and Revilot, we needed someone to put out our next record. We already had plans for a label of our own, Funkadelic Records, and it was starting to buzz. Armen had similar ideas for something called Westbound. One of his early artists was the R&B singer Denise LaSalle, who would have a huge hit with "Trapped by a Thing Called Love." Her success brought more visibility to the Westbound side of the equation, which swallowed up Funkadelic Records in the partnership.

But the first Westbound record was our record. And what was our next record? What was our next sound? We were still into

Motown, still very much responding to their movements, either in imitation or in opposition. We were all huge fans of the Funk Brothers, the group of musicians (including James Jamerson, Earl Van Dyke, and Pistol Allen) who were responsible for the instrumental part of the Motown sound. Somewhere along the way it became clear to me that we had a strong young group of players who were, to us, what the Funk Brothers were to Motown, and because we were so deep into psychedelic rock we started adding the *-delic* to it. The result was Funkadelic. I think I had the idea for the name first, but you'll probably get a debate from two or three others. Everyone knew that it felt right, though. White rock groups had done the blues, and we wanted to head back in the other direction, to be a black rock group playing the loudest, funkiest combination of psychedelic rock and thunderous R&B.

The music scene was ready for us. In the fifties and early sixties, as we were bringing the Parliaments up from Plainfield, soul music and in fact pop music in general were all about singing and showmanship. At some point, pop started to move toward musicianship. There were always players. Jerry Lee Lewis was a hell of a piano player. Chuck Berry could play guitar. But they were in the service of songs and in the service of singing, in the most efficient way possible. And then there was a sea change. I would go to the record store and see Iron Butterfly's "In-A-Gadda-Da-Vida," or these Grateful Dead records that relaxed the limits of song length and went on for twenty minutes. Rock and roll was becoming like jazz had been twenty years earlier, with solos and complex compositions and virtuosos, and all of a sudden kids wanted to know who the guitar player was, who the keyboard player was, who the drummer was. When that happened in rock, it happened mostly only in rock. The major exception was James

Brown. People say that "Papa's Got a Brand New Bag," back in 1965, was the birth of funk, though it's much more complicated than that: there was barrelhouse piano and Texas blues guitar and the New Orleans sound and a hundred other things that came together, came apart, and came together again. But "Papa's Got a Brand New Bag" did start the ball rolling on pushing musicians to the forefront. James would call out to his musicians during songs, make them visible as soloists. But James was the exception. Motown didn't even list its session musicians until 1971, so the Funk Brothers, who were central to the label's success in every way, were also completely anonymous. Motown had been so good at staying ahead of the curve until suddenly they found themselves behind it. If they had recognized that the Funk Brothers were the Eric Claptons and Jimmy Pages of soul music, they could have secured themselves five more years of relevance.

Our shift happened along similar lines. We were already Funkadelic, in a sense, during the last few months of the Parliaments, and especially on "Good Old Music," but we formalized the evolution on our first official Funkadelic single. It wasn't as if we had weeks and weeks to sit around and debate the change, like we were in a think tank or something. "Good Old Music" had broken big—bigger than "Testify," in fact—in Detroit, Cleveland, and Chicago. There was a demand for new music. We got a song together and got it right out, and that song was "Music for My Mother," which some of us also called "Whoa Ha Hey" after the distinctive chant in the chorus. We were already doing that chant live and we built the rest of the song around it. It started with a slinky bass line, with guitar laid over the top, and then opened up into a chant with a rap on it that I said "sound[ed] a little something like raw funk to me."

The song was startling, even to us: it seemed to go back to something before Motown, to hipster jazz or country blues, and also it stretched ahead to something that hadn't happened yet. Tempos were slower, arrangements were deeper, sentiments were more abstract. When you went to parties, someone would put on Cream's "White Room" or Pink Floyd's "A Saucerful of Secrets" and then you would do acid, and when you came back from your trip, the same record would be playing. It was the new jazz and also a kind of dance music for the mind.

When we released "Music for My Mother," we wanted to make sure that we didn't lose the fans we had made with "Good Old Music," let alone the ones who came aboard for "Testify." We had to draw a line between Parliament and Funkadelic, and so we made sure that all the record and concert posters said "A Parliafunkadelicment Thang." The effect was immediate. "Music for My Mother" became the national anthem of Detroit, and it got so big so fast that Armen couldn't keep up with demand. Our second Funkadelic single, "I'll Bet You," reached all the way back into the Golden World years; it was a reupholstered version of the song that Mr. Wingate had asked us to write around Martha Jean the Queen's catchphrase. Theresa's version had opened with hand claps and an up-tempo horn arrangement. We replaced that with thundering drums and a pealing guitar line, and the Motown-style vocals gave way to a multipart lead that was similar to what Sly was doing at that time. On that song, the B-side was "Open Our Eyes," a traditional gospel song in the style of a romantic ballad, though you could still hear the acid guitar buried back there in the mix.

If we were doing our part in remaking soul music, Armen was doing his part taking me around to all the radio jocks. We did all the same events as before, St. Jude's Children's Research Hospital and the others. It's one of the trade secrets of the record business that promotion is everything. Without it, you can have the best record in the world, but you'll have it in cold dead space. Mickey Stevenson was the key to Motown because he got all the records played. He had the key to the jocks. He beat them at pool, brought them some girls. He was so successful that he even got a percentage of the producers' fees. By the time Funkadelic started out at Westbound, Armen was already a veteran at that kind of thing, and soon enough the new band and the new sound was known all over the Midwest and the Northeast.

Devotion to the road helped us capitalize on the momentum of Funkadelic. We signed with Diversified Management, a booking agency from Ann Arbor that handled Detroit-area rock acts like Mitch Ryder and the Detroit Wheels and Iggy Pop and the Stooges. Once we shared management with them, we got booked everywhere, both on the soul circuit we had already visited with "Testify" and in the rock and roll venues that were uncharted territory. Among black acts, nobody was doing what we were doing. Acts like the Chambers Brothers had a chart presence—they had a big hit with "Time Has Come Today" in the fall of 1968—but they were ultra pop. War, which formed in the late sixties with a post-Animals Eric Burdon and then went on without him, had a great sound, but it wasn't exactly straight rock: there was Latin music in there, and even jazz. Even Sly, a genius, was basically running a pop game, aiming straight for the charts much of the time.

We went directly into rock, and we flourished. Right from

the beginning, we had a crazy stage act. Before Funkadelic's first flowering, we were starting to dress in that West Village style, a mod look with bell-bottoms that you might find at a shop on West Fourth Street in the Village. When we went on the road after "Music for My Mother," it was all the way out there, and the sillier the better. We went to a prop store and bought duck feet and rooster heads. There were big floppy Amish-style hats. I started wearing a diaper onstage, sometimes made from hotel towels, and sometimes even from an American flag. And the thing that was most extreme about it is that not everyone in the band dressed that way. Some would, but others, like Calvin, were still in suits. So when you looked at us from the audience, you saw everything colliding all at once, every look imaginable, and even some that you couldn't imagine.

Audiences were in awe. We had two or three guitar players who could go loud like Hendrix and we had Bernie adding in his classical colorings like we were King Crimson. Even up in Canada, where audiences tended to be a little more sophisticated, we got over like a motherfucker. We expanded our base by playing with anyone—old-fashioned R&B bands from the chitlin circuit, new rock acts, whoever had a big pop record. If we were the supporting act, we made it a point to get out there, play our set, and give the stage to the headliner. If we were slated for an hour, we got off in fifty-nine minutes. Because we were so catholic in our bookings, we started to learn how to cater to different styles of audience. If it was a teenybopper crowd interested in the latest dances, we could deliver songs at the appropriate tempo. If we were opening up for Jackie Wilson or Chuck Jackson in front of a mostly black crowd that hadn't yet come around to our new way of thinking, we could keep the songs radio length, or go back to "Testify" and our covers of "Gypsy Woman" and "Knock on Wood." If we were playing a venue like the Fillmore, we might be performing for a crowd that was filled with musicians, and so then we could let Eddie or Bernie show off their chops with solos. The most forgiving audiences were what today you'd call jam-band audiences, kids who were following the Grateful Dead and similar bands. They were musically open-minded and didn't put much stock in costumes or stagecraft. So long as we played with passion, it didn't matter if we were up there in plain white T-shirts.

Once, on the way to a show, we were on the same airplane as the MC5, who were Detroit's loudest and most aggressive political rock band—Rob Tyner was their singer, and they had two great guitarists, Fred "Sonic" Smith and Wayne Kramer. We used to call them the white niggers, because they were legitimately countercultural in their thinking, not interested at all in playing along with the rules. On the plane, everybody was smoking weed, but we were doing it subtly and politely and they were loud and obnoxious. We kept telling them to shut the fuck up. "If the police come on this plane," we said, "they're going to get us because we're niggers." When the plane landed, sure enough, some cops showed up, and during the course of searching Billy and Tiki, found weed in their drawers. This gave them probable cause to search everyone, which was an unnecessary nuisance, especially given that it was the MC5 who was raising all the hell in the first place.

We were kindred spirits with the rock bands in more important ways. We loved the feel of rock and roll, the style. *Creem* magazine accepted us as one of their own: at one point, they wrote an article about how Iggy Pop and I were getting married. That was a sign of respect. *Creem* was like a cross between *Rolling Stone* and *Mad*; they covered music but with a satirical edge, and when they liked you, they wrote something strange about you. Rock and roll was individualistic but also democratic, and we adopted that idea: we were like a tribe or a nation. The idea was off-putting to some people. I remember a conversation I had with Dave Kapralik. When he looked at Funkadelic, he felt something lacking: a leader, a center of attention. He thought we needed a bigger, brighter character smack in the middle of things. He said it just like that. I resisted that for various reasons, some political, some personal. It's hard to come to the forefront of a band in such an aggressive way, to run the show like that, unless you're a Quincy Jones or a James Brown. They had the energy of a motherfucker, from sheer physical exertion on down. I was looking more at models like the Beatles, where everyone could be close to the core, where the whole only existed because everyone played their part perfectly.

For years in the sixties I talked about getting a pig or a skunk. I loved farm animals, pigs and rabbits and that kind of thing. Maybe it was because I was a country boy at heart; if I closed my eyes I could still feel the Virginia ground under my bare feet. People around me vetoed the skunk, and because of that I got more and more serious about the pig. Sometime in 1968, Jeffrey Bowen, who was a producer at Motown, bought me one. It was just a little thing, a piglet, and I named it Officer Dibbles, after the character on the *Top Cat* cartoon. Dibbles went everywhere with us. He was an official band mascot. He would curtsy and show people the diamond bracelet around his neck. Dibbles got treated better than any pig ever had. We kept him on a good diet regimen and scolded people when they tried to feed him scraps. We took him on airplanes when we toured, and even though airline rules required that we check him, like a dog, he was so cute that when we were at the ticket counter the ladies would just tell us to carry him through.

As Funkadelic's reputation spread, it went west and it went east, and some of it went across the ocean. We got booked to play at the Royal Albert Hall in London. For me, that was a dream. I hadn't been to England, but my mind had been there for a year or two, following the music. Just before we got there, they switched our show around. Frank Zappa and the Mothers of Invention had played the Albert Hall, and it had been a crazy scene. His fans tore the place up, and the band desecrated the pipe organ, which dated back to the nineteenth century, by playing "Louie Louie" on it. As a result, the venue wasn't receptive to the idea of rock bands, and our concerts were switched over to the Lyceum. That didn't seem fair, to punish Funkadelic for the sins of the Mothers, so we cooked up a protest stunt. I'm not sure where we found a place to rent us a donkey in London, but we did, and we decided to ride the donkey up to the Albert Memorial in Kensington Gardens as a way of making an ass of the Royal Albert Hall. We went out there in the afternoon, our whole group trailed by reporters and photographers from *Melody Maker* and *New Musical Express*, and we rode up to the statue as planned. There was only one wrinkle: on the way up there, the donkey took a regal shit on the steps. Everyone laughed, and when that happened, Dibbles ran into the middle of the crowd and tried to get attention. He was like a little baby. In the middle of all the commotion, he got excited, or ate something someone threw to him, and he ended up taking a shit, too, a watery bit of skeet. Shutters were going off all around us, and the music papers ended up with pictures of Dibbles and the donkey both shitting right next to the statue.

All through that week in London, I was just like Dibbles, happy as a pig in shit. We played the Lyceum and also played a little club one night, along the way meeting everyone from David Bowie to Rod Stewart to Jimmy Page. We also went around the country a bit, and I was the most taken with Liverpool, where I was like any other Beatles fan. We went to the Cavern Club on Mathew Street, where Paul McCartney's uncle carpentered the stage. We went to Mendips, John Lennon's childhood home on Menlove Avenue. This was less than a year after *Sgt. Pepper's Lonely Hearts Club Band*, so there wasn't the same sense of distant nostalgia there is now. There was a real energy around those sites, because the band was still a going concern.

We reconnected with my old friend Jimmy Miller, who was working with the Stones, and we even managed to get in some recording: we went to Olympic Studios and recorded "Everybody Is Going to Make It This Time" with Ginger Baker's equipment. He wasn't in town, but we asked if we could use the drums, someone went off and made a phone call, and they came back and gave us the green light.

My love affair with British rock followed me back to the States; soon after we returned, I found myself in Boston, tripping my ass off, watching a double bill. Jethro Tull opened the show, and Ian Anderson's flute was a transformative experience. All the good bands from England were starting to experiment with classical elements: Procol Harum, the Moody Blues, and especially the Beatles, through George Martin's production. And the headliner, Led Zeppelin, was as loud as anything I had ever heard but with subtle details, too, a sledgehammer with a filigreed handle. They were taking black American music and feeding it through a white heavy-metal filter. They had great songs and a legitimately dangerous energy. And even though they weren't exactly using classical sounds yet, they had ancient elements that gave their music historical scope. Jimmy Page was playing a thousand-year-old folk song, the same way that Cream was playing off of Greek mythology. My vision of the future sharpened.

All the new energy reflected back on the old responsibilities, not always favorably. Back in Newark, my wife Carol was holding down the home front with the three kids—Donna, George, and Darryl—and a new baby, Shawn, on the way, but our marriage had been through changes. I had toured for too long, worked in too many other places, been distracted and at times unfaithful. I had grown into a different person than I had been when we got together in the late fifties. Carol and I stayed together and maintained our family until we finally got divorced in the early seventies, and I still stayed with them whenever I was there. I loved being with the kids, talking to them about their lives, helping them with their schoolwork. Donna was in her last years of elementary school then, and George right behind her, and both of them attended Catholic school. When I was young, I had noticed that the kids who stayed on the straight and narrow, or at least the straighter and narrower, were Catholic school kids. Carol agreed with me, and we were determined to give our kids that same best chance. Even Catholic schools, though, were subject to the shifts in culture. In the late sixties, there was also a surge of interest in the Nation of Islam and Muslim culture in general.

Muhammad Ali had taken his new name in 1964, explaining that Cassius Clay had been his slave name. Lew Alcindor converted in 1968 and became Kareem Abdul-Jabbar a few years after that. Political consciousness was on the rise, along with the beginnings of what would become the Black Power movement. So there was a strange landscape there in Newark, black American kids getting a Catholic education and becoming increasingly interested in Islam.

Not that it had any effect on pop-music tastes, really. My kids were still listening to the same music as their friends, which meant mostly that they were interested in whatever was topping the charts, whether it was the Fifth Dimension or Stevie Wonder or the Archies. I was going the other direction, moving Funkadelic toward the edge, where I could make sense of where soul was going and where rock was coming from. I listened to radio, because that was still the best way to pick up the pulse of the culture—not just Top Forty radio but college radio, underground radio. And I kept current with all the trade publications. I was a big *Cashbox* and *Billboard* freak, especially. Wherever we were, whether we were home or on tour, I would find a newsstand with the new issues and study them like they were a mix of textbook, sports program, and self-help guide. You could tell by the way records were advertised how much money was being spent on them, whether they were a commercial product or an art project. You could predict the hits for the next month or so, and that gave you an idea of the trends.

When the first Funkadelic singles started to appear, we were a problem for critics and other so-called tastemakers. What it came down to, I think, was race, or how we fit into the narrow ideas of race in music. We were too white for black folks and too black for white folks. We were a source of confusion. And that's exactly how we wanted it. Even if we were sacrificing a mainstream magazine cover or a coveted radio spot, we were staking out ground of our own and making sure we had a stronger bond with the fans who found their way to the band. The people who wanted to see us came no matter what. And the college circuit, which is where we did most of our touring, was perfect for us. The crowd changed every year, and there were always new students who were brave enough to explore music that deviated slightly from whatever was on the charts and responded to our sense of adventure and sense of humor. And they were determined not to rely on the tired old categories: black band is a soul act, white band is a rock act.

One of the companies that had tested those categories earlier in the decade, and in fact remade them, was flailing a little bit. As the world changed, Motown didn't know exactly what to do with itself. For starters, pop music was becoming much more intellectual, in a legitimate way. We were jokesters about it, but there was an undercurrent of philosophy in our music: ideas of self-expression, of rebelling against received norms, that kind of thing. We were also increasingly aware of the world around us, of war and urban poverty and the plight of the black man in America. Motown had built its empire on love songs, with a little bit of self-empowerment thrown in there for good measure, and they didn't want to mess with social change or social issues. And yet there were examples popping up all over the place that testified to the benefits of this new direction. Sly was all the way out there, with San Francisco being in the lead of the peace movement and bands like Jefferson Airplane making it a dominant topic in his community. What ended up happening was that Sly learned to present a polished, funky version of all the intellectual discussion that was bubbling up in Berkeley.

Motown wasn't equipped for change. For starters, Holland-Dozier-Holland, who were among their most forward-thinking producers, left in 1968 to start their own labels, Invictus and Hot Wax. And even though the top Motown artists were starting to grope toward new styles and new substance—Stevie Wonder was, and Marvin Gaye was—it didn't really break through into Berry's consciousness. The politician in him seemed to balk at any thought of fucking with the reality around him.

Without Berry's commitment to pushing the company forward, Motown couldn't really understand either social change or the growth of rock and roll. I gave Sly's records to Norman Whitfield and that resulted in a change for the Temptations, who started to record songs like "Psychedelic Shack" and "Cloud Nine." It was still the Temps, so it sounded fantastic, but anyone who knew what was happening in the world could spot it as synthetic, as jumping onto the path that had been cleared by Sly, or by us. And when Motown tried to break into rock and roll by signing a group called Rare Earth, it ended up sounding like a Motown record. It was really a lesson in limits, and the way in which there were geniuses like Sly, who absorbed everything, and geniuses like Berry, who progressed to a certain point but couldn't see beyond what he had made. Add to that the fact that Berry was starting to pursue a career as a movie producer. He had Diana Ross interested in doing *Lady Sings the Blues*, the Billie Holiday story, which would eventually spur him to move the entire Motown operation out to Los Angeles. The reins of the record label got handed over to the Corporation—to Alphonzo Mizell, Freddie Perren, and Deke Richards—who were writing for the Jackson 5, mainly, and that became Motown's identity. They would have stayed at the top longer if they had understood the importance of getting a little dirt on their hands.

Against that backdrop, Funkadelic became the darlings of the changing culture. In Detroit, we were even hotter than Sly. We were like the Beatles there, the hip thing everyone knew was coming. When we'd play the 20 Grand, we'd see plenty of Motown people in the audience, dressed in their jeans and minks. I might be wearing a sheet with nothing on underneath it, and I would clown them by walking straight off the stage onto their table and pouring one of their drinks over my head, which was shaved bald and decorated with drawings of dicks and stars. They were amused, like kings with jesters. There was a rumor going around that I peed on Berry and Diana at a performance, but that was just the wine running down my bald head and coming off the sheet.

We were hip because we were hippies, and part of that was connected to our understanding of the changing economics of the business. In Sam Cooke's day, the greatest aspiration for an R&B singer was to play the Copacabana or one of the big rooms in Las Vegas. That was the height of all you could imagine. But there were all these rock bands filling Madison Square Garden. Why couldn't we be the Rolling Stones? Why couldn't we be Cream? If it was just the color of our skin, that wasn't going to stop us, not when we had the tightest songs and the loudest guitars and the best singers. Our first album as Funkadelic, which was self-titled, came out with Westbound in 1970, and it was mostly a collection of the singles we had released, a record of our evolution from the Parliaments, along with some longer jams. "Mommy, What's a Funkadelic?" was a founding document, both a declaration of our independence from other forms of music and a kind of Bill of Rights for our fans.

We talked about being not of this world and being good to whoever listened. We were seducing this new audience. We were declaring their readiness along with ours. And while that first record didn't do much nationally, it was a big hit all across the Midwest. Funkadelic was on the launch pad.

When you establish an anti-establishment position that starts to pay dividends, the establishment positions itself near you for a new investment. Jeffrey Bowen, the producer who had bought me Officer Dibbles, had been at Motown with Holland-Dozier-Holland, and he had left with them when they went off to start Hot Wax and Invictus. Right after the Funkadelic singles started to hit—they were number one in Detroit and the surrounding area—Jeffrey contacted me. "Let's restart the Parliaments and do a pop album," he said. He appreciated where we were headed with Funkadelic, but he felt that there was a version of the music that was more radio friendly, more in line with the tradition Motown had established. That made sense to me, though I wanted to be on Hot Wax rather than Invictus, because Hot Wax was run by Neil Bogart, one of the most inventive executives in the business. I was sure that if we cast our lot with him, we'd be a hit act. But Invictus was distributed by Capitol, who had plenty of white rock acts and was hot for a black pop band. So we were placed on Invictus. Almost immediately, we changed our name to Parliament. Back in the doo-wop days, all the names were plural, from the Cadillacs to the Orioles to the Moonglows. But British rock, at least past the Beatles and the Stones, was moving into a phase of singular names that were strong concepts: Cream, the Who, Pink Floyd. Jeffrey was married to a woman named Ruth Copeland, a white British singer, and he understood the importance of being allied with that scene. Parliament was the perfect fit.

The album that came together around that new identity was *Osmium*, which would be released in 1970. We went for the Beatles edge of soul, and tried to keep enough guitar in it to make it sound like American rock and roll. There were songs like "I Call My Baby Pussycat," which was a mildly risqué love song that played off a double entendre. It had two songs that Ruth wrote, "Little Ole Country Boy" and "The Silent Boatman," and another song, "Oh Lord, Why Lord," that she adapted from Pachelbel's Canon.

Making that record at that time, at Invictus, was a comedy of its own. At Motown, Berry's comings and goings had been announced over the company loudspeaker like the weather report; when he came to work, they made an announcement: "The Chairman is in the building." Holland-Dozier-Holland had been Motown's golden boys, and when they left, they set themselves up as untouchables, with Eddie Holland playing the Berry Gordy role. If you were in the room with him and he wanted to tell you something, he would turn to Jeffrey instead and instruct him to talk to you. He affected an authority that came off as arrogant. It never bothered me too much, because we were rebels anyway. I knew that his high-toned ways were a strategy for existing, just like our psychedelic ways. You learned that at the barbershop, when people came to you for a new style, for a way of presenting themselves to the outside world. We designed people's looks back at the Silk Palace, and we designed our own looks as Funkadelic. In truth, underneath the image, I was a much more reserved, centered, circumspect person. In fact, that's why I was able to carry off those crazy looks. It was freedom generated by misdirection, and it allowed me to focus on my real self, the identity I was nurturing away from any kind of spotlight.

Going back to the name Parliament was, in theory, a complication for our use of the Funkadelic name. It wasn't a problem from the Westbound side—Armen Boladian wasn't paying us anything, really. He would get us a van every year and a half or so and let us have access to the studio. That wasn't nearly enough for him to have leverage over us. Jeffrey Bowen, though, subscribed to the old Motown ways, and as soon as we became his Parliament, he tried to block us from going back to being Westbound's Funkadelic. We knew he didn't really have a leg to stand on—the union could prevent certain aspects of a recording, but they couldn't stop us from playing onstage. For that matter, the two bands could continue to function as separate entities, where Parliament was a group of singers backed by a band and Funkadelic was a band backing a group of singers. Still, he tried to muscle us. Jeffrey was a brilliant A&R man, but he had it in his head that good people don't win—we used to drive around for hours arguing that shit—and that made him cutthroat in certain minor ways.

As it turned out, Jeffrey's arrogance solved the same problem that it created, though it sacrificed *Osmium* in the process. We did a big show for CKLW in advance of the album, showcasing our single "I Call My Baby Pussycat," and the distributors who came were so excited by our performance that they put in orders for a large number of Parliament albums, something like fifty thousand. At the same time, Invictus was releasing a single for one of its other acts, Chairmen of the Board. The song was "Give Me Just a Little More Time," and the other side of the single was "Patches." The record company realized that even though "Give Me Just a Little More Time" was a strong enough song, "Patches" was the potential hit. Just as they got ready to put it out, Clarence Carter covered it, and CKLW started playing his version. Jeffrey got very agitated. He told CKLW that if they wanted another Invictus record, they could go to the store and buy it. That next record, the one that got stranded by the "Patches" debacle, was "Pussycat." Instead it went to a little black station, WGPR, which killed it two ways, quick. For starters, it was too pop for an R&B station—it sounded great, but within that narrow context of the radio-friendly pop sound that we were trying for—and then there was the matter of the lyrics. The black community, and especially the church community, pitched a bitch when they heard us singing about pussy. *Osmium*, when it emerged, sold well enough because of the long tail of Funkadelic—everybody knew that it was the same band, and more and more people were signing on for the Funkadelic experience—but by that time I was through with Jeffrey. We remained cordial personally, but our business relationship was effectively over, and they never bothered us again about cutting another record.

Making *Osmium* may not have been a fully satisfying experience, but the cover photo is one of my most vivid memories. We shot it up in Toronto. I wore a sheet and nothing else, and everyone was decked out in hippie regalia. What I remember most is how much acid we were doing at the time. We were eating lots of soul food and steaks, and when you eat that kind of food and drop acid, you start tripping on the meat. You see it pulsating, like it's still alive. That was freaky, but what was worse was how it ran hell on our stomachs. They call LSD acid because that's exactly what it is. It blows up your digestive system and blows your ass out. We spent more time in the bathroom in those days than you could imagine, and there were hemorrhoids everywhere. And while the acid may have given us second sight and opened our inner eye, it didn't affect our sense of smell, unfortunately. We could smell perfectly and that shit was horrible. The shoot took place in a park, in a flower garden, and it was so hot that the sweat and the salt was getting in everyone's ass. Motherfuckers were crying like babies. And then there were bees in there because it was a flower garden, so if it was a movie instead of a still photo, you could see people flinching and swatting, scared as shit.

By then, I was pretty much a Toronto resident. I had gotten involved with a woman named Elizabeth Bishop; Liz and I had met during the first tour that followed "Testify," in Buffalo, where she was a waitress at a club. The next time we came through town, she jumped on board with the band and came on the road with us from time to time. We had a daughter, Barbarella, in 1968, and the three of us, along with two of Liz's kids from a previous marriage, moved to Canada. At first we lived in Forest Manor over by the Bay Bridge in Toronto, and later we moved out to Mississauga. I was officially a Canadian resident for a number of years, though it was in the same way that I had been a Newark resident: I was on the road pretty much all the time. When I had the time to be there, I loved it. Canada didn't seem like a different world to me at all. I was going back and forth so much the border was a street I crossed, Buffalo on the one side and Hamilton on the other. You didn't have to have anything to cross back then, not a passport and half the time not even an ID. Toronto was good for kids, a nice lifestyle, beautiful people, excellent schools. Between 1967 and 1971 it was pretty ideal.

Many Americans went up to Canada to escape the draft, of course, but those weren't my reasons. I was married so it didn't affect me personally. For a little while, you could even say that I didn't notice that there was a war on. I knew all about the army, of course. If you got in trouble in school, the teacher would try to convince you to enlist. They knew you would get a good education and they thought it would straighten you out. But I went off into music instead. Back then, I wasn't that clear on politics, at least in terms of specifics: it was something you couldn't see through and so I looked around it. We were touring musicians, which meant that we didn't always know about things right when they happened, and when we found out about them, we didn't always understand what they meant in the way that you would if you lived in a neighborhood and saw the same people every day. Vietnam was an abstraction until it started to happen to specific people I knew, and even then it was incomprehensible: young Americans being cut down in a distant land for reasons no one could adequately explain. Other events were equally abstract, even when they were thuddingly specific. When Martin Luther King Jr. was killed in Memphis, we were on the road. I don't even know where, to be honest. Could have been Akron, Ohio. Could have been Ann Arbor, Michigan. All I know for sure is that I was backstage, tripping so hard that when a head poked around the door to tell me the news, I couldn't conceive of it.

For me, political engagement in general seemed like a trap. It was too easy to slip into a certain way of thinking and then, once you were there, to lead others into something you didn't fully understand. All I could safely preach was that people should think for themselves. What was funny was that the younger members of our band, the kids like Billy and Eddie, they educated us. My crew, Fuzzy and Grady, we were from the streets. We were trying to be cool, looking like pimps, thinking we were the shit. But once we got on the road with the band, once we pulled into college towns and saw the way that kids interacted with us and with each other, we started realizing that they were dead serious about peace and love, and that took your breath away a little bit. Those kids were brave. They would walk up to a soldier and put flowers in the gun. And they were protected because of their youth. Once they got past eighteen, they were exposed and endangered, like at Kent State. Once the power structure had you on its radar, you couldn't really put flowers into the gun anymore.

When people say the sixties were a revolution, they at least mean that it turned everyone's head around. Everything was getting loose, and boundaries were breaking down faster than new ones could be drawn. One night we were at the Cheetah Club in New York, where the Chambers Brothers were playing. After the show, someone came to the microphone and asked the crowd to sit on the floor, cross-legged. We did, and we watched the stage to see what would happen next. But what happened next wasn't on the stage. All of a sudden, people started standing up one by one in the crowd and singing. "When the moon is in the seventh house," the first one said. "And Jupiter aligns with Mars," the second one said. One of the people standing was the actress and singer Melba Moore, who had been at school with Grady. We didn't know what the hell they were doing, but the harmonies gave us chills. And they were staging it really inventively. Lights cut through the crowd and lit the place up. Strobe lights reflected off tinfoil. As it turns out, they had been rehearsing this kind of thing for weeks, a communal musical that extended into the audience. It was *Hair*, but not quite yet: it was the roots of *Hair*. There was so much happening in those days that it seemed like epiphanies stacked on top of epiphanies. The week we saw the kids singing what would become *Hair* happened to be the same week that Ken Kesey came through town with the Furthur bus. Music and books and films flowed to us through the same channels as sex and drugs. There weren't publicists or managers controlling what you thought. There weren't corporate entities to enforce corporate control. Maybe this is obvious, and maybe it's part of the stereotype of the era, but it's also part of the truth.

Everyone wonders what happened to the idealism of the sixties. As I see it, it ripened into something nearly perfect, and then it began to ferment. Woodstock was the end. Look at what it did to drugs, or to the way that drugs circulated through society. For years, it was a communal scene. You shared drugs with friends. Someone put money into the center of the table and then someone else did and then a third person pitched in, and the fourth swept it all up and went off to buy a lid of weed for everyone to smoke. Nobody talked about selling, really. And because no one talked about selling, no one saw the drugs as a product, and there was no issue of bad quality or bad service. But then, suddenly, it became an industry and the whole thing just flipped to the other side. Quality was a major issue; you heard the announcements over the loudspeaker at Woodstock about the bad acid. Service was an issue; if your dealer was just a middleman retailing a product to you, then you were allowed to demand what any customer would demand. Making drugs a commercial concern was the quickest way to end what was good about them. When the smoke cleared, there were thousands of small businessmen trying to stretch their profit, and they were willing to poison people to do it. Strychnine started showing up in the acid. People were cutting recreational dope with straight PCP. Woodstock may have been the mountaintop but it was also the beginning of the climb back down.

The same thing happened with sex. Free love was fine for a minute. For a while people fell in love innocently, and there's nothing wrong with fucking. We all knew that it wasn't a permanent condition, that people would eventually have to go back to work and get married and raise families. But it was a nice way of thinking until that, too, came to a crashing halt. Diseases started to creep in through the early seventies, more aggressively, more fatally.

All of these things were ways to make sure that societal movements stayed cosmetic, that they didn't really change anything about the power structure. A peace-and-love message was the corniest shit imaginable unless it was coming from someplace special, which it was for a while. The war was going to end. Youth culture was going to be heard. Women were going to be respected. But people higher up on the ladder noticed that the wheels were turning, and they stepped in to stop them. To this day, I am sure that the State Department was involved in trying to end the culture wars. You can see the dossiers they kept on John Lennon, Bob Dylan, everyone else who had similar influence. Freedom's dangerous because it lets you think for yourself, and no one who's trying to protect their power wants a society full of free-thinking people.

OPEN UP YOUR FUNKY MIND
AND YOU CAN FLY

We saw the way that the late sixties were peeling away from the Summer of Love. We sensed the seventies coming. And in that rip in time that had opened up, we made our second Funkadelic album, *Free Your Mind . . . and Your Ass Will Follow*. It dealt with lots of the things that were in the air at that time: issues of social control, self-awareness, the failure of intellectuals to connect their utopian philosophies to what was actually happening on the street. We recorded the album quick, over a matter of days, which gave it a unified feel and a unified philosophy. It was also the first time that I tried to match the power of the band— that mix of hard rock and prog rock, of deep soul and classical composition—with appropriate lyrics, and to write something with deep meaning that gestured toward something larger and more literary. Of course, when I say "deep meaning," all I really mean is a kind of poetry. Lots of people were writing protest songs, from Country Joe and the Fish to Buffalo Springfield to Barry McGuire. Some were better than others, but all of them had a kind of earnest fervor. I moved in the other direction. To me, all the social and psychological content seemed funny, especially the most serious ideas: life, death, social control.

When you stayed there, hanging in the space between comedy and tragedy, between reality and surreality, a kind of wisdom started to come through you.

The two artists who did this better than anyone else, obviously, were the Beatles and Bob Dylan, which is why they not only survived the era but set the tone for everything that came afterward. When the pressure started to mount for them to be spokespeople, when fans and reporters started fishing around for deep thoughts, they had sharp-enough instincts to deflect and say something off the wall. They made an art out of nonsense. Even when John Lennon got in trouble for saying that the band was bigger than Jesus, he was doing it sarcastically and snottily, to make a point. He wriggled so you couldn't catch him. It got into his art, too, and you can see it clearly in a song like "I Am the Walrus." Was it deep because it showed how shallow everyone else was? Was it making fun of the idea of being deep? Was it just a matter of opening people's heads up a little wider than they had been before? It was the same with Bob Dylan, though it took me longer to understand how he was operating. At first, he seemed especially sincere: just a guy out there with his guitar, singing in a nasal voice about love and politics. But when I started seeing his interviews, and then especially when he broke out of that troubadour mold, I saw more clearly what he was. He was a poet, and he was using language to open things up.

Those two influences fed me during that first phase of Funkadelic, along with many others. I was also doing lots of reading: Black Power books, novels, pulpy shit, underground comics, and then all those bestsellers that people now think of as the classics of the hippie era. One of the most influential books of that time was Erich Von Däniken's *Chariots of the Gods*. Everyone had a copy of it. He had a theory that the greatest achievements of human history, from the pyramids to crop circles, were the work of aliens. They had come down from outer space and given the gift of advanced civilization to humans. Why else would the Egyptians embalm somebody to last so long and put all their belongings in the tomb with them unless they thought that they'd be collected later on? Maybe the aliens were coming back for the pharaohs. It was an intriguing idea that didn't seem entirely crazy on its face. It seemed like something to explore. These ideas of serious wisdom, these intriguing theories that bordered on historical conspiracy, they all got mixed together in my head. Or maybe it's more accurate to say that they were dissolved in acid. *Free Your Mind . . . and Your Ass Will Follow* was written almost entirely on LSD. You can hear it in the guitar sound we got, and the way we produced it, and you can read it in the lyrics and the song titles.

It was also the true beginning of another phase in black music. There had been hints of social awareness a year earlier, when songs like "Cloud Nine" found the old guard moving tentatively into this new space. But that was nothing compared to what was starting to happen. In the summer of 1970, Marvin Gaye went into the studio to start work on *What's Going On*. Later that year, Sly and the Family Stone started recording what was essentially their answer record, *There's a Riot Goin' On*. *Free Your Mind* was released right at the head of that new trend. I felt the same obligation they did, probably, but I dealt with it differently. We were tripping like this, and so when we turned the tape on and the band started to play I started to improvise lyrics, monologues, and slogans. The title track begins with pings and hums and the sound of a radio tuning. Then I come in with the title chant.

There are lots of voices there, some that sound like children, some that sound like women. It's not until about two minutes into the song that the music arrives: a funky guitar part and then a highly distorted sci-fi organ on top of it. It would set a kind of pattern for Funkadelic, for a little while at least, to kick off an album with an abstract manifesto. After that, there are more traditional funk-rock songs. "Friday Night, August 14th" is a paycheck and party song, getting your income-tax refund and going to town with it, though there's a dark undercurrent. "I Wanna Know If It's Good to You" is a fairly traditional love song with poetic lyrics ("You make my heart beat sweeter than / the honey that replaced the rain"). There's a track on there called "Fish, Chips and Sweat" that's a Funkadelicized remake of "Headache in My Heart," which I had done back at Golden World with a group called the Debonaires. *Free Your Mind* was sung all over the place, in the sense that lots of different people took lead vocals. Billy Nelson did "Friday Night, August 14th." Eddie Hazel did "I Wanna Know If It's Good to You." Even Tawl Ross had a lead on "Funky Dollar Bill," which was a deeply funky piece about consumerism and capitalism, how they distorted the social fabric and erased real responsibility.

There are people who say that the album is antireligious because of the way the title song talks about the kingdom of heaven, and because of the spiritual overtones of the last song, "Eulogy and Light." Musically, that song is another collage, with backward playing and vocals, disembodied noises, and just about every other effect you can imagine. But thematically it's a close cousin to "Funky Dollar Bill." I was seeing the beginnings of a kind of materialism springing up around me, and it was at its worst where people had the least. I couldn't see how it made sense for the poorest communities to plant the seeds of self-destruction.

> *Our father which art on Wall Street, honored be thy buck*
> *Thy kingdom came, this be thy year, from sea to shining sea*

For the backing melody, we used "Father, Open Our Eyes," a song from the mid-fifties by the Gospel Clefs, a group that used to practice in our barbershop in Jersey. It was one of my favorite songs, and the fact that they were locals only strengthened our connection to it. But it was an inside joke rather than an outward gesture. When we used gospel songs, it just confused people further: were we mocking divine music, suggesting some alternative system, or directing it toward sincere ends? Legitimate soul musicians might have had some right to draw upon gospel, but did freaked-out, psychedelically wrecked black rock and rollers? I liked to play with those references because I had no answers. And the monologue that accompanied the music was a parody of the Lord's Prayer, which tangled things even further. When you parody something, you have to pay attention. When you pay attention, you're taking something seriously. So isn't parody the most serious form of imitation?

Right around the time that *Free Your Mind* came out, Jimi Hendrix died. That was the end of an era as certainly as anything else was. He had come up to Toronto in May of 1969 and gotten busted. They had opened his luggage and found drugs right there. I just assumed that it had been planted. Why would he be so stupid as to leave it right on top like that? And so when I heard that he had died, I took it for granted that he had been killed. To me, the music he was making was far too great a threat to the establishment. It was generating questions that no one wanted to answer, and the only other way you can quiet a question is by quieting the questioner.

During the mid-sixties, at Golden World, I got comfortable in the studio, but it was a comfort of its time, with certain limits to what a studio could do and what a label could release. With records like *Free Your Mind*, studio technology had caught up to the sounds in my mind, and I was finally able to make records that were heavy, warped, and weird. We weren't getting paid very much for the records, but we were making enough from them that Armen left us alone in the studio. I was using it as a creative laboratory, trying to capture all the energy of the psychedelic era. There was lots of weather outside—the souring of hippie culture, inner-city rot, both legitimate and illegitimate mind expansion—and lots of weather inside, and it all came together toward the end of 1970 when we went back to United Sound in Detroit to record the third Funkadelic record, *Maggot Brain*.

The leadoff track, which is also the title track, was one of the first things we got down on tape. It opens with a spoken-word piece:

Mother Earth is pregnant for the third time
For you all have knocked her up

What did it mean to taste the maggots in the mind of the universe? Well, it meant all of it: the lack of self-knowledge outlined in "Free Your Mind," the consumerism and short-sightedness in "Eulogy and Light." It was writing that moved away from prose and even poetry into a kind of sloganeering. That made it compact, mysterious, and memorable. But the song's immortality came from Eddie Hazel's guitar solo, which occupied most of the rest of the ten-minute track. I remember recording the solo, of course. It's possible I'll never forget. Eddie and I were in the studio, tripping like crazy but also trying to focus our emotions. There was a band jam going, a slow groove I knew he could get into, and we were trying to launch his solo. Before he started, I told him to play like his mother had died, to picture that day, what he would feel, how he would make sense of his life, how he would take a measure of everything that was inside him and let it out through his guitar. Eddie was the kind of player who rose to a challenge. If you gave him instructions or a prompt, he'd come around to it. And when he started playing, I knew immediately that he understood what I meant. I could see the guitar notes stretching out like a silver web. When we played the solo back, I knew that it was good beyond good, not only a virtuoso display of musicianship but also an almost unprecedented moment of emotion in pop music. That was the missing ingredient that arrived in time for that song; it was maybe the first time that our emotional ability as artists matched our technical ability as players.

But there's a science behind the art. It's one thing to hear that kind of performance in the studio, and another thing to communicate it on a record. We had other engineers with us, people with more training than I had, people who had been doing it longer and had better professional credentials, but I was the one who knew that things needed to be different. When Eddie played originally, it was over a more traditional slow band jam. I took all the other instruments off the track and then I Echoplexed everything back on itself four or five times. That gave the whole thing an eerie feel, both in the playing and in the sound effects. There's a noise at the beginning of the song that's a chattering or chewing, and people sometimes ask if it's the sound of maggots feasting on the brain. I can't say that it was. I was just trying for something fucked-up and novel. Many groundbreaking effects happened that way. Sly and the Family Stone had recorded a song called "Sex Machine" a few years before, and it sounds like Sly's vocals are electronically processed. In fact, he was singing through a toilet paper roll covered with paper and feeding that through a wah-wah pedal. Back at Motown, they used to stomp on Coke boxes to get percussion noises. I was doing that with the mixing board, and all along trying to monitor how it was making things feel.

Throughout the production of that song, the other engineers who were working there with us, the professionals, stood down—or rather, they got up from the board. They heard things through professional ears, how in some places it would just overload and crack. They weren't willing to say it would work, but they also wouldn't say that it wouldn't, and they weren't all thrilled about having their names on it. "Maggot Brain" didn't necessarily seem like something you'd want on your résumé. As it turns out, though, it's been durable and then some. More than forty years later, I was in New York, playing at B.B. King's Blues Club and Grill with the 2013 version of P-Funk. We didn't play "Maggot Brain" at that show, which was more of a party atmosphere. But that same night, just across the river, there was an electronic music event at the Brooklyn Academy of Music organized by Questlove of the Roots. They had a two-act program that mixed piped-in music with live performance, and it covered some of the giants of European and American composition: Pierre Schaffer, John Cage, Raymond Scott. There was a Stevie Wonder song, "Look Around," which he recorded for *Where I'm Coming From*. And then, closing the first act, there was "Maggot Brain." Since the show was about electronic music, they cut and pasted my opening monologue, sped it up, leaned heavy on the bass. Then that gave way to the guitar solo, Eddie's eternal solo, which was played by Kirk Douglas, the Roots' guitarist. The song's essence—that sense of loss and powerlessness, that spirituality of despair, the slight surge of hope when your feet touch the bottom of the ocean—came clearly across the decades, undimmed.

For the rest of the album, I tried to keep the same sense of scale. My first drafts were usually about personal matters—a romantic injury from a woman, my own feelings of inadequacy or fear. But before I put songs on a record, I tried to transform them into something universal or philosophical. On the one hand, I wanted Funkadelic to reach upward and outward. That was the band's charter. But I didn't want to go for something small and finely observed, because that meant that I'd be going head-to-head with the kinds of songs that Smokey Robinson had written, and I knew that was a battle that I'd lose. That's what helped shape a song like "Can You Get to That," which was a reworking of a Parliaments song called "What You Been Growing." The original was a fairly straightforward love song in the Northern Soul mode. For the *Maggot Brain* recording, I fed it through a kind of philosophical filter, adding a descending acoustic guitar line that put it roughly in the company of soul-folk songs like "For What It's Worth" and emphasizing the universal meaning in the lyrics:

I once had a life, or rather, life had me
I was one among many or at least I seemed to be

Later on in the song, there's a quote from Martin Luther King Jr.'s "I Have a Dream" speech that borrowed the metaphor of the checkbook, of—in a social or romantic relationship—writing a check promising love or devotion or freedom that would come back stamped "insufficient funds." The idea of social progress came to the fore. The idea of romantic vows receded. That gave the whole song the feel of a manifesto about civil rights and civil justice.

At that time the band was basically Eddie and myself, at least for the process of figuring out the hooks, and then Billy and Eddie would flesh out the music as I worked on the lyrics. I had gotten the band into all-out psychedelia over the years, and what had been an implication before was now a master plan. On "Super Stupid," we were trying to write a new kind of rock and roll song that kept the bass foundation of soul music while absorbing some of Hendrix's innovations. "You and Your Folks" was built around a stage chant that was actually a nursery rhyme I had picked up from my mother. "Back in Our Minds," which I did with Tawl Ross, was our imitation of the English rock groups of the period. And "Wars of Armageddon," the closing track, was a sonic collage with elements of free jazz, though we didn't think of it as jazz in that sense. When Miles Davis heard the drumming on the track, he loved it so much that he came and took Tiki from us to drum with his band for a little while. That's one of Tiki's claims to fame. The other is that his drum part from "Good Old Music" is the second-most-sampled break in the hip-hop era, trailing only Clyde Stubblefield's work in James Brown's "Funky Drummer."

Maggot Brain also has what might be our most notable early album cover. The first Funkadelic album had a kaleidoscopic portrait of the band. *Free Your Mind* had a woman praying, and then when you opened it up you saw that she was naked. *Maggot Brain* was going places that black groups hadn't gone, into questions about whether America was still on the right path or whether the promise of the late sixties had completely evaporated. One of the first ideas we came up with was a picture of a vampire with pearl fangs and a glass of blood. When you looked closer you could see that the blood in the glass came from squeezed-out tampons. That turned out to be too extreme, even for us. And so we compromised on the final image, the screaming face on the front that turned into the skull on the back. That's the version of the idea that we thought was more acceptable. Can you get to that?

WOULD YOU LIKE TO DANCE WITH ME? WE'RE DOING THE COSMIC SLOP

One night in Cincinnati, Mallia Franklin, one of the vocalists with Funkadelic, told us that we had to go see some young musicians. She said they looked like us, with the same style and the same attitude. We played that night at a club called Graveyard, kind of a hippie place, and after that we went with her to check out these young guys.

The two musicians she wanted us to see were a bassist named William Collins and his brother, a guitarist named Phelps Collins. William, who people called Bootsy, and Phelps, who people called Catfish, had been in a local group called the Pacemakers, and they had done sessions with various stars, including James Brown. One night in Jacksonville, James got in a dispute with his band, the Famous Flames. They thought that monies were owed. James disagreed. Rather than negotiate, he got on the phone with his management and extended an offer to the Pacemakers, who quickly became his new band, the J.B.s. They recorded and performed with James during the lightning-in-a-bottle year of 1970, which produced songs like "Sex Machine," "Talkin' Loud and Sayin' Nothing," and "Superbad," not to mention one of the most towering funk instrumentals of all time, "The Grunt."

But the relationship with James didn't last: he was still the same authoritarian bandleader, and money was still a problem, and the Pacemakers were evolving personally. The Collins brothers left James and started a new group called the House Guests that released a pair of funk singles, one called "What So Never the Dance" and the other called "My Mind Set Me Free." They were moving in the same thematic circles that we were, fully aware of the counterculture and psychedelic styles.

That first night we met Bootsy, I recognized that kindred spirit, though it wasn't much more than a recognition. We didn't talk that much—I acknowledged him and he acknowledged me. Then a little later, someone brought him around in Detroit, and we had a more involved conversation. At right about that same time, some of the younger players in Funkadelic were leaving the band for other projects: Eddie and Billy went off to go work with the Temptations, and Tawl was in and out as a result of his issues with drugs. We had outbound musicians, and the Collins brothers were inbound traffic, so we brought them on. By that point, the widening group of musicians around us also included Garry Shider and Boogie Mosson, from United Soul, both of whom would be instrumental to our growth over the coming decade. Funkadelic had always been a hybrid of other things—at first, of the original Parliaments and the psychedelic rock that was happening all around it—and the second wave of musicians reaffirmed my belief in the way to grow. Absorb youth and you will be absorbed by youth. Take on new influences without fear and you need not fear what is new. Change the people around you by changing the people around you.

★

Funkadelic kept barnstorming. We pretty much lived out on the road, because it didn't pay for us to bounce from city to city for one-night stands. Instead we did ten days in Detroit at the 20 Grand, ten days in Boston at the Sugar Shack, ten days in New York at the Apollo and other theaters. Bigger stages meant bigger backstages, with more access to girls and drugs. I was funny about the girls, or rather they were funny about me. I had such a dark image from Funkadelic that they were scared of me more than anything, and in those rare cases when women would want to be with me . . . well, I was scared of those women. One night we were out on the road, and I was tripping my ass off, with crazy paint all over my face. A girl walked right into the room and announced, to no one in particular, "I'm going to fuck a Funkadelic." Then she looked over at me and said, "But not you." Bootsy and Catfish started calling me Prez, as in the president of the no-pussy-getting club. And I guess it was a role I relished. My favorite thing to do, frankly, was to chase people out of the club with bizarre noises or makeup. That let them preserve the idea they had of me and let me get back to recording and writing.

Drugs were everywhere. They were part of the time, part of youth culture, and part of the musician's life, and we were at the intersection of all three. It was mostly weed; cocaine was a little pricey, though sometimes someone would bring it around, a guy from a record company or a dealer looking for new customers. Whatever the drug of choice, everyone in the band was using acid all the time, still. It cleaned everything up. When you were tripping, you didn't do coke or even drink.

Most of us were users rather than abusers. After 1970, sometimes there would be a bad trip that resulted in a man-down situation. Once Eddie passed me a sherm, a joint laced with angel dust. Angel dust is a pitiful, morbid drug, and that didn't work for me at all. I was so out of it that we played the whole show and then, at the end, took a bow and went right back to the beginning. The band was so high that they didn't notice either. We did two and a half more songs and then I crumpled to the ground, out cold. When I came to, everyone else was standing over me, making sure I was okay. Everybody had one or two episodes like that, but they weren't horror stories, for the most part. The exception was Tiki, who didn't know much about psychedelics or how to control intake; he would fall out high in some corner of a city where we couldn't find him. At times he couldn't work with the band at all and we hired Tyrone Lampkin, a trained jazz player who had a group called Gutbucket in Connecticut. Tyrone was tremendous; he came right in and helped remake the band's sound: louder, both looser and tighter, depending on the song, funkier. Tiki and Tyrone alternated for a few years, traded places in and out of the band.

America Eats Its Young, the double album that Funkadelic released in 1972, is one of the richest stews we ever made. It has the emotional-male anthem "We Hurt Too," the straight funk anthem "Loose Booty," and even "That Was My Girl," another remake of an old Parliaments song. The title track was the third in the trilogy that had started back with "Free Your Mind . . . and Your Ass Will Follow"; like "Maggot Brain," it was a kind of sermon that worried that people were getting out of touch with human rhythms ("A luscious bitch / It's true / It's not nice to fool Mother Nature"). "A Joyful Process" offered an unromantic look at black life in America. "Biological Speculation" pointed forward to sci-fi concept albums like *Mothership Connection* and *Clones of Dr. Funkenstein*. And then there was "Pussy," which we had recorded before as "I Call My Baby Pussycat" on *Osmium*. That more profane title lasted through some of the vinyl pressing, but then Westbound backed down and put the long title back.

As a writer, I was digging deeper into puns and wordplay. I had done it before, but on *America Eats Its Young*, I was doing it all over the place, compulsively. There's a song called "If You Don't Like the Effects, Don't Produce the Cause" that, even in its title, reverses cause and effect. It was a way of bending people's minds and showing them that what they took for granted might not be the truth at all. In other words, it was classic psychedelic thinking, in the sense that you didn't take no—or yes—for an answer, instead tunneling down a little bit to see what else might be there beyond the binary. Most of all, that kind of punning was in keeping with the temper of the times: slang was increasingly popular because of drugs and Black Power and inner-city talk. Smokey Robinson had achieved precision in his writing. He wrote the way that Shakespeare had, with occasional detours into Ogden Nash. The stars of the early seventies took it in another direction. Listening to Sly Stone was like taking a master class in brilliant nonsense. You could talk to that motherfucker for twenty minutes and not understand a word of what he was saying, though you also understood that he was saying everything. Sly, of course, was building on an old tradition of hepcats and jazz speak, going all the way back to Cab Calloway and continuing through Lord Buckley, but he was doing it in the early seventies, when black America was onstage in a different way. When Sly went on Dick Cavett and acted too cool for school, when he clowned the white establishment by mumbling, that was power politics in the purest sense. Smokey was "You Really Got a Hold on Me," but Sly was slippery.

We were starting to rotate in our new members. Bootsy and Catfish, along with the rest of the House Guests—Chicken Gunnels on trumpet, Rob McCullough on tenor sax, and Kash Waddy on percussion—appeared on "Philmore," which Bootsy sang in a more traditional style than he'd later become known for. It's uptempo funk rock, with a little bit of James Brown in the precision, and a lyric ("Everybody's got a problem but you don't even give a damn") that was either about scorned love or social awareness or both.

The cover is an illustration of a (funky) dollar bill that showed America as it really was: corrupt and debauched, consuming resources in a way that benefited the rich at the expense of the poor. The liner notes were equally philosophical. There was a group called the Process Church that had been founded by a British couple as an offshoot of Scientology, and in the late sixties they started hanging out with the band, mainly in Boston. They would feed the kids in Boston Common and they ran what was basically the first day-care center that I can remember, offering to watch children when mothers went to work. We ended up excerpting some of their thinking in the *Maggot Brain* liner notes, which seemed fine at the time—it was a form of self-actualization, not an uncommon or unpopular philosophy at the time. We did the same thing for *America Eats Its Young*, but with far different results. In the summer of 1969, a career criminal (and part-time songwriter) named Charles Manson led a band of followers on a killing spree in upscale residential neighborhoods in Los Angeles, murdering a number of people, including Roman Polanski's wife, Sharon Tate. The killers were under the influence of a crazy-quilt mythology that somehow tied together the Beatles' "Helter Skelter," race war, and Satan worship. There was some thought that Manson had drawn on some of the writings of the Process Church. I thought there was a difference—he talked about something called the Final Church of Judgment, and the group hanging around with us was the Church of Final Judgment—but this was probably too fine a distinction for a public still trying to get a handle on a killing spree. *Rolling Stone* gave us a hard time for the association in their review.

There were real-life consequences, too. Right around the time we finished up this record, we were out in California. Half of the band must have gotten the same pussy, so one by one they went off to the clinic. Fuzzy Haskins had a bad reaction to the shot, and having heard on the radio all day about the Family murders, he started rambling about the band right there in the clinic, explaining how we weren't connected to Manson at all but somehow, in his not-entirely-coherent monologue, making it seem like maybe we were. We were strangers in California at that time. People didn't know shit about us. We looked weird, and we had weird ideas. The notion that we had anything to do with Manson caused a tremendous problem for a little while.

California was a rarity. For the most part, we were back East and in the Midwest, touring hard as always. One night, Calvin was driving and I dozed off. When I woke up, the grass was parting in front of us and trees were whizzing by on the left. Calvin was still in the driver's seat, but with his head down on one shoulder, snoring lightly. I couldn't reach the wheel, so I started to whisper to him so he wouldn't wake up alarmed. He resurfaced with a look in his eyes that was so calm that it must have been desperate, took the car up the embankment, fishtailing like a motherfucker the whole way. Fuzzy and Grady woke up, too, and they cheered him on: "You got it, Calvin." Heads were hitting the ceiling of the car, but we ended up right back on the highway, like we had never left.

A little later on, we hired a girl named Sharon to drive us from show to show. One evening she lost control of the vehicle. "Uh-oh," she said. And then just like that, the car rolled over three times, amusement-park style, and landed right back on its wheels. She turned to face the rest of us, not fazed in the least. "You all fine?" she said. She was something else, Sharon. We all thought she was corny and lame. We used to mock her behind her back and maybe a little bit to her face. "I know you all don't think I know anything," she said. "Why don't you come to a party with me?" She took us to a party with Bobby Orr of the Boston Bruins. It was a hell of a thing. Someone took a Pepsi-Cola bottle and pushed it up inside this girl and then the girl couldn't get it out and no one else could either. The suction was keeping it in there. They had to find a metal rod and smack down on the bottle, which was hanging out from between this girl's legs. Right after the bottle broke, I looked over at the other guys from the band and raised my eyebrows. They knew what I was thinking: Damn, Sharon may be lame, but she has some hardcore friends.

Out on the road, we were still playing with a wide range of groups, extending our reach by meeting new audiences. We didn't have any trouble, for the most part, as a black band playing to largely white crowds. The only time I can remember any problem at all was during a show where we opened for Black Oak Arkansas. They were popular at the time, and we knew that meant we'd have to prepare for a certain amount of heckling that had nothing to do with race—if you go on before the Stones, you have to know that you're delaying a crowd's access to the Stones. But this crowd got dark quick. They started singing "Dixie" and wouldn't stop. Bernie bailed us out. He was on the organ and he played a version of the song that was epic—it wove through classical music, rock and roll, the roaring twenties, even Gregorian chants. He took those motherfuckers on an expedition. By the end, they were laughing. He just wore them out.

When we'd come off the road and go home to Canada, we'd check our fan mail. Some of it was negative—people who still wanted to worry about the Process Church, people who thought black musicians should leave rock to the white musicians—but much of it was supportive, and many of those letters were from like-minded fans who were themselves artists. Around 1972 or so, we started to get letters from a young artist in Chicago named Pedro Bell. He doodled these intricate, wild worlds, filled with crazy hypersexual characters and strange slogans. After a few months of delivering Pedro's letters to us, the Postmaster General wanted to know if I was involved in some kind of subversive organization, because he was certain that these marginal drawings couldn't be part of conventional society.

Pedro's correspondence gave me an idea for how we could move Funkadelic up a notch, how we could take what we were doing musically, and onstage, and capture some of that anarchic energy in the album packages. Up until that moment I had done the gatefolds myself—I had worked with photographers on *Maggot Brain* and *Free Your Mind*, and with illustrators on *America*

Eats Its Young—but when I looked at Pedro's letters I started writing him back, and then calling him, to discuss the ideas that were circulating through the band, this idea of highlighting certain problematic aspects of American society but doing it with a sense of humor. They were crystallizing into our next record, which we were calling *Cosmic Slop* after its title track, which was a deep, funky song about a woman who turns to prostitution to support her family. Lots of soul and rock acts were engaging in social commentary at that time, as the hangover of Vietnam changed the way the nation thought about itself. A song like Marvin Gaye's "Inner City Blues," while brilliant, was more digestible by the mainstream: Motown artists were staying more or less in the soul pocket, coming out slightly to the contemporary rock crowd with a wah-wah pedal. We were accustomed to ranging so far and wide that we couldn't see the place where we had started from, and even if "Cosmic Slop" couldn't possibly be as extreme as "Free Your Mind," it wasn't as conventional as "Papa Was a Rolling Stone," either. We wanted both the chromatics of Jimi Hendrix and a realistic shot at the radio.

I talked through the title song with Pedro on the telephone, and his mind translated it into a strange vision, told in a half-visual and half-verbal language. When he sent us his interpretation, I was blown away—it included pimps and hos, some of which were drawn as aliens with little worms coming out of them. It was nightmarish and funny and beautiful, a perfect fit for the music we were making, and it became the cover art for *Cosmic Slop*. Even then, Pedro didn't really want to take too much in the way of payment. He had a day job at a bank in Chicago, though he doodled constantly on his clothes. His mother used to tell me, "George, will you explain to him that this is reality, that this is life?'" He saw the bank as a way of earning wages and the art as a way of expressing himself, and in his mind there was no overlap.

To this day, Pedro's covers are many people's point of entry for Funkadelic albums. When people talk about *Cosmic Slop*, for example, they talk as much about the cover art as anything else: the way that the screaming face is inset into the woman's Afro, her vampire fangs, the map on one nipple and the stereo dial on the other, the strange yellow bug off to the right of the woman with Pedro's signature along its body. Or at least I think it's yellow. I'm color-blind, and many of his finest drawings are so close together value-wise that I can't really make them out. I've had them described to me a thousand times by fans and other band members, and maybe that's no substitute for the original art, but as another song from *Cosmic Slop* explains, "You can't miss what you can't measure."

The rest of that album worked within the tone set by the title song—in strangeness, in style, in broad scope and gallows humor and visionary imagination. There's "Nappy Dugout," a vicious, low groove that Boogie brought us wedded to a lyrical idea I got from something a girl said to me about pussy: "You're just trying to get some nappy dugout." Lots of ideas arrive along that route, from what you hear somebody say or what you think you hear them say. Boogie's track was so funky that I didn't have to add too many words to it; my job was to make my point and get out of the way. The final step was to let Bernie take his shot at it, add his keyboard parts around the bass. Bernie, like Sly, liked Bach quite a bit, and both of them used his theory of counterpoint, which is about setting melodies up on top of one another to create something larger. Bernie's understanding was a bit more classical than Sly's, but both had a way of making different parts that wove in and out of each other.

Cosmic Slop also included one of our most direct protest songs, "March to the Witch's Castle," which dealt with the plight of soldiers returning from Vietnam. It was structured like a sermon, or a news report followed by a benediction.

We were hippies, sure, and we were opposed to the war—most of youth culture was—but we never had anything against the soldiers. They did the bravest thing imaginable, and we had known some of them. "March to the Witch's Castle" was a song that reflected the headlines—the album came out only months after the start of Operation Homecoming, which brought back the first POWs—but also one that reached far back into pop-music history. In 1959, a soul singer named Dee Clark released a song called "Hey Little Girl (in the High School Sweater)" on Abner Records, which was a sublabel of Vee-Jay. The B-side was a ballad, "It Wasn't for Love," with a high, keening melody, and I used it for "March to the Witch's Castle." But when you take something, you have to treat it right. We had a guitarist in Funkadelic named Ron Bykowski who had started as a roadie but learned to play on a Les Paul guitar, which has what guitar players call sustain—once you get a note, you can hold it forever. When I brought around "It Wasn't for Love," he took it right up and turned it into something completely new. He's also on another song on the record, "No Head, No Backstage Pass," where he has an amazing solo. He played it forward but it sounds backward. That one has become a hip-hop staple: Public Enemy sampled it and Rakim did, too.

Cosmic Slop was an example of how we could only get to political songwriting through outré songwriting. Straightforward political messages came with risks: risks of being ejected from the pop realm, risks of resistance, and so on. Marvin Gaye largely

Even from the beginning, I looked like I was coming out of the
Mothership.

The father of the father of funk: my dad, also George Clinton.

The Parliaments, letter sweaters and all, in 1955.

Funkadelic in 1970, Armen Boladian at right.

Music for your mother: me, my mom, and my brothers.

With the family, in the seventies.

At home with Liz, Barbarella, Kim, and Tracey in 1972.

The fur is flying: me in full regalia, at the height of P-Funk.

Casablanca promotion head Cecil Holmes, two gentlemen
from the House of Lords—the other Parliament—and me,
holding my spokesperson.

Emerging from the Mothership.

What's more dapper than a diaper? Onstage with Garry Shider.

Stretchin' out with Bootsy Collins at Disneyland.

14

The nose knows: me in Sir Nose garb, in the seventies.
That's not Elvis in the background.

15

Up against the wall,
you mothers: the band,
including Garry Shider
and Eddie Hazel.

Bernie Worrell, Debbie Wright, and me.

Funkadelics on parade: with Grady, Fuzzy, Boogie, and Eddie.

Touring *Funkentelechy* in the late seventies: Gary "Mudbone" Cooper, skinny me, Larry "Sir Nose" Heckstall.

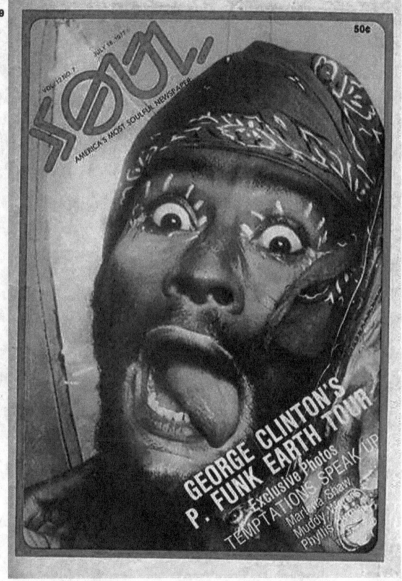

I'm no numerologist, but I like this *Soul* magazine cover from the
seventh month of the seventy-seventh year.

Black is the brightest color: patchwork in 1977.

Has anybody seen Sir Nose? P-Funk artists Pedro Bell
and Overton Loyd, the men who made the images that
made the images that made the men.

Blonds have more fun: at the microphone with Garry Shider.

Michael "Clip" Payne goes under the sea, with one of the *Motor Booty Affair* tour costumes designed by Larry LeGaspi.

Military men: Archie Ivy, Nene Montes, Raymond Spruell,
and me, as General Chaos.

The General in his chambers.

backed off of protest songs after "What's Going On." Curtis Mayfield remained topical but detoured into film soundtracks. There was one principal exception to that rule, and he was a principal exception to every rule: Stevie Wonder. If you were Stevie Wonder, you could do anything you wanted. He had started young enough to be able to absorb lessons from everyone else: Marvin, Smokey, Ray Charles, James Brown, and so on. He could do a soul cover of Dylan's "Blowin' in the Wind" when he was a teenager, and then start to write his own socially conscious material, never losing sight of the pop market.

As we evolved, other black music icons were in transition. It was a strange time for James Brown. He was still doing it like he did, but he was mostly about singles, which were a dying market. The only consistently impressive thing he put out during that period was the 1972 live Apollo record. Onstage he was that motherfucker still, even in his forties, and I saw plenty of bands who spent their entire careers trying to tap into that same energy. Other bands were regional stars: Dyke and the Blazers in Buffalo, Chuck Brown in D.C., the Meters in New Orleans. I kept track of all those bands, but because of my interest in reaching a broader audience, I was thinking as much about rock acts like Led Zeppelin, the Who, and Jimi Hendrix. Jimi was on my mind constantly during the time we were recording *Cosmic Slop*. I thought about where he started from and how far out he had gone. He had gone so far out, in fact, that he had to come back to earth a bit, first with *Electric Ladyland* and then with *Band of Gypsies*, which was a hell of a record but was more conservative, his take on contemporary R&B. Jimi wasn't the only one. Eric Clapton came back from Cream and started making traditional rock and roll, which turned into roots music. Sly went out there, but he couldn't stay out there long. We got out there, nearly, with *Cosmic Slop*, and the view was breathtaking, but the air was thin. So we came back, too, following Isaac Newton's most basic principle: for every upstroke there is an equal and opposite downstroke.

EVERYBODY GET UP FOR
THE DOWN STROKE

Neil Bogart was an East Coast guy like me, and like me he had drifted into the Midwest during the sixties. He was a singer at first, and he recorded a few singles that made the chart, including one called "Bobby," but a few singles didn't make for a career, and Neil stayed in the record business by becoming a big shot on the business side. He ran the Midwestern offices of the Cameo-Parkway label before the feds shut it down for stock fraud, and then he went back to New York to head up Buddah Records, where he was a master of radio pop. With bands like the Ohio Express and the 1910 Fruitgum Company, he practically invented bubblegum. In Detroit, we knew each other around town, liked each other in style and substance both. When Jeffrey Bowen had called me about the record that became *Osmium*, I had dreams of pairing with Neil, who was distributing Hot Wax, but we ended up at Invictus instead.

Soon after Funkadelic released *America Eats Its Young*, I heard that Neil was putting together a new label with the backing of Warner Bros. He wanted to call it Casablanca, which was a typical Neil move. It had always been his favorite movie because of his last name, but it was also opportunistic because the movie rights resided with Warner Bros., which meant he could use the name without fear of legal repercussions. He always had a vision, and his plan for Casablanca involved complete radio dominance. Interestingly, though, he imagined that it would happen through bands who were making types of music that weren't quite on the radio yet. He signed Kiss (they came on at the same time as we did) and Donna Summer (she arrived a few years later), and within a few years Casablanca dominated seventies radio in multiple categories: heavy metal, disco, and, of course, funk.

But what was funk? More to the point, what was P-Funk? After the *Osmium* record, and Invictus's mishandling of it, the Parliament name drifted back to us. At the very least, Invictus was in no position to do anything if we started using it again— they had more or less fallen apart as a label. I was ready to restart Parliament for Casablanca, though this time around I had a different idea about what the band would sound like. In the *Osmium* era, Parliament had been an outlet for the Motown side of our personality, the place where more traditional material went, and Funkadelic had been our chance to stretch out—in length of songs, in subject matter, in philosophy and image. But the message got a little muddled by the weaker production style. From the start, the second-generation Parliament was conceived as something a little different. I wanted to do a record in the style of the Beatles—horns, strings, complex arrangements—but also aim straight for radio R&B. It was like jazzy James Brown, or a pop Pink Floyd. We had a huge stable of musicians at this point and we were learning to use everyone properly, figuring out who could contribute riffs, who was best at decorating existing songs, who could come up with the best slogans.

When I brought the idea to Neil, he was excited, but he had one major stipulation. If we were going to move forward with Parliament, we needed a more traditional front man. He was as clear about this as Dave Kapralik had been in the *Osmium* days. Though this was an extremely conventional model, it was radical for us. Funkadelic was a band that was sprawling and democratic. We moved out in all directions, stylistically and otherwise. We used the wings of the stage. Now we were being told that if Parliament was to be reborn on Casablanca, it would need a clear focal point. I agreed, somewhat reluctantly. I didn't necessarily see things the same way as Neil. But I also knew that Neil was the only record man who could get on board with our ideas, and even advance them. He was that energetic, that innovative, that committed to his artists. The trick, then, was to find a front man. Bootsy was still a few years away from being able to do that for us. He was a Bootsy-in-waiting, really: a William still. So the responsibility fell to me.

Fairly quickly, we realized that a band aiming for the radio needed a killer song: more than that, a title song for the first album. We hadn't gone that route before. When we put out *Osmium*, we were still in the frame of mind of album artists. There was no song called "Osmium" because there didn't need to be. And while Funkadelic had plenty of title songs, from "Maggot Brain" to "Cosmic Slop," they weren't exactly commercial singles. I was thinking along those lines when, in the middle of a jam session, like "Testify" before it, I thought of "Up for the Down Stroke." The riff was something we had been toying around with, and all of a sudden the lyrics came to me. It was everything all at once: sexy, paradoxical, and even a little political, if you looked at it a certain way. Most of all, it was catchy as hell, the kind of thing an audience would chant if a band was playing it onstage.

Like many of my ideas, it probably would have been lost to time if it hadn't been for the people around me, especially Archie

Ivy. Archie had started as a journalist who first hung out with the band in the *Maggot Brain* years, when he was reporting for *Soul* magazine. He was from Los Angeles, though his cousin had been close to Eddie Hazel in New Jersey. I liked having Archie around, and other people like him—Tom Vickers, from *Rolling Stone*, was another one—because I understood that they were the message makers, the designers and disseminators of what we liked to call "impropaganda." Archie became a regular in the P-Funk camp and then a member of the inner circle. When we restarted Parliament for Casablanca, he became essential, in part because he was the one who wrote down all the crazy ideas and began to organize them into a coherent message. If I made a joke or a pun, if I spouted a slogan just for fun, Archie would get it down on paper, where it started to take on a more profound significance. It's a good thing, too, because my handwriting and my spelling were awful. I could have had every good idea in the world, and no one would have been able to find them for shit. Archie's official title was personal manager, which increasingly meant confidant and soundboard and brain annex.

The rest of the album followed in the footsteps of "Up for the Down Stroke," though much of it was an exercise in listening to old tracks with new ears. There were some songs from the old Parliaments catalog that we hadn't been able to do—or do justice to—as Funkadelic, so we picked them back up and remade them with our new sound in mind. We redid "The Goose (That Laid the Golden Egg)." We redid "All of Your Goodies Are Gone." And, of course, we redid "Testify." Why not? Even though it had been a big hit for the Parliaments, the conventions of the time had hemmed it in. Finally, on *Up for the Down Stroke*, I got to record it the way I had originally imagined it. We had Bernie. We had

Bootsy. We had Tiki. We had a half decade of constant touring and the momentum of new ideas. It was like a painter going back to the same river bridge and creating another canvas.

The cover of *Up for the Down Stroke* tries to deliver on all the consolidated innovation. It's a blurry photo of me surrounded by a trio of women, and I'm wielding a whip. The idea came from Cholly Bassoline, our manager at that time, and fit in with other things that were happening in R&B around that time—especially the S&M-themed covers of the Ohio Players, a Dayton soul and funk group that had been a labelmate of ours at Westbound. Our imagery was more theatrical, with more elaborate costumes, and maybe it was more comic than dark, but I didn't exactly love it at the time. It wasn't the visual match for our music that I wanted. We even did a video for that album, though it was more like a commercial. Joyce, Neil's wife, who was very involved in the imagery of the label's bands, went with me to the West Fourth Street basketball courts and made a short film that showed me dancing up and down the street in tall boots with a boom box on my shoulder that was playing "Up for the Down Stroke." Now they show it as a video on YouTube, but at the time it was a commercial that ran on TV.

The single quickly became our first top-ten R&B hit. You heard it everywhere: I think I was in Los Angeles the first time it came on the radio. But the record business was never easy. Just as Neil was putting out the album, Casablanca and Warner Bros. had a falling-out. Warners was having trouble with the manufacturing side and couldn't focus on promotion and other aspects of the business, so Neil went to Mo Ostin, the chairman of Warners, to complain, after which Mo released Neil from the deal. Casablanca went out into the world as an independent label. This was great news for freedom, though slightly more worrisome for finance. To make money, Neil came up with a scheme: he bought up the record rights to *The Tonight Show with Johnny Carson* and released a double album of highlights, which he distributed through a new deal he struck with Polygram. It didn't do as well as Neil had hoped, and things were a little rocky there for a while, but I never lost my confidence in Neil.

The way he handled us on tour was proof of that. We revisited all the spots in the Northeast that were part of our regular circuit, but he also focused on a new set of cities: Chicago, St. Louis, Nashville, and especially Washington, D.C. Neil made sure that we were doing promotional work in all formats—R&B, rock, pop. Funkadelic had been popular mostly with FM rock stations and college programmers, but "Up for the Down Stroke" brought us back to R&B for real. I started hooking back up with lots of the DJs I had known in the mid-sixties, people like Butterball Jackson in Baltimore and Frankie Crocker in New York. In fact, playing off the personas of the black radio jocks would become a central part of Parliament's identity. One thing about Neil and the people he worked with—Jheryl Busby and Cecil Holmes, especially—is that they never separated R&B from pop when it came to promotions. There was a division at the radio level, so at most labels there was a competition between different parts of the staff. Would the song break pop or break R&B? Who would get credit? Neil had a very diverse roster and he made sure that all promotions staffers were able to move freely between categories.

What did it mean to have a hit like "Up for the Down Stroke"? The easy answer is that it meant everything, that it was a dream come true, the cherry on the sundae of the fifteen years I had spent making records. The true answer is that it didn't feel like a big deal at the time. I was always so busy pushing forward creatively, trying to come up with the next big thing, that chart success changed my immediate surroundings without affecting my destination. The success brought more money in the short term, which increased the number of hangers-on and improved the quality of drugs. But even that wasn't as drastic as it was with some other bands, largely because when we made money, we spent it on new sessions, new equipment, tour props. That arrangement seemed to work for everyone. Neil never even minded that we were maintaining our existence as Funkadelic at the same time that we were blowing up as Parliament. I would let him come in and listen to the tracks, and if there was one he felt strongly about keeping with Parliament, I'd let it go that way.

Handling it like business—if a song sounded like Parliament, it was Parliament—actually helped us maintain our split personality. The very same month that *Up for the Down Stroke* was released, we released *Standing on the Verge of Getting It On* as Funkadelic. It was the least Parliament-like album imaginable, an exercise in guitar excess. By this point, most of the core Funkadelics had been in and out of the band more than once, and *Standing on the Verge* was a kind of reunion for me and Eddie. We wrote alongside each other for almost the entire record. On the original pressings, those songs are credited to me and to Grace Cook, who was Eddie's mother; he used her name because he didn't want to get hit for the publishing rights. But it was a blazing guitar record from door to door. We picked up one of the Invictus songs, "Red Hot Mama," and set it on fire. And the title song: man, watch that thing go. That's Eddie, primarily, but he taught the part to Garry Shider and Ron Bykowski so that everyone could play in concert.

It was like one of the jams we did onstage, finally captured on record: loud, sloppy, undeniable. I didn't think of it as an anthem, necessarily. It just came out that way. Eddie played his fingers off on every song. You know that old western *Bad Day at Black Rock*? *Standing on the Verge* was a good day.

It was also the growth of Funkadelic as an idea, or a way of life, or a cult, or a comedy troupe, or however you want to see it. I started to hear the way that we were carrying on the legacy of people like Jimi Hendrix and even extending it into a new black rock and roll. That meant that we were off in another country, and we had a language of our own. Ron Bykowski was credited as "polyester soul-powered token white devil." I was "Supreme Maggot Minister of Funkadelia; vocals, maniac froth and spit. Behavior illegal in several states." We used computer-altered vocals more and more, throwing in shit that no one else was doing in pop records. At one point you can hear me, in a squeaky voice, call someone a fat motherfucker. That was Armen's right-hand man, a guy who weighed about four hundred pounds. He pulled his shirt up while we were recording; he was always there doing something gross and nasty. When he wasn't being disgusting, he was responsible for bringing around contracts for assignment of publishing rights. They were usually blank; we were told specifics would be filled in later. We didn't think enough about what we were signing. We were preoccupied with the art, not to mention that we were always at a point where somebody needed money fast. That's how it goes for working musicians, and it wouldn't always work out to our advantage.

If *Standing on the Verge of Getting It On* had some of our most uncompromising music up to that point, it was also a high-water mark for Pedro Bell. His cover was a work of art in every respect.

I told him I wanted a vehicle and a biological entity combined, some sort of living spaceship. What he did with those instructions was staggering. He designed something that was truly visionary, years before any *Robocop* or teledildonics. He drew terrifying monsters and eerie alien landscapes and a line of little tiny characters in the front parading with a flag that reads UNITED STREAKERS FRONT. It was a combination of Ralph Bakshi and Samuel R. Delany and Superfly and Fat Albert and Philip K. Dick and Krazy Kat and Flash Gordon, all mixed together in Pedro's brain with some kind of blender that hadn't even been invented yet. On the back, there's a winged warrior in a chariot, and he's saying, "There's nothing harder to stop than an idea whose time has come to pass! Funkadelic is wot time it is!"

We toured for that album without Eddie. He was flying somewhere, and while he was sitting in his seat waiting for takeoff, he heard something in his ear telling him to get off the aircraft. He was doing so much angel dust that he was higher than the plane. He thought there was a radio in his teeth. He flipped out and struck an air marshal, who arrested him. When the tour stopped in Cleveland, someone came backstage after the show and told us that there was a seventeen-year-old in town who could play "Maggot Brain" like he had written it. We went to his house and saw him play. He played the whole solo. That was Michael Hampton. A few days later, we contacted his family and asked them if he could come out on the road with us, and that went so well that he became part of the permanent band. It was both strange and familiar to have a kid around—it was like a throwback to the days when Fuzzy, Grady, Calvin, and I had to drive around with Billy and his friends in tow.

Mike was part of a repeating phenomenon of bringing in the youngest and the best musicians, because they kept the rest of us young. Even so, it wasn't easy. We were a bigger band by then, with more access to everything both good and bad, and Mike was beside himself at first: sex and drugs and rock and roll, you know. We had to bring in a guy named Lodge, Mike's cousin, to be a chaperone. Lodge ended up working with us for years in management. Even with a chaperone, Mike couldn't hold off all the temptations, and early on that got him into some tough spots. Part of the problem was that he ran with the younger half of the band, Eddie and Billy and Tiki. Tiki was always the furthest out on any ledge. He would drop acid with Mike, and as soon as they were high, he would steal Mike's money or even his clothes. "We forgot to tell you," we told Mike. "You got to protect yourself. When you walk around naked, you ain't got your pants on."

Parliament was, from the start, intended to capture mainstream attention and bend the ear of the radio. Paradoxically, that led me to investigate heavier ideas. For starters, thoughts weren't bitter when they went down candy-coated. You could do things with humor and a nice horn part that you couldn't with an assaultive rock guitar and a twelve-minute jam. That's what ended up pointing me into the heart of the second Parliament album, *Chocolate City*, which came out at the beginning of 1975.

One day, sitting around the house, I heard someone on the news saying that Washington, D.C., was 80 percent black. A little light went on in my head. Damn, I thought, we got the vote. By the rules of any sane democracy, we've already won. And on the heels of that came other thoughts. Sane democracy? That was the blackest black comedy. I started jotting down slogans like "You don't need the bullet when you have the ballot." We had a black mayor in Newark in those days, Kenneth Gibson, the first black mayor elected to run a big American city, even though many of the Black Power people thought he was a patsy who didn't understand the real workings of power. I didn't have any huge amount of admiration for Gibson, but his color was a fact, and that meant that some version of that same situation was about to wash up on the shores of other American cities. I kept taking notes and kept making jokes, and I ended up imagining it forward, all the way to the White House: "They still call it the White House, but that's a temporary condition, too." By the end of the first few pages, I had signed and populated an entire imaginary federal government: President Muhammad Ali, Education Secretary Richard Pryor, Arts Secretary Stevie Wonder, and so on.

The rest of the album didn't quite deliver on its promise. It's not that it was a bad album at all—it's one of my favorites—but it wasn't a fully executed idea the way I wanted it to be. The politics, or the topical commentary, tapered off after the title song. We were a half step away from figuring out how to do that part of it more comprehensively.

On the other hand, the record was a landmark for how it expanded our sound, and much of that expansion came courtesy of Bootsy Collins. His megastardom with his Rubber Band was still a few years off, but *Chocolate City* was really his breakout record. There was a company out of New Jersey called Musitronics that was founded by a guy named Mike Beigel, and he had spent time at another company developing a synthesizer that ended up being abruptly unfunded. He had nowhere to go with his technology, so he rebuilt it as a guitar-effect pedal and went to Bob Moog, the synthesizer pioneer, to help get a patent. That was the Mu-tron

III, and Stevie Wonder used it, and Bootsy used it, too, feeding his bass through it and getting this incredible wah-wah sound. "Ride On," the second song on *Chocolate City*, after the title song, is maybe the best example of Mu-tron funk on that record. It's basically a dance song ("Put a hump in your back / Shake your sacroiliac") with a little detour into questions of personal liberty and integrity ("It ain't what you know, it's what you feel / Don't worry about being right, just be for real"). But the real draw is the bass, which is wah-wahed into outer space, just undeniable from the beginning of the song right up to the end. "What Comes Funky" is like that, too, a solid funk foundation underneath lyrics about dancing and freedom ("I don't need approval to be a mover").

From a bandleader's point of view, Eddie Hazel's accomplishments on that album were spectacular. When you think of how out there he was on *Cosmic Slop* or *Standing on the Verge of Getting It On*, and then look at the control he had as a player on *Chocolate City*, it's mind-boggling to imagine that both styles came from the same person. Much of what he was doing on *Chocolate City* was influenced by Sly and the Family Stone. Sly's bands were never heavy in the rock sense—Freddie Stone, his brother and lead guitarist, never played like Jimi Hendrix, but instead went for a big pop sound. Eddie could move in either direction, and he did. It was like an old-fashioned football player who went two ways, lined up at receiver and then came back as a defensive back.

As the musicians found their voice, the writers and producers worked out a band strategy. In general, Bootsy and I laid down the basic track and then Bernie revised and extended it. Other songs were more conservative, genre numbers basically. "I Misjudged You" came straight from Motown. We had written that at the Brill Building years before for Jobete, and even recorded it as a demo. And then there's "If It Don't Fit (Don't Force It)," which is one of those rare cases where Bernie and I just sat down and cowrote from beginning to end.

Because Parliament was mainstream, because "Chocolate City" was aiming for radio, I made sure to wrap the political statement in humor and a kind of theatrical cloak. It was my way of protecting myself. When I saw artists who stepped out without that cloak, I was scared for them. I was scared for Bob Marley for a long time. He was saying things of import and consequence, and saying them in a straightforward way. That was very dangerous in Jamaica, very dangerous. Over the course of his career as an artist and activist, he crossed wires with legitimate politicians who were mixed up with power brokers and gangsters. It was all high-level shit, world domination and social control. That kind of shit will get you killed. I never wanted that responsibility, not the responsibility of a political spokesperson like Malcolm X or Martin Luther King, and not even the responsibility of a musical spokesperson like Bob Marley. He was almost like a Dalai Lama. Critics and fans were thrusting him into that position even before he knew he was in it. We went the other way, played so crazy that nobody wanted to be connected to us at that level.

As a band, the Wailers were something else. They had transcended just the reggae groove, and they were playing everything from doo-wop to straight pop. Around *Chocolate City*, we crossed paths with Bob fairly often. There was a story going around that Bob had been born in Delaware—that his mother, Cedella, had come up to the States to make sure that her baby was an American citizen. Whenever we saw them on tour, I would call Bob "Delaware," which drove him crazy. We would needle each other about weed, too. He would roll joints that also had tobacco in them, which was the English style, and mock me for being "bougie" and having the money to smoke straight weed. "They got you fucked up wanting that shit," he said. "You've been programmed." Somewhere in the mid-seventies, there came a point where we didn't see him around very much anymore. At the end of 1976, gunmen broke into his house and shot Bob, his wife, and his manager. He wasn't seriously injured, just minor wounds in his chest and arm, but it was a scare. And then after that he had a bad toe injury, which turned out to be an early sign of cancer. Whatever happened to him, in my mind, was a consequence of how big he got. I just felt certain that there were forces trying to take him down, and they weren't going to stop until they had. The same thing happened to John Lennon. The Beatles were a British version of ghetto kids, smart as hell. But peace and love was a dangerous platform. When you talked about it too often, and too prominently, you messed shit up for all the businesspeople in the world who made money off of chaos. If you come in peace and love, they will get rid of you.

★

Once again, we were thinking in pairs: every Parliament album had a Funkadelic twin. In 1975, we delivered our babies in spring—*Chocolate City* came out in March and then, a month later, Funkadelic put out *Let's Take It to the Stage*. When we made that record, we were in the process of extricating ourselves from Westbound and moving over to Warner Bros. I wasn't done with Funkadelic by any means, but our time on Westbound wasn't working for us anymore. It wasn't a financially profitable situation—we would just make a record and Armen Boladian would put it out. We didn't get tour support, really, and he wasn't a creative partner in the way that Neil was. Our attorney, Ina Meibach, along with our manager, Cholly Bassoline, started looking for a new deal for Funkadelic, and found one at Warner Bros.—which was, ironically enough, the label that had parted ways with Casablanca just as *Up for the Down Stroke* was coming out. Leaving Westbound wasn't very complicated. We agreed to finish up with Armen, at which point we'd be free to release new Funkadelic material on Warner Bros. It wasn't even a contractual matter, since we never had a proper contract. The only questions that made it sticky at all in a corporate sense came from the Warner Bros. side: they needed proof that we were free of all prior obligations, that Armen wouldn't turn around and make any claims on us.

Sometimes bands approach the final records they owe a label as a tiresome duty. Funkadelic wasn't that kind of operation. "Good to Your Earhole," the opener, is straight-ahead heavy funk, with one of our best chants: "Put your hands together. Come on and stomp your feet."

We also reinforced our straight funk bona fides with a track called "Stuffs and Things" that we recorded with a drummer named Barry Frost, a white kid who was in an Oakland funk band called Leon's Creation. We shared management with them, and Tiki wasn't there the day we recorded, so we briefly created a kind of hybrid band, a ParliafunkadelicmentLeon's Thing. Another song on that record, "Be My Beach," is maybe the first appearance of the Bootsy character, the high elastic vocals, the elaborate metaphors. It's kind of an early sketch for the underwater boogie that would later turn up on *Motor Booty Affair*, or for that matter on the B-52s' "Rock Lobster." There are tons of puns and references to other songs, like when Bootsy says, "I'd just like to be your bridge over troubled waters, mama / Dig . . . while I smoke on it," which somehow pulls together Simon & Garfunkel and Deep Purple. And then there's the title track, which has all these old nursery rhymes and dozens-style blue humor:

> *Little Miss Muffet sat on her tuffet, snorting some TAC*
> *Along came a spider, slid down beside her, said, "What's in*
>   *the bag, bitch?"*

Andrew Dice Clay used much of that material later, and made quite a bit of money with it. But for us it had a deeper significance. There were always rivalries with other bands, and never more so than when we started to take off. Groups were starting to get jealous of each other. We were on a double bill with Earth Wind & Fire once, and they prevented us from playing. "Let's Take It to the Stage" means "We ain't got to argue and fight— I'll meet you on the stage." In the process of settling scores, we gave those other bands ridiculous names: we called James Brown the Godmother instead of the Godfather, said *Sloofus* instead of Rufus. We even called out Earth, Hot Air, and No Fire. We would end up doing that more and more in Funkadelic, keeping up a line of patter about other pop culture, taking good-natured shots at competitors, the kind of thing that would become popular in hip-hop fifteen years later.

One day we were at Hollywood Sound in Los Angeles, cutting "Get Off Your Ass and Jam," one of the rock-guitar showcases on the record. Eddie Hazel wasn't there, and Michael Hampton, who was the guitarist on the song, was playing on a stack of Pignoses— that's the type of amplifier—rigged together for the rhythm. We finished one take, took a smoke break or something, and noticed that a white kid had wandered into the studio, a smack addict. We didn't know him at all, but he said he played a little guitar, and he wanted to know if he could play with us and pick up a little cash in the process. "You got something I could put a solo on?" he said. "Just give me twenty-five dollars and I'll do it." I guess I could have been offended, or laughed it off, but I figured it differently. As far as I was concerned, if he had enough nerve to say that, to offer his services to Funkadelic, I wanted to see what he could do. So this boy went outside and got his guitar, which didn't even have a case. We set him up, started the track, and he just started to play like he was possessed. He did all the rock and roll that hadn't been heard for a few years, and he did it for the entirety of the track. Even when the song ended, he didn't stop. All of us were up there goggle-eyed, saying, "Damn." We had agreed on twenty-five bucks, but I gave him fifty because I loved it. He pocketed the money, walked out, and that was that. When we played the track back, I was even more impressed. "Get Off Your Ass and Jam" smoked, and over the years it's proven to be one of the most enduring songs from that record. I tried to find the guy and put him on another song, but he was gone. He never resurfaced. We never heard from him. He's not credited on the record because we have no idea who he was.

THERE'S A WHOLE LOT OF
RHYTHM GOIN' ROUND

Our thought, always, was to release albums in twin-like pairs, a Parliament record accompanied by a Funkadelic record. But we were making so much music at that point that we were outpacing the plan. And so in 1975, along with *Chocolate City* and *Let's Take It to the Stage*, we birthed a triplet at a slight delay. The record was called *Mothership Connection*, it arrived in December 1975, and it quickly changed the landscape for all of us.

Chocolate City had set the table for Parliament. It let us see that we were on the move. In its wake, I started to sense that a bigger feast was on the way, in part because I heard what was happening in the music, and in part because I knew that the Casablanca team would put us across. The title song not only became part of the vernacular, but also the name of a spinoff label at Casablanca: Cecil Holmes ran it, and signed artists like the New York City Players, who would soon be known as Cameo. With *Chocolate City* under our belt, Bootsy and I went into the studio and laid down track after track. Some of them sounded like they were Parliament hits, which was a category we were starting to understand: bouncy horn part or smooth R&B ballad or big bass funk.

As I sorted through all the tracks, I knew that they needed a unifying idea, too, not just a theme but a kind of plot. *Mothership Connection* was that idea. Now, with almost forty years of hindsight, people can look back and take it in stride: a concept album based around a crazy alien funk mythology. But at the time, it was harder to understand exactly where the idea came from. Drugs may have had something to do with it: they furnished confidence and momentum and sometimes turned sparks of ideas into bonfires. But it was also the natural—or, if you'd prefer, unnatural—step in our thinking. In *Chocolate City*, we had imagined a black man in the White House. That would take thirty-four years to come true. For *Mothership Connection*, we went even further afield and imagined a black man in space. Joyce Bogart, Neil's wife, had a slightly more limited idea of the concept, which was that a ship had come down from outer space and landed in the ghetto. In fact, that's what she wanted to call it: *Landing in the Ghetto*. In their mind there was a black-liberation dimension, alien beings coming down to save all the poor people. I saw it differently. To me it was pimps in outer space, the spaceship as a kind of high-tech Cadillac. Space was a place but it was also a concept, a metaphor for being way out there the way that Jimi Hendrix had been. Imagining a record in space was imagining artistry unbound, before it was recalled to Earth. I did love science fiction, of course, especially *Star Trek*, because it moved along on its ideas. They came up with some brilliant concepts and developed amazing realities. Plus, they personified the idea of teamwork. Kirk needed Spock. Spock needed Kirk. They both needed Bones, Scotty, and Sulu. All of them together made an entity that could cope with almost anything. They personified the idea of teamwork.

As much as it was a space album, *Mothership Connection* was also a radio album. At the time, radio stations were changing radically. They had been these independent businesses, underground tastemakers. They worked to bring new artists to listeners, and they were as important in shaping the sixties as drugs or free love or any other part of the culture. So in my mind, the concept of *Mothership Connection* wasn't just *Star Trek* in the ghetto, but pirate radio coming in from outer space. It's not thought of in that way as much, at least anymore, but that's at the heart of the album. In fact, it wasn't until I recorded "P-Funk (Wants to Get Funked Up)" that the concept really came together in my head. For that song, and all the ones that followed, I wrote lyrics that were raps, not in the hip-hop sense, exactly, but raps in the style of the Last Poets.

I say the Last Poets, but there are other influences in there as well, Frankie Crocker and Rod Serling and Lord Buckley and Wolfman Jack and dozens of other voices I had heard over the years. Radio was magic. It could transport you to a place without moving you at all. That monologue required a certain voice, and that voice became a character—Lollipop Man, also known as the Long-Haired Sucker.

Mothership Connection refined what we were doing on *Chocolate City*. For starters, we were leaning more heavily on brass. Horns had always been part of soul music, but they were all over rock and roll in the mid-seventies, from Chicago to Blood, Sweat & Tears to Tower of Power. Bootsy knew Fred Wesley from working with James Brown, and Fred brought in Maceo and Michael and Randy Brecker, who were just starting out as the Brecker Brothers after playing with everyone from Aerosmith to Horace Silver to Billy Cobham. It was just unbelievable what we could do with those guys added to what we already had.

In the title song we introduced Star Child, another character, who was an alien who brought funk to Earth. I folded in the *Chariots of the Gods* mythology, sprinkled some contemporary science fiction on the top, and stirred it all together.

> *We have returned to claim the Pyramids*
> *Partying on the Mothership*

There was a great chorus there, too: "If you hear any noise, it's just me and the boys." Neil's appreciation for bubblegum, our musicianship, these new expansive lyrics: I could feel that it was all coming together into a sound that no one else had. I started to see how it could dominate the charts.

The third major song on *Mothership Connection* first occurred to me when I heard the David Bowie song "Fame," which is itself a James Brown–style performance. We had a new drummer, Jerome Brailey, who had come over from the Chambers Brothers, and he was with me when "Fame" came on the radio. "Remember that beat for me," I said. He did, and that's one of the reasons that he got a cowriting credit on that song. Back in the studio we fired up that beat and built it back into "Give Up the Funk (Tear the Roof off the Sucker)," which incorporated chants that we were already doing in concert. With those three songs nailed down, I went into the vault of unreleased tracks and began to retrofit the strongest ones to this new concept. "Unfunky UFO" was a funky track that I knew I could link to the same theme. "Night of the Thumpasaurus Peoples" was an undeniable chant. And "Handcuffs" is a track left over from *Chocolate City*, but we updated it for *Mothership* by adding those alien accents, accelerated voices and such. I had a collaborator on that song, sort of: Janet

McLaughlin, a girl I was seeing in Los Angeles. She had come out from Chicago with a group of young women. They were just out of college, all of them, but they were getting close to stars; one of the girls in her circle was Janis Hunter, who ended up marrying Marvin Gaye. They had this hip Chicago rap, talked about how they were living, how they were making it, and one of the ways they described getting their hooks in men was handcuffs. I liked that idea, so I used it in a song and gave her a cowrite. That was always my theory: give them credit for whatever bullshit they were talking, especially when it was an interesting turn of phrase. That was better than nabbing a star, wasn't it? Publishing credit stuck around long after the man departed. It was real bank that you could count on. And what was the alternative, really? One morning I came out of bed and saw Janet making pancakes. She was pissed off at how I wouldn't ask her to marry me, mumbling angrily to herself loud enough for me to hear. As I got close to the kitchen, I heard her say, "Motherfucker jumping up and down on me for free." It was the funniest fucking thing I ever heard.

★

For the cover photo of *Mothership Connection*, I wanted a spaceship. Who doesn't? Cholly Bassoline went straight to one of the prop stores in Los Angeles, and the next thing you know, we had the actual ship from *The Day the Earth Stood Still*, a classic sci-fi movie from the early fifties. It was your basic flying saucer, classic round, little doorway near the top, and we took a series of pictures sitting on it or near it. And there it was, the first fully mature Parliament record: songs all nailed down tight, concept worked out in advance, artwork in service of the larger idea. It came out in December of 1975. I remember some of the other headlines. The observation deck at the World Trade Center had just opened. There was some news story about China: I think President Ford was visiting there, and they were returning the remains of two navy pilots who had been shot down in the sixties. Our record wasn't the only thing happening in the world, but it was in the world, happening.

We picked "P-Funk (Wants to Get Funked Up)" as the first single. We were all in agreement: everyone in the band, and everyone at Casablanca. It was an R&B record, basically, with slippery horns and a strong hook, and it started killing at the R&B stations immediately. The song was big in the hood. A little while after we released it, though, pop stations got onto "Give Up the Funk (Tear the Roof off the Sucker)." I have to say that none of us saw it coming, though I see in retrospect how it could happen. The song had a catchy pop melody, a memorable catchphrase, and that light and bouncy chant. It wasn't really deep funk like "Mothership Connection." Pop programmers had one little idea. They wanted us to take the chant off the front, the part that said "Tear the roof off the mothersucker," because it bordered on profanity, and they said that if we did it they'd promote the record like crazy. Once we did, and once they did, the effect was immediate. It was like Motown putting out a new Stevie Wonder record, or Atlantic with Aretha. That thing moved like nothing I had ever seen. You could turn on two or three stations one after the other and they all would be playing it. It was in Philly. It was in Detroit. It was in Los Angeles and St. Louis. After a while, even if we were in West Virginia, going through the mountains, and we turned on the radio, there it was, "Give Up the Funk." It reached the top five on the soul chart and got to number 15 on the pop chart. That was the year of "Silly Love Songs" by Paul

McCartney and Wings and "Don't Go Breaking My Heart" by Elton John and Kiki Dee, and we were right there with them. It was such a big hit, in fact, that it temporarily cast a long shadow over Funkadelic, which was the DNA of the entire enterprise.

On and off again over the years, we had shared bills with Mother's Finest, an Atlanta-based funk-rock band. They played great, had a great look, wrote real nice songs. I liked their whole operation. At one of the shows we played with them in the early seventies, they had a little rocket on a string that used to shoot up from off-stage and pass right over people's heads. It was just a firecracker, nothing more than that really, but it was exciting to the people in those smaller venues. I took note of it. When *Mothership Connection* came out, and especially after "Give Up the Funk" took off, I went to Neil and told him that I wanted a real spaceship. I didn't know how much it cost to have one. I didn't know anyone else who had one. I just knew that it suddenly made sense for me. Many label heads would have balked. Neil wasn't a balker. In fact, he jumped at the idea, and came right back at me with an idea of how it might be financed. Neil was always having creative ideas for how to finance things. He knew how to move money around. When he released a record, for example, he would go to the bank and get a loan to press the discs, and then sell them to a distributor and go back to pay the pressing plant. He could have $10 million in his bank account at nine o'clock in the morning and then be a hundred thousand overdrawn in the evening, or the other way around. And so when I said "spaceship," Neil just nodded and set up a million-dollar loan for me.

As it turned out, that was the beginning of a bit of trouble—

my management took commission on the loan, which you're not supposed to do. And a good deal of the spaceship money also went to buy cars for everyone connected to the band. Cholly got a Jaguar. Boogie and Calvin got Sevilles. Garry got a Thunderbird. Ray got a Thunderbird. Bernie got a Volvo. I think there were twenty-six cars in all. I didn't need a car. I didn't drive. I just wanted my spaceship.

What I had in mind was big: bigger than the Beatles at Shea, bigger than *Tommy*. There was nothing to compare it to at the time, and it would be years before bands like Boston came along with comparable arena-rock props. Ina Meibach, our lawyer, put us in touch with Jules Fisher, who was one of the premier lighting designers on Broadway. He had done *Hair*. He had done *Jesus Christ Superstar*. We explained the concept to him and he got it right away. He had the idea to add a little one. He wanted us to arrive in it. The idea was that the small one could fly over the audience, sort of like the Mother's Finest firecracker, and I would be inside the big one, which would descend to the stage.

Even before *Mothership Connection* appeared in stores, I was already pushing ahead to the next album. That's how we worked: overlapping recording schedules, ideas spilling into new ideas. We had to maintain cruising altitude and velocity.

In the fall of 1975 I was in Dallas, at the airport, following a show at the convention center. The system of shuttles between terminals had just opened, and I was the only one on the train that morning. Right there on the seat next to me there was a book called *Clones*. I picked it up and read the first sentences, which said something like, "Steve Swanson had docked spaceships on planets, but he could never get used to the train at the Dallas airport." The book was fiction, but it was talking about the very same train that I was on. That was strange. Even stranger was the fact that when I got to Portland, Oregon, the first thing I saw in every magazine stand was the same *Clones* book. It was just being launched. But so was the Dallas inter-terminal shuttle system. How could a new book have a reference in it to an equally new train?

I had always liked science fiction because of how creative the ideas were, and this particular book seemed to be sending me a message. If it wasn't fate, exactly, it was at least coincidence, and sometimes that was good enough. After I checked in to my hotel in Portland, I went to the public library, where I checked out H. G. Wells's *The Island of Doctor Moreau* and some other books about cloning. They summarized the thinking about genetics and what constitutes original life, though the librarian explained to me that if I wanted access to the actual experiments the government had conducted, I would need to go through the Freedom of Information Act. That intrigued me even more. I was always open to new concepts, and when I started reading around about cloning, it really resonated with me. In a way, that's what I was doing. It was true in a narrow sense in the way that the Parliaments became Funkadelic became Parliament—we transplanted personnel and grew a new organism—but it was true in a broader sense of all art and all ideas. You take a piece and you replicate. That's what we were doing back at the hula hoop factory, grabbing a strip of plastic, twisting it, and stapling it together. Each strip exactly resembled the one before it and the one after it. They were products that retained more than a shimmer of the original idea; they carried the entire idea, perfectly. Along with the commercial implications, there was a spiritual part of the equation. In one book, there was an anecdote about how a woman in a lab had created a hundred salamanders from a single cell. That seemed amazing and futuristic. But it also tied back into something I had been thinking about since *Chariots of the Gods*, which is that death can be defeated by science. If you're in ancient Egypt and you're embalming someone, keeping them in that state forever, that seems like a hope that you'll see them living again one day. Cloning was cutting-edge science that answered age-old questions about mortality.

The resulting album, sparked by the book and the ideas that were circling around it in my mind, came together quickly. "Children of Production," for example, looked at the beings that might result from a process like this.

"Do That Stuff," which turned out to be the single, was a blazing funk song. "Gamin' on Ya!" had that elastic Bootsy feel that we had perfected back on *Chocolate City*. But the title song was where I started to sketch the outlines of a more elaborate and internally consistent P-Funk mythology. On *Mothership Connection*, we had introduced Star Child, an interplanetary being who helped bring funk to Earth. (Decades later, there was an archaeology initiative called the Starchild Project that dealt with a prehistoric skull found in Mexico.) On *Clones*, we added Dr. Funkenstein, who was my alter ego. He was Star Child's boss, a kind of emperor of intergalactic funk, and he introduced himself via song: "Call me the big pill, Dr. Funkenstein, the disco fiend with the monster sound."

Dr. Funkenstein was me. I was Dr. Funkenstein. Expressing myself through characters was comfortable to me. More than that, it made good sense, creatively and financially. I had always liked cartoons, the anarchic humor and the clear lines and the redundant, almost archetypal plots. I always thought I connected to them on a deeper level, but I wasn't sure how. One day, watching TV around the house, I saw a special on Mickey Mouse, and that's when it hit me: I liked cartoons because they were some of the purest examples of characters, and characters were the closest that humanity came to immortality. People aged, but characters never did. You could work with them forever, adapt them to the time, reupholster them to reflect the changes in society. Once again, this tied back into the anxiety I had felt as far back as "Testify," that we were just a guitarist, a drummer, and an old fool. Adopting psychedelic styles for Funkadelic temporarily took the edge off. But Parliament had put us back in the crosshairs of the popular imagination. We were on the chart, and that meant that we were in grave danger of slipping off the chart. Characters prevented that problem permanently.

Neil supported us through all of it. I'm not sure he understood the band very well at that point, but he had our back, both because he was a promotions man and because there was no arguing with success. It reminded me of the Beatles a little bit, and how they had such an easy time for their experiments. Once they got on a roll, once they were the Beatles with a capital B, everything they did mattered and every thought they had was valid. People were predisposed to listen to them: more than that, they felt left out if they didn't listen. But before an artist is on that kind of roll, it's a completely different story. If I had shown up at a label executive's office in 1966 and announced that I wanted to do a funk concept album about clones, I would have been thrown right out the door. It's possible that I wouldn't have made it past the word *funk*.

The Clones of Dr. Funkenstein was recorded at United Sound, and most of it was recorded quickly. The template for the music was basic funk—a little more fundamental and straightforward than some of the other records from that time—although it's also a high point for how we used the horns. Fred and Bernie went wild with the horn arrangements on that album. They would do the same song: one would do half, and the other the other half. Bernie hated to do stock arrangements. I would tell him to do it artsy-fartsy, jazzy. Fred was going to be funky no matter what he was going to do, based on his training. That gave the whole project real color, a chromatic diversity.

In keeping with the feel—fast, dirty ideas taking precedence over budgets—I designed the cover photo myself. I set up a doctor's office and used tinfoil to get that space-alien look. It shows Dr. Funkenstein making another Dr. Funkenstein in the laboratory, and it's supposed to be reminiscent of clone armies. *The Boys from Brazil* had come out that year, not the movie with Gregory Peck and Laurence Olivier but the Ira Levin novel it was based on, and I was playing off that kind of thing.

If *The Clones of Dr. Funkenstein* was a shot in the arm for Parliament, there was still the matter of the broader P-Funk empire, and what other characters might rise out of the democratic murk of Funkadelic. How would the funk be cloned and cloned again? What were the productive mutations? One of the answers was right under my nose the whole time.

In the months after *Chocolate City*, Bootsy and I had started wearing rhinestones and studs in our jeans, dressing in the fashion of the times, though we made our clothes ourselves. Over the summer, we were in New York, going to see our lawyer Ina

Meibach. Much of our day was spent walking up and down the avenues, looking at girls and buildings, making jokes and puns, and at some point I came up with a little lyrical hook: "Stretching out in a rubber band." I didn't think of it as a group name, a Rubber Band, but more as an image, an image of exploration and permissiveness. Bootsy picked up on it, and soon we had an expanded version, "Stretching out, kind of hanging loose, in a rubber band." When Bootsy added his little flourish— "Hallelujah!"—we knew we had the foundation of a hit. When we left New York, we went straight back to Detroit and cut it at United Sound. The character was in place from the start, largely because of Bootsy's vocals. But there was also a strong shift in the lyrics toward a kind of innocent sexuality, something that was childlike without being childish. Where Parliament was complex and cutting-edge, sometimes nerdy, sometimes sleazy, Bootsy was almost like a human cartoon, but with a true-believer kind of evangelism about the power of the funk. The very beginning of that very first song is a pretty straightforward manifesto.

Hallelujah! They call me Casper!
Not the friendly ghost but the holy ghost! Dig!

In that first phase of presenting Bootsy, there was another little nod to Mother's Finest, just as there had been with the Mothership. They had a bass player named Jerry Seay who went by the name "Wyzard," and he had such an outsize personality and look that it made sense for him to be out in front of the rest of the band. Bootsy took this to a new level. Since he was such a great live performer, I knew we would have to develop a character for him that could translate to the stage, a pose, an outfit, a style. Even back when he and Catfish had been in the House Guests, they had dressed like the most outré Funkadelics, so he had that sense of style: the on-the-edge outfits, the not-of-this-world affect. As it would turn out, the most important part of his costume was the star-shaped glasses. I got him those somewhere in New York. At first the lenses were littler, the size of John Lennon's glasses but in the shape of stars. Later, we had a pair made with larger lenses, and they became his trademark, as important as Mickey Mouse's ears or Popeye's biceps.

Bootsy's emergence as a solo artist was a long time coming. Ever since I first saw him in Cincinnati, when Mallia Franklin brought us around to meet the Collins boys, I knew there was a character in there waiting to get out. The concept was blurry at first, but it got clearer on *Chocolate City* (where he contributed Mu-tron-powered tracks like "Ride On") and on *Let's Take It to the Stage* (when he started doing that gentle, cartoony falsetto on "Be My Beach"). But Bootsy wasn't just about Bootsy. As luck would have it, there actually was a Rubber Band, and they took center stage on that first record. They were basically Bootsy's group from Cincinnati—him, Catfish, and Frank Waddy—and we added in lots of P-Funk personnel: Garry Shider and Glen Goins and Bernie and myself. Boogie, who played bass in the main group, switched over to drums on some of Bootsy's recordings. It was a hell of a band. His singers were unbelievable: Robert "P-Nut" Johnson and Gary "Mudbone" Cooper. They brought the whole enterprise into the stratosphere. We had met them in Baltimore when they were touring with an R&B singing group, so we knew how perfectly Bone could do all the Sly and James Brown tricks and anything else that was happening in early-seventies R&B. Pat Lewis, who I had worked with since the

Golden World years, was on to him at once. She saw how versatile he was, how committed he was to trying (and perfecting) new techniques. She was right to spot that trait in him, and she was right that it mattered. Shit was always evolving. You don't want to be standing on a second when the clock moves. And Gary was the best there was at almost everything: he could sing, play, arrange, whatever. He had played with Shirley Caesar and lots of other gospel groups back in Jersey.

That first Rubber Band record came out in August 1976, at exactly the same time as *Mothership Connection*. I saw them both for the first time in Bimini, where I went with Bootsy. We were surprised as hell to see that *Mothership* was out, because we had just finished it a week before. The record was the culmination of lots of the experiments that we were doing. We used tons of novelty effects, voices that were sped up and slowed down, arrangements that shifted briefly to gospel and then returned to traditional R&B. We had been doing so much crazy shit with Funkadelic that this was almost straight by comparison, but it had a commercial clarity that Funkadelic didn't. The songs we wrote for him worked out beautifully. The first single released was "I'd Rather Be with You," a ballad with a bare minimum of the trickery, and radio took to it. Even though it was silly-serious, it was a love song, with a clear message. Then we released the title song, "Stretchin' Out (in a Rubber Band)," an anthem that announced the new band's arrival. There are also songs on there that are pretty far out there, like "Psychoticbumpschool," the third single, which was pretty much a Funkadelic composition filtered through Bootsy's band. Even though we had singles, we weren't thinking in terms of singles. We were still thinking back toward artists like Jimi Hendrix. He sold albums, and Bootsy was doing the same thing, but with R&B as the foundation rather than the blues and a Mu-tron bass rather than the guitar. This album also marked the first time I truly understood what people like Neil and Dave Kapralik had been telling me: that art needed something bright to pop so the people could see it. For years, I had been saying that I understood it, but when I saw that picture of Bootsy on a motorcycle with a white suit and those star glasses, the force of it hit me all at once. It was iconic and breathtaking. It was easier to get your mind around than Funkadelic. I guess I was a slow learner. Right from the start, Bootsy brought in younger fans, who we started to call "geepies." Fans liked his persona, the way he came on like a cross between a blaxploitation movie character and a Saturday-morning cartoon. He had a shy psychedelic cool that drove them wild, and that helped us inch closer to total demographic domination. Bootsy was bringing in the preteens while we maintained our hold on the rest: the teenagers who had jumped on during *Chocolate City*, the adults who had been with Funkadelic since *Maggot Brain*, and even the gray-hairs who remembered us when we were the Parliaments.

PUT A GLIDE IN YOUR STRIDE AND A DIP IN YOUR HIP AND COME ON UP TO THE MOTHERSHIP

We spent the fall of that bicentennial year up in Newburgh, New York, with the entire population of the P-Funk nation. We traveled with thirty or forty musicians then, plus our crew. We commandeered a local motel and set up shop. We were in Newburgh as a prelude to our fall tour, and we needed all the time we could get to prepare. We had a tremendous amount of material to rehearse: *Clones*, for starters, and Bootsy's first record, but also *Tales of Kidd Funkadelic*, which would truly be our final Westbound album, and *Hardcore Jollies*, our Funkadelic debut for Warner Bros. But mostly we were there to figure how to play alongside the actual Mothership, the one that I had imagined, that Jules Fisher had built, and that sat smack in the middle of Hangar E at Stewart Airport in New Windsor, about fifteen miles west of Newburgh.

An airport hangar is a strange place to rehearse, even if you do have a spaceship. It was absolutely cavernous, to the point where Bootsy could be down at one end with his band and we could be at the other with the spaceship, and we could both be playing and we wouldn't interfere with each other. Down on our end, we had basically built the stage out to look as it would on tour. The P-Funk stage equipment had come from Aerosmith, who had retired it in 1976. We had a kind of indirect history with them: Bernie had played with Joey Kramer in Chubby and the Turnpikes, and we ended up having the same manager for a minute. I saw them as a funk band, strangely enough—they played loose and with rhythm, which you can hear in a later song like "Rag Doll." The only other rock band capable of that was Led Zeppelin, and only onstage: when they went into the studio they started tinkering with effects and complexity. And the ship—well, it was all I had hoped for and more. It looked like some kind of unholy cross between an American car from the late fifties and early sixties, a piece of equipment from a children's playground, and a giant insect. It was awesome. I went into a black box, sort of like a magician's cabinet, at the base of the ship, came up via an elevator, and then, as smoke and lights went crazy, appeared at the top of the steps. It made for quite an entrance. Soul music had never seen anything like it—for that matter, neither had rock and roll. It was like a Broadway show in the most elaborate sense, or what Las Vegas would become decades later.

To pay off the stagecraft, we had to make sure that we were just as impressive musically. In Newburgh, we rehearsed with a degree of professionalism and commitment that was, at least in our history, unprecedented. After four Parliament albums and half a dozen Funkadelic albums, we were genuinely kaleidoscopic, capable of everything from doo-wop to heavy rock to jazzy horn arrangements. Luckily, we had Maceo Parker overseeing the band, and he's one of the best in the world at that. He had done a superb job with James Brown's band, and if you can make it there you can make it anywhere; to say that he was very good at organizing rehearsals and getting musicians to master new material would have been an understatement. You could go to him with a brand-new song that you had never played before, and within fifteen minutes he'd have everyone up on it. Down on the other end of the hangar, Bootsy was doing the same thing with his music, and he was almost as good as Maceo. He rehearsed his band until they all had music coming out of their nose.

Rehearsing P-Funk for the Mothership tour was like deploying an army. Because of all the equipment, all the lighting cues, and the complexity of the staging, it was important to hit certain spots in certain songs at exactly the right time. That stretch spent in Newburgh was really hard, both physically and creatively taxing. We had a tradition of thinking of our music as a living thing, an evolving conversation, and I tended to go off script and improvise while I was onstage. Our new approach cured me of that, quick. What we were doing was more like staging a play. You couldn't be as crazy high as you used to be, in the psychedelic sense. You couldn't get carried away. Because of the way the show was choreographed, we started to focus more attention on Garry Shider and Glen Goins. That was fine with me: they were photogenic and energetic, and Glen was particularly important for the Mothership—we needed his strong gospel vocals to call the ship down from the heavens to the stage. Once again we were emphasizing the young guys in the band, which proved to me that we were headed in the right direction. That's how we kept our currency.

Along the way, up there in Newburgh, we managed to finish up our record for Warner Bros. There wasn't much of a concept for *Hardcore Jollies* other than what the title says: it's about playing the shit out of your instrument and getting your jollies—or, if you'd prefer, getting your rocks off by getting your rock and roll on. That's why I dedicated that record to "the guitar players of the world."

Finally, after weeks of rehearsing every song and every stage cue, after nailing down every second of the production, we were ready to kick off the P-Funk Earth Tour. It debuted in October 1976 at the Municipal Auditorium in New Orleans. That first show went the way Jules Fisher imagined: the little ship flew over the head of the audience and transformed, via the magic of misdirection, into the big ship. But in following Jules's blueprint, we learned an important lesson, which is that it was impossible to follow the ship. Everything that happened after it arrived seemed like an anticlimax. We performed the entire show in its shadow.

After New Orleans, we knew that the ship had to come on at the end of the show rather than early on. Doing so at the second tour stop, in Baton Rouge, proved that. It was so powerful—and such a perfect way to cap off the concert, with Glen calling the ship down—that it took your breath away. Every night we packed the whole assembly onto seven trucks and set out for the next stop. All the shows through Louisiana and Mississippi were impressive, but Houston, the fifth stop of the tour, showed us what we really had. I got to the venue, the Summit, early enough to see the stage before people came in. The place looked like a megachurch without a congregation when it was empty; as the stagehands arranged the stage for the show, it began to look like a circus. But by the time of the show, the circus looked like a church again, this time full of parishioners. Sly was opening

for us, backed by a new Family Stone that included Lynn Mabry
and Dawn Silva, who would become the Brides of Funkenstein.
He played a great set, and then Bootsy stepped out there and the
crowd went crazy. When he left the stage, we came out and tore
through Parliament hits like "Do That Stuff" and Funkadelic hits
like "Cosmic Slop." Sly's band came back to join us for "Night of
the Thumpasaurus Peoples."

Even in a perfect show like that, there were things that bothered me: dropped cues, slight glitches on the soundboard or lighting rig. And then there was the matter of the small Mothership,
hanging out there over the heads of people who were paying
good money to see us, throwing off sparks. Who could promise
that the thing wouldn't fall into the crowd and injure our fans?
As soon as I got it in my head that the small ship was a potential
liability, it wasn't long for this world. Besides, it only worked in
certain venues anyway. It was great for the Garden, the Forum,
the Spectrum, but as soon as we got outside in a festival setting,
it was useless, and any smaller stage posed a problem, too. After
about twenty shows, we retired the small ship. But that wasn't
the strangest hiccup on the tour. In Norman, Oklahoma, about a
month into the tour, we were playing "The Undisco Kidd (The
Girl Is Bad)" when it came true. A woman walked right up the
center aisle onto the stage. She was smoking a joint and wearing
overalls, and she hit the button of one strap and the overalls slid
right off. There she was, completely naked, nappy dugout and
everything. She turned around, waddling on account of her pants
were around her ankles, stuck the joint up her butt and blew three
smoke rings. Every time we tried to start the next song, people
were laughing so hard that we had to stop. We kept jamming,
kept trying to find our way into the next song, but it was no use. I

talked to her about twenty years later on the telephone: she knew someone who knew someone. By then she sounded old and tired. "Did I really do that?" she said. It didn't seem like the kind of thing you'd forget.

We had the records. They had the ear of the radio. We had the stage show. It had the eyes of the audience. And after a few months on the road, we had the full force of Neil Bogart's promotional genius. He hired a lieutenant from the air force to travel around with us. They toured us through NASA facilities: Huntsville, Alabama; Hampton, Virginia. We even got the entire band into NORAD—the North American Aerospace Defense Command in Colorado Springs—for a blink. The Mothership was almost a band member in its own right, subject to quirks and tantrums like anyone else in the band.

That first wave of shows went through me like an electrical current, recharging me and showing me what a rock show could be if it had the full participation not only of musicians but of set directors, choreographers, and prop masters. We were putting on the equivalent of a touring Broadway show. I was so fascinated by all the moving parts that it was sometimes hard to concentrate on the message in the music. When I was reminded that there was a philosophy behind it all, the idea sometimes came as a shock, and never more so than when the Black Muslims developed a special interest in the show. The Mothership, of course, had a rough precedent in Black Muslim theology and mythology. In the biblical book of Ezekiel, there was a prophetic vision that some believed was a story of alien visitors. The Honorable Elijah Muhammad, the leader of the Nation of Islam, wove that into a much more elaborate idea that was later explained by Louis Farrakhan:

The Honorable Elijah Muhammad told us of a giant Mother Plane that is made like the universe, spheres within spheres. White people call them unidentified flying objects. Ezekiel, in the Old Testament, saw a wheel that looked like a cloud by day but a pillar of fire by night. The Honorable Elijah Muhammad said that that wheel was built on the island of Nippon, which is now called Japan, by some of the Original scientists. It took $15 billion in gold at that time to build it. It is made of the toughest steel. America does not yet know the composition of the steel used to make an instrument like it. It is a circular plane, and the Bible says that it never makes turns. [Excerpted from "The Divine Destruction of America: Can She Avert It?" (1996)]

I had heard plenty about the Black Muslims from my kids and other kids their age, and I remembered shards of the Mother Plane story from my customers in the barbershop back in the fifties. But to me, it was just another mythology to draw on, no different from stories of mummification in ancient Egypt, from sci-fi movies and their vision of outer space, or from cloning. That's why it was such a shock to look out into the crowd in Philadelphia and see all these guys with bow ties in the front row, shouting up at me. "Teach the knowledge, Brother George," they were saying. The knowledge? Holy shit. It suddenly struck me that they were serious. When I looked at their faces, they were bowing down, praying almost. I started looking directly at them and saying, "Ain't nothing but a party." I started making more jokes about money and pussy, to make sure that everyone in the crowd, bow ties included, knew that I was getting paid for entertaining people. I wasn't interested in promoting an eternal truth of any kind.

I was leading a rock and roll band. The prospect that our music might be used for dogmatic purposes or associated with true believers of any stripe, well, that hadn't worked for us back with the Process Church, in the early days of Funkadelic, and it wasn't going to work with the Black Muslims.

Plus, the show itself was its own kind of high. Our faith in our ability as a live act is one of the reasons that we never went on TV shows like *Soul Train*, or anything else that required artists to lip-synch or play along with a prerecorded track. We didn't want to do pantomime. TV was all about little ticky-tack speakers, which meant that it depended upon an artist's ability to create intimate moments. Al Green could sing soft and pretty, so he worked in that medium. Sly could sit at the piano, play "If You Want Me to Stay," and break your heart in the process. We were closer to Led Zeppelin, big enough that there was no point in shrinking ourselves to fit inside the box. We stayed big, stayed in arenas, and documented the tour on *Live: P-Funk Earth Tour*, a double live album that we taped in January at the Los Angeles Forum and the Oakland Coliseum. The set list was made up of *Mothership Connection* and *Clones of Dr. Funkenstein* songs, mostly, with one Funkadelic song ("Undisco Kidd") and two new studio tracks, "This Is the Way We Funk with You" and "Fantasy Is Reality," a song from our Invictus days that we recut. Back then it had been a piece of pop soul, with fuzz guitar in the left track. For the live record, we redid it more grandly, with dripping piano chords and doo-wop vocals. The new version sounded older, maybe, but less dated, and the sentiment was the same.

Fantasy is reality in the world today
I keep hanging in there, that's the only way

The *P-Funk Earth Tour* album mainly documented Parliament. But that was only part of the P-Funk story, and it didn't tell how all of our other artists were helping to create a new genre. The most important, of course, was Bootsy and his Rubber Band. In the studio, all of us worked on the Bootsy records, but when he played live, he took the stage with a stripped-down group—just him, Bone, and P-Nut. Most of the time I only saw the Rubber Band from backstage, because I was getting ready to go out and follow him, but one night I went out in front of the audience to watch Bootsy's set. When he came onstage, he didn't move for two solid minutes. He just stood there in the dark with this thumping beat behind him, only his silhouette visible, and the crowd went crazy. I was so overwhelmed I could hardly stand it: the loudness of the people was something I had never experienced. He hadn't made a sound yet and the place was vibrating. And then he said, "Hallelujah," just a single word in that cartoon voice, and what was already exploding in the crowd exploded again.

We had set up P-Funk like Motown, at least in the sense that there were shared musicians and shared songs, and so if you were the act that had the current hit record, then you had the upper hand. Bootsy's debut went top ten on the R&B chart. The title track was a top-twenty single. "I'd Rather Be with You" was a monster ballad that could be heard at radio stations and dances everywhere throughout the summer of 1976. When Bootsy took the lead on the charts, everyone inside the organization started telling me that it was only fair to make him the headliner. I agreed. And so we let him top the bill one night. Rick James was playing with us, and he was complaining all afternoon. He felt even more trivialized. He didn't want to go out onstage at all. We followed

Rick, and our set closed, as always, with Glen calling the Mothership down. When we wrapped our set, we went offstage, and as we passed Bootsy it was clear that he was quaking. Nobody could follow the spaceship. He had been nervous that night before the show, and he was worse afterward. He would have been worse still the next night if we hadn't moved him back to his middle position.

As an experiment in character, as an expansion of P-Funk, Bootsy worked like a charm. For a while there, he was the hottest thing going. We had succeeded so well at building him a separate identity that for many people he was the only P-Funk name they knew, the only individual who had an existence independent from the group. Still, he was more or less a quiet guy. When his star ascended, he had to shoulder lots of the burden of being the public face of P-Funk. It wasn't easy for him. But you couldn't argue with success.

There were others, too. I knew we had to do a solo record for Eddie Hazel. He was a Jimi Hendrix type and most of his playing didn't fit within the confines of traditional songs or even traditional labels. Most record companies were willing to go about as far as an artist like Ernie Isley, who was a hell of a player but stayed part of the Isley formula. Anything more extreme wouldn't have worked—and in fact when Ernie did a solo record, *High Wire*, a little later, it was too daring and unexpected. Like the Isleys, Funkadelic was a safe place for Eddie. We kept R&B and funk in there for him as a foundation, and so he was able to get away with it. When it came time for Eddie's solo album, though, we knew he was just going to play his heart out, and so we had to find another way to anchor him. Our solution was to pair him with existing rock and pop songs. I put him on to a Beatles song, "She's So

Heavy," that we used to do to death onstage. We used to tear that one a new asshole. And he got to the Mamas & the Papas' "California Dreamin'" through some work he did with Shuggie Otis, who was the son of the bandleader Johnny Otis and a psychedelic folk artist in his own right. Those were both known pop songs, so Eddie could just work his magic on them, and they made up the spine of his album, *Game, Dames and Guitar Thangs*. Many of the tracks were from Bootsy, which was ironic, because the two of them never really played together. They were great friends, but each of them was creatively elbowed out of place by the other. We had to get Eddie out of jail to do the record. He was in prison up at Lompoc after his altercation with the air marshal, and some guys at Casablanca were able to pull strings and get him out. He rode back with us, did the album, and then went straight back to prison.

We also made an album for Fred Wesley and Maceo Parker, which we credited to Fred Wesley and the Horny Horns. Fred and Maceo wanted their own project, and they had helped us plenty, so we helped them. I got tracks from Bootsy, along with covers of existing P-Funk hits like "Up for the Down Stroke." Much of the challenge of that record was getting Fred and Bernie to work together, encouraging each of them to arrange the horns in their own style and then weaving the two together. The result was more about the talent of our musicians than aiming for the charts. There were commercial concerns, of course—you want to eat—but there was also a real artistic agenda, too. I respected Motown and I wanted to tip my hat to that. I respected the English groups and their take on American blues. I respected show tunes and vaudeville music. With all the players around me, all either finding their voice or finding ways to use the voice they already knew they had, P-Funk was painting with all the colors and then some, on a canvas that was getting bigger and bigger.

Commerce fed art, and art fed right back into commerce. The radio was on fire with our music: Bootsy had his hits and we had *The Clones of Dr. Funkenstein*, which went top twenty and also had two big singles, "Do That Stuff" and the title track. It happened so fast we didn't have time to really let it sink in. What we did have time to do was to build a business infrastructure to preserve our momentum. Much of this came from our live shows. When bands toured, it was the same drill. Artists worked with radio stations and promoters. Radio stations talked up the show on the air. Promoters brought acts to venues. Acts appeared on radio stations in advance of the show. DJs came onstage during the show to promote their stations. But we had a unique arrangement. We were a package deal. We came to town as a unified army, Parliament and Funkadelic and Bootsy all rolled into one. That meant that we could come into town firing on all cylinders: one radio station would have a promotion with Bootsy, another would have Parliament, another would have Funkadelic. When it came time for the DJs to appear onstage, we required that they all come out together in space suits and stand next to the Mothership. We weren't about to stop the show three times for promotional announcements.

We instituted another innovation, too. The traditional system divided financial responsibilities and financial gain between promoters and DJs; radio jocks weren't supposed to actually promote concerts. We taught them how to circumvent the system, mainly by getting their wives promoter's licenses. This was something I remembered from the mid-sixties, from when Armen took me around to stations in the Midwest. If DJs set their wives up as promoters, they didn't have to pay a deposit to a promoter. We didn't let them pay us less than a promoter would, but we didn't ask for more, either. This empowered DJs and made them more than happy to work with us.

And yet there were problems, minor controversies. As we started to tour with the Mothership, as it became clear that we were a major concert draw, there were people who started to lament what they perceived as a lack of fairness. Much of it centered on race. A group in Atlanta hired the civil rights activist Hosea Williams to picket our show because we didn't have a black promoter. He came by to check up on us, put a briefcase up on the table, and started to ask questions about our business practices. We told him something about them that he didn't know: when we started doing big arena and stadium shows, we had also started donating twenty-five cents from each ticket to the United Negro College Fund. We had been doing it for years, and since shows were bringing in tens of thousands of people, the money added up. When Hosea Williams found that out, he just closed his briefcase and left. "We ain't got nothing here," he said.

That didn't stop the carping, though. White promoters got upset in the other direction, worrying that we were going to cave in to the pressure of picketers and hire only black promoters. To placate everyone—and, at the same time, to keep doing exactly what we wanted to do—we hired the team of Darryll Brooks and Carol Kirkendall, a black man and white woman with a company called Tiger Flower based out of Washington, D.C. The first show they promoted for us, I think, was at the Capital Centre in

Landover, Maryland. We explained ourselves on radio and then I went out and talked to the guy who was picketing us. Once it was clear to him that there wasn't any more juice in protesting against P-Funk, he offered his services to us to help manage any future protestors. Almost any political alliance works that way. You can have someone fucking with you or you can defuse and co-opt them. It's all a matter of realizing that everyone wants their bread buttered on a certain side. Years later, in the nineties, there was a summit meeting at the home of Joe Jackson, Michael Jackson's father. They were upset with Janet Jackson for the same reason—too many white promoters—and there was talk of a boycott. We got there, listened for a few minutes, and then Archie Ivy went to the podium to speak. "We'd love to go along with this," he said. "We're for black business, of course. But as I look around the room, half of you motherfuckers owe us money so I find it hard to go against Janet and deny her the freedom to make the choices she wants to make."

Race was an issue on the sidewalk outside the theaters and are-nas, and it was an issue on the radio, too. Just as Funkadelic had tried to carve out a space for black rock, Parliament was rede-fining the way people thought about funk. Suddenly, it was part of the mainstream pop-music conversation. This had happened before, on a more limited scale. Sly had crossed over to pop star-dom. But Sly was both a trailblazer and a genius, so he didn't ex-actly create a category around him. In the mid-seventies, in fact, nobody wanted to be funk, or at the very least they didn't want to be called that. Everyone wanted to be pop and crossover because the budgets were adjusted for category. The English rock groups had come over and heightened the budgets. If you were a black act, the budgets stayed relatively low. We got decent advances for

Mothership and *Clones*, but nothing approaching the rock bands. We called it the "junior budget."

After *Clones*, the money started to come more easily. We were proven as a chart performer. Everyone assumed that the next Parliament record would up the ante again. But even in this new environment, some bands couldn't quite take advantage. The Ohio Players, for example, were a band I loved: they were supremely talented, with smoking grooves and the ability to really put it across onstage. But in their formative years, they didn't play in front of large crowds with any regularity, and so when they started to have big hits and get more money to make their records, they couldn't adjust to being a bigger live presence. They knew how to play to people standing right before them, when they could see the crowd with their eyes and feed off the energy. But when we played with them at the Summit in Houston, they showed up with these small column speakers that echoed when you shook them. They insisted on using them no matter how big the house was. It was like putting a high school gym in the middle of an arena.

We had rivalries with other bands, to some degree, or at the very least we were careful to always look around and keep track of the competition. The biggest black group other than us was Earth Wind & Fire, though we were profoundly different operations. They had decided early on that they were going to abandon hard funk for crossover pop, although that didn't stop them from hiring Jules Fisher, the same guy who had made the Mothership for us, to design pyramids for their stage show. There were up-and-coming acts like Cameo and Rick James, who toured with us, along with veteran soul groups like the Bar-Kays, who remade themselves as funk bands.

The one place we didn't really have any rivals was inside Casablanca. The label had no staff producers, the way Motown had. Giorgio Moroder produced Donna Summer. Kenny Kerner and Richie Wise produced Kiss. We had our people. Since there wasn't overlap, there wasn't competition in the Motown sense. Instead, the other acts were like colleagues. We bumped into each other a little bit in the office, congratulated each other, watched with admiration as Kiss took over hard rock and Donna took over disco. I mostly credited Neil for creating the kind of environment that made all of it possible. He was so fast and so smart that no other label could keep up with him, and he had an infrastructure of veterans, from Cecil Holmes to Gene Redd, who had more knowledge about the record business than almost anyone else around.

The operation felt like a real triumph—creatively and financially and in every other way. That included drugs, of course. Casablanca was nothing but drugs. You answered the phone with cocaine in your nose. But it wasn't like we were doing anything strange for the time. Cocaine was the diet of the day. Hollywood was doing it. Wall Street was doing it. Main Street was doing it. You'd go to lunch with a record executive, and midway through the meal he'd take the little bottle of coke from his pocket and empty it onto the table and do a line. You could be at a lunch table or fully out in the open: I remember being at the Bud Billiken Parade in Chicago with a well-known syndicated morning show DJ, snorting coke up on top of the float. It got to the point where you didn't even pay attention anymore. It's like looking at a painting of a forest and noticing that there are trees.

Coke wasn't the only drug. Most musicians smoked weed regularly, and a few did harder shit like heroin or dust. The best drug of all was quaaludes. That was Casablanca's main drug besides coke, and it was nothing but pussy. That drug made you want to fuck, and if you were lucky enough to spend an evening with it, fucking is exactly what you'd do. You'd end up with a pretty young secretary or a backup singer or maybe even someone you thought was ugly until the minute you took the quaalude, a piggly wiggly, and you wouldn't care a bit. It was almost like being drunk, but without any of the performance drawbacks: you could get a hard-on in a second or come without a hard-on. And girls loved it, too. When you saw those little pills with "714" printed on them, you knew you were going to have a good time. And then, all of a sudden, it was gone. You could not find it anywhere. There was briefly a Mexican substitute called lemons, but that didn't live up to the standard of bona fide quaaludes. I can't help but feel that the government made it disappear. Anything that works that good, it goes away.

Drugs definitely had genres, just like music did, and the two were closely related. Rock and rollers had one kind of drug, a little down and dirty, either to come down for a show or expand your mind or get loose with a girl. Around that time, though, disco started to emerge—Casablanca was on the leading edge, of course, because of Donna Summer—and I noticed immediately that the disco people were a different type. There's a difference between funky people, who tended to be poor people, and disco people, who were rich partiers. Some of them were straight, many were gay, but most were materialistic. When rich people start partying, it becomes decadent. You have so much money. You can pay for anything you want. You start getting too much, and then you get desensitized, and the high isn't about the drugs or the sex. It's about access and entitlement. That's what I started to feel as disco emerged. You saw Mercedeses and Lamborghinis parked four deep at parties, and when you saw the people doing drugs, you noticed that they were demanding in every way: they wanted the best sex and drugs and they wanted them right away. Their preference ran toward things like poppers. We had done them once or twice back in the barbershop, because you could buy them over the counter back then. It was a heart drug, amyl nitrate. If you didn't know it was coming, you would think you were going crazy. It made you sweat and opened up your pores. You got a big bang for thirty seconds. In the hands of the disco crowd, it was a fuck drug—but not cool and sexy like quaaludes. It was hard-edged, a little vicious. Drugs made for straight freak behavior.

At heart I was still a hippie and disco left me cold, even though it also amused me sometimes. I was staying with Cholly Bassoline right up on top of King's Road on Hollywood Boulevard, and we would hear these insanely loud predawn fights, some rich chick out there at four in the morning screaming, "I want cocaine!" There was one girl in particular who did it all the time, and she was down the road from the house of Paul Lynde, the comedian. He would open up his window and with the maximum amount of gay attitude shout right back at her, "Shut the fuck up, bitch!" Cholly and I used to wait up for her outburst and Paul Lynde's return fire. I took it all in with interest, because I wasn't only in the music business anymore, but also in the business of creating characters. I could make better cartoon characters in my music by watching the people who were acting like cartoons in real life.

Drugs was one problem, but it wasn't a problem if you didn't see it that way. The same was true of sex. At that time, everyone started to get worried that they were subject to unnatural perversions or passions, and they investigated by going to see high-priced shrinks. That was the hip thing in Hollywood. People would talk to one in the hopes that something was wrong with them. I went to one myself, a Hollywood sex psychiatrist, mainly to have conversations and trade stories that might help me with my songwriting. It turned out that she was a bigger freak than anyone she was treating. She was privy to all these insane situations and circumstances, and when someone told her an especially crazy story, she got off on it. I can't say her name. Patient-doctor confidentiality.

Sex, check. Drugs, check. Rock and roll, check. The only thing that really got under my skin was the materialism of the time. I had always lived a gypsy existence. I didn't even own a house—all I had was a two-bedroom apartment in Detroit, on 8 Mile. Ownership struck me as vaguely silly. Once, around that time or a little later, I ran into Satch, who played sax and guitar for the Ohio Players. The record company had bought him a $35,000 bracelet that read OHIO PLAYERS in chip-diamond lettering. He was showing it off proudly, and I just didn't understand it. What were you going to do with a thing like that? Years later I went over to his house, and that bracelet was on his mantel, but he wasn't in the group anymore. For me, that was a symbol of how priorities could get twisted. When I got money, I didn't think about jewelry or cars or houses. I thought about experiences. Again, some of them were sex, and some were drugs, but most of them were rock and roll. I kept studios running all the time. I cut tracks with all the artists I knew and shaped them into songs, which in turn were shaped into records. What did I need with possessions? I had a spaceship and that was going to be enough for a long while.

★

Bootsy's second Rubber Band album, *Ahh . . . the Name Is Bootsy, Baby!* came out in January 1977. The first record had been a success, but it was still a tentative step, like any debut. On that second record, the Bootsy character snapped into focus. I understood that it was a version of what Parliament would have been had we made it big in the late sixties. It was still doo-wop, in a sense, still classic romantic R&B ballads, but with a surreal and futuristic twist, and funnier than Parliament. I had real inspiration for writing that record. In late 1976, I went to Hawaii with Stephanie Lynn, my new girlfriend. Stephanie and I had met on tour, and fairly soon after that she had started coming on the road with us. We got close fast, and then it was off to the islands, where the two of us relaxed in the sun and watched all the other lovers running on the beach and diving off the cliffs and hang-gliding. In that paradise, I wrote about a dozen of those ballads. The vast majority went to Bootsy.

The Bootsy program was simple at that point. It was clear that we had to extend him further into cartoon land, while keeping him legitimate as a romantic figure. We had talked about Casper the Funky Ghost on the first album, and we did more of that kind of thing, with broader strokes and stronger hooks. And when there were straightforward love ballads, we made sure to give them outrageous titles, like "Rubber Duckie," so that someone scanning the track list wouldn't think they had accidentally stumbled on a Teddy Pendergrass album. We were also building the larger P-Funk myth, brick by brick, though we didn't always know it at the time. There's a song called "The Pinocchio Theory," which introduced the notion that funk represented some fundamental emotional honesty: "If you fake the funk, your nose will grow." Later on, that would help me to develop one of our most famous P-Funk characters, but on Bootsy's album it was just an isolated idea. At the time we recorded it, Bootsy didn't even know who Pinocchio was. When he saw the movie a few months later, he thought Walt Disney was copying us.

Of all the albums I worked on during that time, *Ahh . . . the Name Is Bootsy, Baby!* is one of the highlights. It was the first P-Funk album to hit number one on the *Billboard* R&B chart, and it made it into the top twenty of the pop chart. That record was far ahead of its time, and it's an almost perfect example of how to combine commercial music and artistic music. For me, it fulfilled a promise I had made to myself after "Testify," which was that I wasn't going to let anyone put me in a bag. Self-expression was the only real point. It helped to have two groups, of course, and it helped even more to have three or four.

WHEN THE SYNDROME IS AROUND, DON'T LET YOUR GUARD DOWN

We had been told that movie studios were looking at us for a film like David Bowie's *Ziggy Stardust and the Spiders from Mars*, a documentary that would combine onstage footage and backstage looks. Originally, it was going to be directed by Robert Downey, but he dropped out and a new group came around that included a guy named Sy Libinoff and another one named Nene Montes. Nene had a slick seventies look, casually fashionable and counterculture, like a kind of Serpico figure. The first thing he did when he came into the room that day we met him was pull down a bottom eyelid and say, "I'm an outlaw." The second thing he did was get rid of Sy, who committed the cardinal sin of confusing me and Bernie. That was embarrassing for someone who wanted to make a movie about us, and Nene took notice of it and disposed of him. Maybe they never had Sy attached anyway. Maybe it was a Hollywood ploy. Who knows? The point was that we suddenly had this new guy, this outlaw, attached to the band.

Nene was constantly filming footage, but very quickly he established himself as more than a cameraman. One day in 1977, we were scheduled to play at the L.A. Coliseum. Fans were lined up around the block starting at noon. In the early afternoon, a strut gave way and the roof partly collapsed. They called me immediately at the hotel and told me the show would have to be canceled. There was handwringing and wailing. All those tickets, and nothing could be done. It wasn't safe for crowds and it wasn't safe for the band. It was a catastrophe. I got in a cab and hurried down to the Coliseum, and by the time I got there, there was a crane holding the roof up and the promoters had calmed down significantly. There was no more handwringing and wailing. It was going to work. I asked around and found out that no one had been able to solve the problem until Nene stepped up. As soon as he saw the roof collapsing, he ran down the street to a construction site and paid a guy a thousand dollars to bring a crane over. The guy came by and put his equipment to use holding up the roof of the building. It worked perfectly. Prince was in the audience for that concert, and neither he nor anyone else had to deal with a falling roof.

In the wake of that Coliseum brainstorm, Nene became indispensible. He was very aggressive and very smart and went after everyone in the camp who wasn't pulling their weight. For example, there was a special plug in the Mothership that I was paying a thousand dollars a show to use. Nene went in there with a pliers and rewired things. I didn't need the special plug, so I didn't need to pay that guy anymore. There were dozens of examples of that kind of thing. Nene had called himself an outlaw at our first meeting, but as time went on he called himself a janitor, and that was probably closer to the truth. He cleaned up messes.

I was so grateful at first that I didn't notice how fond he was of the divide-and-conquer strategy. After the Coliseum incident, for example, it wasn't enough for Nene to take credit for going to get the crane. He also had to make sure that I knew that everyone else wasn't taking the situation seriously, and to prove it by showing me film he had taken of the promoters standing there, pointing up at the partially collapsed roof and laughing. Every job Nene did came with something else attached to it, usually the implication that other people didn't have my best interests at heart. The situation was complicated by the fact that Nene refused to take a salary. He stressed that he didn't work for anyone. That seemed strange, but I looked past it at first, especially since he had no problem running up a huge fucking expense account. But as time went on, something about his unwillingness to be straightforward unnerved me. If someone isn't taking money, they're taking something else, and it's probably something you can't see.

In the late sixties and early seventies, whenever I got ready to move into the next P-Funk project, I convened what I called a Funkathon: a rambling, open conversation about the ideas circulating that would eventually produce an album. We talked through all aspects and concepts to ensure that we didn't miss a trick. By 1977, the Funkathons were a little different for me. The early years of strategizing and brainstorming had gotten me too much in love with Eddie, Billy, Tawl, Tiki, and Calvin. We were too emotionally tied together. As they left, one by one, I found I couldn't do it anymore. I had great admiration and affection for the new band members coming in, Michael and Tyrone and Garry, but that first ring had been so tight around me, like family, that it was like my heart was broken. I didn't make a big announcement about how I couldn't participate. I just stopped doing it.

Nene noticed that I was withdrawing a little from the group

and took it as a sign—or an opportunity. He started taking the lead in introducing new ideas and challenging me to think through the various things that were circling in my brain. He was pretty new to the P-Funk world, but he had a talent for establishing himself quickly. One day, Nene brought around a guy who was a famous Santeria priest. This priest had observed P-Funk from afar and decided we were into all kinds of voodoo and black arts. We were meeting with him to talk it through, put his mind at ease, maybe learn something. During that meeting, Nene passed me a note that said "entelechy." That's all. One word. I asked him what he meant and he said that he would explain it later. A few minutes later, he passed me another note that said "placebo." In a way, I had to admire him. He had figured out that we made our things according to information and ideas, and he wanted in.

Entelechy, as it turned out, was about potential: it was a word coined by Aristotle to explain the process by which a species becomes most itself. And a placebo, of course, was a sugar pill. I started to think my way around in those concepts. Man has a need to improve, but how does that improvement happen from within a society that numbs you with fake pills? We had investigated politics on *Chocolate City*, communication and social justice on *Mothership Connection*, and individualism and groupthink on *The Clones of Dr. Funkenstein*. So what would this new album do with these two new ideas? Maybe funk itself was a form of evolution. Maybe if you refused to participate in it, you were holding yourself back. We had already created and deployed Star Child, an agent of interplanetary funk. Did he have the secret for improving the species, funkateer by funkateer? There had always been a strain of self-actualization in our music, though it had also always been sharpened by humor and irony and dirty jokes.

After I jotted down pages of lyrics and ideas, I went looking through the tracks we had accumulated and found that there were pieces of new songs already in existence, fragments we had been playing live or had laid down in the studio. "Got to get over the hump" was a popular concert chant that Bootsy and Bernie and I built on; it was a feel-good experience when we played live, and I knew that it would work well in the studio. The song I wrote was about the Bop Gun, a weapon that thwarted any resistance to the funk. The lyrics also touched on everything from Otis Redding ("Turn me loose") to Martin Luther King Jr. ("We shall overcome").

The singer was Glen Goins, and he did some serious work on that one. He got an epic gospel sound. As soon as we got onto the idea of a Bop Gun, we built a big prop gun, and we used it for what would become the cover photo for the record. The photographer we hired had a stop-motion camera, and he wanted me to move around a little as he got multiple exposures. I ducked down and spun around, and somehow they got all that in one shot, a collage of four or five of me in my Dr. Funkenstein outfit. I'm also the figure off to the left. I had just come from Rutgers, where my daughter Donna was graduating. I put on a suit to go to the ceremony, though I hadn't dressed up like that in a decade. Even at the time, people didn't really think that the figure to the left was me, not only because of the suit but because I'm so thin. We added in the waves from the Bop Gun to show how Dr. Funkenstein was shooting a dance ray at the straight George persona.

That was one of two songs we thought of as singles. The other one was "Flash Light." When Bootsy brought me the basic track, it sounded tremendous, but it was a traditional arrangement, guitar and bass. I kept the guitar, but took the bass off and replaced it with Bernie mimicking the sound on three connected Moog keyboards. The result was a bass bubble, a real eye-opener: it was like the beginning of Stevie Wonder's "Maybe Your Baby," but after six months in the workout room. That Moog circuit turned the song from straight James Brown to something more bubblegummy, the Jackson 5 but with a deeper bottom. Bootsy switched over to drums, which was something that didn't happen often, but that worked well on this one. When we played it back to people inside the band, everyone got up out of their chair.

As with every album, there were songs that held the concept together, glue tracks. "Placebo Syndrome" was the main one for *Funkentelechy*. Ever since *Chocolate City*, I had been moving toward a complete, comprehensive funk opera. In my mind, I was thinking all the way back to Davy Crockett, and then through the Beatles, through Motown, through *Hair*. Why couldn't soul or funk music be just as sophisticated, just as wide-ranging, just as artistically successful? All the younger guys in the band were on board immediately. The only people who resisted were Grady and Fuzzy and the rest of them, the older singers who had been with me since the Parliaments were a new idea. It was hard for them to come out of the suits in the first place, and so it was hard to change from one thing to the next so quickly. Plus, I'm sure they thought I was becoming the center of the group in a way that was too obvious and self-serving, though the truth was that Neil and Casablanca Records wanted it that way. *Funkentelechy* was a collection of funk anthems about the anthemic power of funk. It described the illuminating power of the music using, as metaphors, common tools of illumination (a flashlight) and power (a gun). Almost everything on that record was about that record and the records that came before it. "Bop Gun" includes one of the best examples of this strategy:

> *When the syndrome is around*
> *Don't let your guard down*

This kind of self-referential writing made the entire experience extremely satisfying for hardcore fans, along with showing new fans that they had to learn their lesson before coming to class.

We used each new album to introduce new characters, and the character that sprung up on *Funkentelechy vs. the Placebo Syndrome* was one of our most enduring. Back in Plainfield, there was a kid named Berkeley Othello Noel. Noel was a nice-looking guy. Girls loved him. He was in a singing group, Sammy Campbell and the Del-Larks, that was our main competition; in fact Ray Davis, who eventually became one of the core Parliaments, was the bass singer in that group. As nice a singer as Noel was, that wasn't his distinguishing characteristic. You could say that he was a little crazy but he was so much crazier than that. He would carry a straight razor for gang fights. Once he was roller-skating backwards down the street, and he passed by a girl and just flicked that razor out and sliced her skirt right off. Another time, he was sweet on Barbara Ford, the sister of my best friend, Ronnie, but he had a funny way of showing it. He drew a picture of her and hung it all around the neighborhood, along with a message that said ANOTHER ONE OF OUR SISTERS HAS DIED and collection cups hanging underneath every sign. Ronnie's mother saw them and said, "Where that motherfucker Noel?" She could tell from his drawings that it was him.

The best thing about Noel was his voice, which was a high Peter Lorre–like quaver. Once, Ronnie and I were at a house party, lights low, cool dancing, and the next thing you know there was a scuffle. Noel and Billy Johnson, who had danced with Barbara, were fighting like mugs. The next thing we knew, Noel was hitting away at Billy with a paper bag, but it wasn't just a paper bag—there was a glint of metal, and we could see that there was a hatchet in the bag. Ronnie shoved Noel back. Noel pushed past a group of boys and ran out the door, shouting, "Ronnieeee, why'd you do this to meee? I love you like a brother!" Another time his car stopped in front of the barbershop one day, just cut off. He jumped up on the hood and in that same high, wobbly voice, said, "I haaaate you!" to his car before he started stabbing it.

Noel, or at least Noel's voice, became Sir Nose D'Voidoffunk. He was an extension of the principle we sketched out on "The Pinocchio Theory" on Bootsy's second record: if you fake the funk, your nose will grow. But he was also the first real enemy in the P-Funk universe, the nemesis of funk emissaries like Star Child. Sir Nose only cared about his look and his presentation. He was too cool for everything real: too cool to dance, too cool to play, too cool to swim. Sir Nose was even too cool to fuck. It messed with his pimp shit. What I want with jumping up and down on a bitch? But Sir Nose was only fooling himself. Everyone likes pussy. Even pussy likes pussy.

Sir Nose was in "Flash Light" (where we taunt him by saying, "Dance, sucker," and "Get on down, Nose"), but he also had his own song, "Sir Nose D'Voidoffunk (Pay Attention—B3M)." That song scared every motherfucker in the group. It was Bernie and Fred, both independently doing horn arrangements, coloring around the singing and the rhythm track. The lyrics extended the idea: Star Child was going to make Sir Nose dance no matter what, and his weapons, apart from the Bop Gun, included jokes, philosophy, and persistence.

Sir Nose was one of our most popular characters, to the point where we couldn't even get fans to go along with us as we cracked on him or shot him with the Bop Gun. That was especially true in New York, where they booed us for mocking him. They loved the idea of the pimp. Being cool was the most important thing there, even more important than the pleasures of funk.

At around that time, Ronnie Ford started working with us more closely. He cowrote "Wizard of Finance," which is a folky soul ballad on the record. I don't know if I ever told him specifically that Sir Nose was based on Noel because I didn't need to. He knew it immediately. Everybody knew it. It was unmistakable to anyone who grew up in Plainfield, except maybe Eddie, who was one of those kids who wasn't allowed to come out of the house. We didn't keep in touch with the actual Noel. He got into more trouble, ended up in jail. He appeared in the movie *Scared Straight*, in fact, which came out just after *Funkentelechy*, and he's since passed on. But he lives forever as Sir Nose.

As usual, we needed visuals to complement the music. Around the time of *Mothership Connection*, we met a young guy named Overton Loyd; he used to draw caricatures of us as we came out of nightclubs. Overton started drawing for us, and his cartoonish, energetic artwork was a great counterpoint to Pedro's elaborate mythology. Over time, Pedro became more closely associated with Funkadelic, and Overton sort of took over the look for Parliament, although we didn't maintain a strict division internally. For *Funkentelechy vs. the Placebo Syndrome*, Overton created an eight-page comic book that was an origin story for Sir Nose. His first idea of the character was a little different than it ended up, slick but darker. Neil got a look at it and had him redo it to be brighter and popper, more like a Saturday-morning cartoon. But he kept his personal touch in there—if you look right on his shoes, you'll see a little sign that says "Ouch." That's a perfect example of Sir Nose being cool at the expense of comfort.

Anything like that—the comic book, the growth of Sir Nose as a character, the way that we settled on a Parliament logo to match the Funkadelic skull logo that was already pretty popular—was a breeze for us, in the sense that many of our people came from editorial. Archie Ivy had been a reporter and an editor. Tom Vickers had, too. Neil respected us for our ideas and as long as we didn't cost him money or get in the way of the band's success, he was completely on board. Or mostly completely on board. When he first heard what we wanted to call the album, he rolled his eyes. "*Funkentelechy vs. the Placebo Syndrome?*" he said. "I'm telling you that no one's going to get it. They won't even read it right. Some kid is going to come up to you at a show and call it *Funkadelic and the Place-Bo Syndrome.*" I told him he was underestimating our fans.

The same week he passed me the notes that led to the creation of *Funkentelechy vs. the Placebo Syndrome*, Nene took us to see *Star Wars*. He must have known someone, or at least said he did, and he got us into the premiere. Twenty-five of us walked right in through the side door. That was one of the first big movies to use the Dolby four-track stereo system, and it blew my motherfucking head off. During the opening sequence, when the writing is going across the top and then you see the taillights of the spaceship, everyone stood up and applauded, not just because it was a cool image, but because they couldn't resist the sheer physicality of the sound. Later on, when I saw the movie again in a smaller theater, it was softer, not as visceral or as dynamic. I liked *Star Wars* fine as a western. The robots were cute. But it didn't have the kind of philosophy that I was looking for. I wanted space movies to answer my questions about where our world came from. Did aliens come down and help Egyptians build the pyramids? Were they going to come back later and pick us all up, whether or not we had our thumbs up to hitch a ride?

Later that year, there was a movie that did more of that kind of thinking, and we got into the premiere for that one, too, and almost into the actual movie. That was Steven Spielberg's *Close Encounters of the Third Kind*, which we found out about from Julia Phillips, who had produced it along with her husband, Michael; Julia knew Nene because the two of them had developed a Che Guevara project together. It was Julia's third hit in a row, after *The Sting* and *Taxi Driver*. She was a huge name in Hollywood and also a huge nightmare, and if you asked around enough you'd hear plenty about her temper and her aggression and her appetite for cocaine. I mostly knew her as a hotshot producer, and like all good producers, she kept her finger on the pulse. One day her office called us up to ask if I would come in for a meeting.

We met at her place; Julia told me about *Close Encounters*, describing it so vividly that I almost thought I was watching it. She went through the scene where Roy, Richard Dreyfuss's character, sees the flying saucer on the highway. She told me about the Devil's Tower obsession. Then she told me that she wanted us to do a funk version of the John Williams theme song. People were calling the movie CE3K; she wanted to call our version CE3funK. I wasn't sure about the title, but I was pretty sure that a song was a good idea. Why wouldn't I want to make good on the space funk I had started back on *Mothership Connection?* Plus, we had just started recording *Funkentelechy*, which was scheduled to come out the same month as the movie.

People now think of *Close Encounters* as one of the all-time greats, but back in the fall of 1977, the powers that be were anxious about its prospects. Spielberg had shown it to a preview audience somewhere in Texas, and they hadn't gotten it. It went over their heads or under their radar. He went back into production for another month or so and fixed up what he thought was wrong. Finally he was ready, and Julia called me back and invited me to the premiere.

The movie had events all over the world. There was a New York premiere; I think Bruce Springsteen went to that. There was a London premiere with Queen Elizabeth and a Tokyo premiere with the Japanese equivalents of Springsteen and the queen. But we were in Los Angeles, which meant that we had a Hollywood premiere, an event at the Cinerama Dome with a red carpet and plenty of stars. After everything I had heard about the movie, I wasn't sure what to expect: I knew almost too much about it, and for the first few minutes my head wasn't clear. But I got into it. By the time they got to the theme music, I had a good understanding of the broader concept. Those notes weren't just there for the enjoyment of the audience. The characters heard them and, more to the point, the aliens played them. It was the music from their world, their way of communicating basic needs and ideas.

Julia had invited us to a party at her house after the premiere. We stood outside the theater for a few minutes, unsure about the protocol. Who went into what limo? One car
and then another pulled away, and eventually it became clear
that we all had to fit inside the remaining car. Julia went first.
Some actor I didn't know went second. Then there was a guy
who seemed like he worked for the studio; he had his shirt open
almost to his navel. Then I went, and then two girls, and then
there was no more room. We knew there was no more room
because the next person out on the street got one leg into the
limo before it became clear that he wasn't going to be able to
get the other one in. "We have to go," Julia said to the driver.
We drove off without the poor guy—and by poor guy, I mean
Ringo Starr. We left the Beatle there on the curb and drove off
to Julia's house.

At the party, everybody filed in, already high, ready to get
higher. Nene had warned me about Julia's predatory ways.
"Bring Stephanie," he said. "Otherwise, I can't protect you from
her." When I walked in the front door, Julia pulled me into the
bedroom and showed me a picture of myself on her wall. It was
two or three weeks old at most. "This is how much I love you,"
she said. I figured that she was trying to impress me so that I
would do the song for the soundtrack. There wasn't any funny
business, at least not as far as sex. She did offer me some coke, of
course. I shook my head and pointed at the chain I wore around
my neck, and specifically at the little bottle that dangled from
the chain. I called it my Casablanca bottle. "No, thanks," I said.
"I'm all set." Julia wrote about that incident in her memoir, *You'll
Never Eat Lunch in This Town Again*, and though most of the rest
of the book is spent burning bridges left and right and running

people through, I somehow earned a compliment. I had the good manners to bring my own blow.

We ended up doing the disco version of the theme. When we cut the song, it was for a new group I had in mind called the Brides of Funkenstein. It was led by Lynn Mabry and Dawn Silva, both of whom had been singing backup for Sly through the mid-seventies, and who also sang backup for Eddie's solo album. Lynn and Dawn had tremendous range and innovation in their vocals, like the Pointer Sisters if they had come to Earth from another planet. In fact, that's where the idea for the Brides started: they were part of the story we developed for *The Clones of Dr. Funkenstein*. They sang great, and Bernie went absolutely fucking crazy on the keyboards. I loved the sound we were getting. As it turned out, after all that, Julia didn't use it. Hollywood. I brought it to Neil, who loved the song but thought the concept was too dark. Instead he wanted Casablanca to sign a different girl group we were developing for some of the other backup singers: Mallia Franklin, Jeanette Washington, and Debbie Wright. It was called the Parlets, after a group I had started way back in the doo-wop days. That was what you did in those days: you took your male group and feminized the name. Bobettes, Primettes, that kind of thing. So we worked it all out. The Brides went to Atlantic and Neil got Parlet. The P-Funk world expanded further.

★

Funkentelechy vs. the Placebo Syndrome came out Thanksgiving week in 1977, and it started to get the gravy immediately. "Bop Gun" was the first single, and the R&B stations jumped right on it and started to play it regularly. But our promotions guys were working the other songs, too. We had a guy who did promotion for us, Henry Mayer—he was a local, a corner kid who was friends with many of the DJs—and he went to one little station in Detroit, WGPR, where he talked to a jock who called himself the Electrifying Mojo. Mojo's real name was Charles Johnson, and he had started out in Little Rock, Arkansas, before coming to WAAM in Ann Arbor and then to Detroit. When he started at GPR in 1977, he had nothing, really, just seven P-Funk records and an idea about what a perfect radio show should sound like. He didn't hold to any existing formats. He might play a new song, then an old one, then talk for twenty minutes, then go back and play another song by the same artists he had already played. He bought his own time on the station so they couldn't tell him how to do his show, and almost immediately he started to develop a local following.

When Henry went to Mojo with *Funkentelechy*, Mojo started playing "Flash Light," and after that, Henry went to JLB, the big urban station, where Donnie Simpson had started out. Henry's contact there was Al Perkins, a big Detroit DJ who was one of the leaders of the national consortium of black jocks. Al liked power games, so he William Telled (or is it William Told?) Henry his conditions for jumping on board with "Flash Light": he said, "Let me shoot the cigarette out of your mouth and I'll put that song on the radio." Henry was so crazy that he let him, and "Flash Light," with Mojo and JLB behind it, started shooting straight up the charts. Later Al told me, "That guy was crazy. I was drunk as a motherfucker." It was almost an exact repeat of what had happened with *Mothership Connection*: release a strong R&B single, watch as a few other stations find their way to a pop song elsewhere on the album, sit back and let the charts draw us on up into the top ten. "Flash Light" went right to number one on

the R&B chart—the first song by any P-Funk group to do that—
and even made top-twenty pop. Everything exceeded my expectations. Well, almost everything: there was one afternoon when a
fan buttonholed Archie to tell him how much he liked our music.
"Man," he said. "I especially love that new record, *Funkadelic and
the Place-Bo Syndrome.*"

★

We had made fine records before. We would do it again. But if
I had to pick one P-Funk record to take to the moon, I'd take
Funkentelechy vs. the Placebo Syndrome. It did certain high-
concept things with such a nice light touch, and the music was
tight as a motherfucking drum. Almost everyone was responding to our sound, to the tradition we were creating. One of the
biggest soul songs that year was "Float On" by the Floaters; it
was written by James Mitchell from the Detroit Emeralds, which
was a Westbound group. Artists in every other genre fell into
line, too. George Duke, who had primarily been a jazz player
up to that point—though he had worked with Frank Zappa—
moved squarely into the funk world, releasing songs like
"Reach for It" and "Dukey Stick," both of which were cook-
ies from our cutter. New artists were another great way to measure influence: every week we'd see some young band springing
up, trying to make (or fake) the funk. Once again, the only artist who truly remained surprising on his own terms was Stevie
Wonder. When he recorded *Songs in the Key of Life* and *Journey
through the Secret Life of Plants*, he was gone for real. He left
the planet in a way that nobody else could do, and while I used
to get upset that he didn't do more funk songs, he had a different kind of ear. He was already way ahead. He was a composer

in the classic, and maybe even classical, sense. He was writing instant standards.

Right on the heels of *Funkentelechy vs. the Placebo Syndrome*, Bootsy released his third album, *Bootsy? Player of the Year*. If the first album had been an establishing shot and the second one a confirmation that he was a star, this one was all about him being ready for his close-up. The cover had a giant image of his trademark sunglasses, and they were actually a cutout so that kids could wear them. The songs on the album followed that script: the production of product, the oddity of commodity. "Bootzilla," the single, imagined Bootsy as a toy, "the world's only rhinestone rock-star doll." This was long before *Toy Story*, but it was the same idea: he was there to be played with, to entertain kids, and he even had a chip on his shoulder about the value of other toys: "Teddy bears and Barbie dolls can't boogie down."

Bootzilla, the toy, was futuristic (he came equipped with "stereophonic funk producin' disco inducin' twin magnetic rock receptors"), but he was also rooted in American pop culture, in the kind of hunger for novelty that had led to Davy Crockett, to hula hoops, to Motown, to the British Invasion. The fact that he was a fictional toy made little or no difference. "Bootzilla" rose into the highest heights of the R&B chart, where it replaced another song at the top. Let me check which song it knocked out. Oh, that's right: "Flash Light." It was a combination punch: hit 'em with the right, and while they're reeling, get 'em with the left.

The second single from *Bootsy? Player of the Year*, "Hollywood Squares," came at the same idea from the other side, arguing that celebrity was a game but one that had to be played with a certain amount of sincerity: Bootsy's alter ego, the Player, has a kind of romance with Hollywood itself. Other songs were more straightforward love ballads, but they became product, too, by virtue of their titles. Take a song like "May the Force Be with You." We wrapped a contemporary slogan around a timeless idea and the whole package looked a little brighter. That's how factories operated, by taking tried-and-true products and reworking them for the modern era.

We were reworking our own product, too. At the end of 1977, we hired a new management team: Steve Leber and David Krebs, who had been with Aerosmith and also managed Ted Nugent and Mahogany Rush. We knew we were in that rock space, and we thought they could help us navigate. Around that same time, most of the original Parliaments left the band: Calvin, Grady, Fuzzy. They hadn't been fully happy in years, and I could understand why. In the early years they were out in front, getting all the attention, all the girls, and then the spotlight shifted over to musicians like Billy and Eddie. Those guys were like their little brothers. They had sponsored them out of Plainfield. Those younger guys were brats and it was hard for the older guys to stomach them. Plus, when new members came in, like Bootsy, their stars shot right up past those original guys. They always had the nagging feeling that things could have gone in another direction, that they could have been on top of the elevator instead of inside it. They were wrong, of course, but you can't always control for right and wrong. In the music business, like in everything else, so much dissatisfaction has to do with outsize dreams. When people start out in groups, everybody imagines making it, but no one thinks hard about what that means. Does it mean being a star, staying in the top hotels, headlining arenas? Or is it enough to be able to do what almost no one in the world does, and sustain a career as a professional musician? The mere fact of surviving in this industry is a huge victory. But survivors forget that the alternative is annihilation. They think that the choice is between a good career and a great one. They reach for stardom. And those unrealistic expectations are compounded by creative ability, or the lack of ability. People don't have a clear idea of what they can and can't do as artists. I knew my limits. I knew what I couldn't do. I couldn't play an instrument. I couldn't sing as well as some and I couldn't arrange as well as some others. But I could see the whole picture from altitude, and that let me land the planes.

The live shows were getting even liver. We had everything that the *P-Funk Earth Tour* record had going for it, plus "Flash Light" and "Bop Gun." It was like topping off a skyscraper. Because of the success of "Flash Light," we added a stage effect. When the Mothership landed, five hundred lightbulbs exploded on either side of me. That was rock and roll but not just rock and roll. It was theater but not just theater. It was a kind of transformative moment, a secular religion, a level of experience I had never before imagined, and that few bands—the Who, Led Zeppelin, the Rolling Stones—ever reached. Crowds were starting to become hysterical. They were also helping us to understand how we were being understood: there was a level of membership and participation that was almost like a *Rocky Horror Picture Show* thing. At a show in Richmond—it was the same night when we almost couldn't take the stage because our costumes were late— they turned off the lights in the arena before the show and the crowd looked like a field of stars. Everyone was holding flashlights, which was something we'd never ever considered. The next show, in St. Louis, people were standing on the streets on the main road that led to the arena, selling light sabers for people to wave around in the dark. By the third show, we were selling both flashlights and light sabers ourselves. We were making as much money on lights as we were on T-shirts. In Washington, D.C., a cab driver who picked us up asked if we were Parliament. We were. "I'm pissed at you guys," he said. "I had a flat tire last night and I couldn't find a flashlight in the whole goddamn city."

Our official merchandising was handled by Billy Sparks. In Prince's *Purple Rain* movie, there's a rotund little chipmunk of a guy who plays the owner of First Avenue. He's always walking around in a tracksuit, talking to Morris Day, or sitting at the bar wearing a Detroit Tigers cap. That's Billy, and seven years before *Purple Rain*, he was the P-Funk merchandiser. Billy was the son of a guy named Diamond Jim, who had worked for Armen Boladian in Detroit, and they all were part of a crew that included the Electrifying Mojo and the promoter Quentin Perry. Before every show, we'd do a walk-around, check out the scene, and during that tour we started to see an increase in bootleg merchandise: T-shirts, posters, pins. We also noticed that some of the bootleg stuff looked nicer than the official merchandise we were selling. It was product that came from one bootlegger in particular, a guy named Slim Goody. Not only was his product good, but he had a gift of gab: he really connected with audiences, made them feel like they were buying a part of the group's excitement when they bought his merchandise. Billy wanted to shut him down because he was stepping on our profits, but I told Archie to cut a deal with him and make him an official bootlegger.

The tour rolled on, picking up momentum and picking up

new fans in the process. Very little dropped off, except occasional pieces of the Mothership itself. We had a side rig on the stage set that included a few giant props connected by a light truss: one of them was a sneaker about nine feet high. The whole piece of equipment was heavy as shit, a ton but for real, and the roadies got tired of putting it up for each and every show just to take it down again. It broke their backs. One day, they took it off the truck and just left it on the side of the road in North Carolina. We didn't notice that it was missing that night or the next. In fact, we didn't notice for six months. That tour was so complete that you could take away from it and it would still have been everything.

SO HIGH YOU CAN'T GET OVER IT

In the course of two years, we had released two Funkadelic records, three Parliament records (including the live set), two Rubber Band records, and side projects from acts like the Horny Horns and Eddie Hazel. Other groups might have taken a break. We opted for breakneck instead. We really felt like we had found our sound, and we kept rolling right into the next Funkadelic album, *One Nation Under a Groove.*

Funkadelic was the senior band (senior to Parliament, though junior to the Parliaments), but it was in a strange place. *Hardcore Jollies*, the first record we had done for Warners, was a hell of an album, but it had been folded into the big Mothership tour and then *Funkentelechy vs. the Placebo Syndrome*, both of which were overwhelming. It wasn't that Funkadelic was becoming an afterthought, exactly, but there was no denying that Parliament, both on record and onstage, was so massive and bright that it was hard to look away from it.

As we got ready to go back into the studio as Funkadelic, we added some new personnel. The most important arrival at that time was Junie Morrison. Junie had been one of the cornerstones of the Ohio Players, a band that had been around even longer than their name: in the early sixties, they had called themselves the Ohio Untouchables and backed the Falcons, a Detroit vocal group featuring Wilson Pickett. Junie had joined the Ohio Players in the early seventies, and I had introduced them to Armen, who signed them to Westbound. Junie was one of the main songwriters during that period, responsible for hits like "Funky Worm." Junie left before the Ohio Players went on to Mercury Records and even greater success, with songs like "Fire" and "Love Rollercoaster," but he was known around the music world as a brilliant guy capable of doing almost anything: writing, arranging, playing keyboards, preparing a band for a tour. He came aboard as musical director as we started to make the new Funkadelic record. In fact, you can hear his first day on the song "Doo-Doo Chasers"; that's him saying, "Which one is George Clinton?" That was kind of a joke that was going around at the time, because Bootsy was such a public face and I was a little less recognizable out of character.

Junie was a fascinating person to work with. He could do it all, and if you weren't careful, he would. When he made a record, his preference was to put down the bass, then the guitar, then the keyboards, then the drums. That was fantastic for demos. He could do brilliant things while you weren't looking. But it also meant that the finished product, at least when he was off on his own, could sound a little characterless. Just because you can play all the instruments doesn't mean that you should; you have to be mindful of which instruments sound like something special coming out of your hands, which ones have a distinct character, and you also have to play off others. That's how you get chemistry, by mixing elements. Junie wasn't the only one in danger of disappearing into the solitary-genius bag, of course. Sly had been like that before him. Prince would be like that after him. Even with them, there was a danger: if you don't go back to a group environment now and then, you start to lose your juice. With Funkadelic, he put himself back in the group environment, and it started to pay dividends immediately.

★

The title song of *One Nation Under a Groove* became one of our most beloved anthems. I didn't think of it that way at first. It was just another song, sparked by something two girls said to me after a concert in Washington, D.C. The girls, LaTanya and Darlene, came up to the car. "That's the greatest concert we've ever seen," they said. "It was like one nation under a groove." Junie and I wrote a song around that idea, and we went right into the studio and cut it. That day we had just gotten some new equipment, and we opened the boxes and went to town. It was the last song that we all played in the studio together, live and loud. There was such a feeling of togetherness in the room that it put the lyrics across. It was all of us, all the guitarists, all the keyboard players, all the drummers. Plus there was a dude playing the banjo who we didn't even really know. Years later, I ran into the girls who suggested the slogan. One of them was married by that time, and when I met her husband, he said, "How close were you and George exactly?" I said, "Man, that's a hell of a question to ask after seventy years."

Other songs pushed the concept forward. "Promentalshitbackwashpsychosis Enema Squad/The Doo-Doo Chasers" looked at funk from the other side, outlining all the horrible (and unsanitary) things that could happen if you didn't possess the clarifying power of funk: mental diarrhea, mental constipation, anything logical, illogical, or scatological.

The rhythms were leisurely and hypnotic, for the most part. One of the prettiest songs on the record, "Groovallegiance," was kind of an anthem for newcomers to the funk nation. The melody was taken from a Latin song I had heard back in the fifties. I had remembered it, and I'd always wanted to incorporate it into a P-Funk song. At one point, Nene had someone in Cuba go to the library and research the original lyrics, and it turns out they were about a spaceship landing in Havana, and the aliens getting out and dancing the cha-cha-cha. That clinched it for me. When I brought the song to the session, Bernie knew it instinctively. I sang the first few notes and he was able to finish it, exactly as it was in the fifties.

It's not the only time on that record that we used older songs as inspiration. "Who Says a Funk Band Can't Play Rock?!" took its melody from a church tune. Inspiration in these cases is unavoidable—there are only seven notes in music—and it's not even desirable to avoid it. Every Led Zeppelin song is an old blues. The Beatles lifted the famous solo in "Revolution" directly from Pee Wee Crayton. Living things find nourishment where they can. The point of music is to take what exists and to make it matter again, in your own style, with your own stamp. To talk about "original" and "unoriginal" is as unoriginal as talking about genres or categories. You never want to be in a bag, let alone someone else's bag. Music is music, and bands become what they are. They play because they want to, and audiences sense that and listen because they want to. That's what "Who Says a Funk Band Can't Play Rock?!" tried to explain, in fairly direct terms. It was a kind of encyclopedia entry, a sequel to "Mommy, What's a Funkadelic?" And while "One Nation Under a Groove" is thought of as the anthem from that record, "Who Says a Funk Band" is just as anthemic.

One Nation Under a Groove came out in September of 1978, with a bonus EP for the fans that included one extra song ("Lunchmeataphobia"), a second version of "Promentalshit-backwashpsychosis Enema Squad/The Doo-Doo Chasers," and a live version of "Maggot Brain" we had recorded in April in Louisiana.

★

We had toured with the Mothership for two years, and we were exhilarated but also exhausted. When *One Nation Under a Groove* came out, we headed off on what we called the Anti-Tour. We had no big stage set, just stripped-down equipment. We weren't playing huge venues, but rather smaller theaters. We even switched the bill around so we weren't the headliners of our own tour; we were opening for the Brides of Funkenstein. The band called the tour the chitlin circuit. Some of the new members made fun of the idea, though for the older musicians it felt like a throwback. We had been there before, driving overnight between cities just so we could play a short set to promote "Testify." We emphasized the basic-training feel by outfitting everyone in fatigues. It wasn't exactly U.S. Army issue, but it wasn't quite Maulana Karenga's U.S. Organization either. Most people had private rank, though Roger was an admiral and Junie was a general. In a way, it was a rebellion against what we had been told since the late sixties, that the band needed a brightly colored focal point to succeed. We were going back to democracy: that was the one nation.

At the start of the tour, our participation was kind of a secret, which meant that it was hard to fill venues. Sometimes I would go out into the street in front of the theater and pretend to sell the comp tickets: "Yo, man," I'd say, "five dollars for these? I'm just trying to get some dope." People looked at me strangely, not sure what my game was. They would whisper, "Is that George Clinton?" or, "Is he crazy?" We ran the Anti-Tour across the whole country, P-Funk and the Brides, barnstorming. We had new musicians like Jeff "Cherokee" Bunn, who played bass for the Brides, and we had part of Bootsy's band, too, though Bootsy himself wasn't there. By that point, he was starting to think a little bit like a solo act; he was booked into venues as himself, separate from the rest of us. During his very first show, they had to call me because he got shingles. He had people stationed outside his dressing room to guard him from fans and other musicians. Even Maceo couldn't go in there. It looked like he was pulling star attitude, though I think it was more a case of sunstroke. He was starting to feel a little like Icarus, getting too close to the sun, wings melting down, not certain how far he would fall or whether there was a net to catch him anymore.

As Funkadelic went under a groove, Parliament went under the water. I had been fishing my whole life, from the time I was a little boy. I loved the peacefulness, the way it took you away from the rest of the world. Starting in the mid-seventies, I started visiting Miami and chartering boats, sometimes to take us all the way out to Bimini. We were on the same boat, the *Sea Spirit*, for years until they took it out of commission and used it for *Miami Vice*: it was where the alligator lived. I started to notice that there was an entire genre of fishing signs, these cheesy, friendly, sometimes almost cartoonish posters and cards hawking bait and explaining etiquette. There was a lure named Mr. Wiggles with a funny little worm drawing. There was a place named Number One Bimini

Road. That world became the basis for the next Parliament project. We had been in the ghetto, electing a black government. We had been in the lab, making clones. We had been in space. Now we decided to make a concept album about raising Atlantis in the name of the funk: *Motor Booty Affair*. The title is a layered pun: "motor booty" instead of motor boat, and also instead of Motor City—it was an illustration of the way that the Detroit sound had evolved since Motown. I wrote about regular dolphins and card sharks, made celebrity puns along aquatic lines (that album has the immortal Howard Codsell). I had fish jokes for days, so many that I saved some of them for a later solo record, *You Shouldn't-Nuf Bit Fish*.

The album also expanded the P-Funk character gallery. Star Child had come along for *Mothership Connection*. Sir Nose showed up on *Funkentelechy vs. the Placebo Syndrome*. For *Motor Booty Affair*, the new character came directly from the signs I had seen at bait shops. It was Mr. Wiggles, the worm. We populated the ocean of *Motor Booty Affair* with mermaids and fish and everything you'd expect to see, but also with tribes from Africa who left the plains and went into the ocean. Mr. Wiggles was another clone of Dr. Funkenstein who had decided to become an underwater emissary for the funk. He was the one who threw the party.

I'm Mr. Wiggles the worm
These are my ladies Giggle and Squirm

There wasn't much filler on any of the Parliament albums, but *Motor Booty Affair* was particularly consistent. "Mr. Wiggles" phased right into "Rumpofsteelskin," a variation on the butt-centricity (and self-empowerment) of the album title:

Rumpofsteelskin, he don't rust and he don't bend
He's got dynamite sticks by the megatons in his butt

"(You're a Fish and I'm a) Water Sign" was a lush love song left over from my Hawaii writing session. "Liquid Sunshine" was a pop song, almost psychedelic, the kind of thing you might have heard back in 1968, but with a funk twist. And "Deep," which runs more than nine minutes, poked into pretty much every remaining corner: political organization, NIMBYism, and raising Atlantis to the top.

The biggest song on the album, though, was "Aqua Boogie (A Psychoalphadiscobetabioaquadoloop)," which came together in the same way as other signature Parliament songs like "Give Up the Funk" and "Flash Light." It has a burbling bass line that Bernie translated from a classical cello part, and crazy bird calls that I was doing (from the old Tarzan movies—they all had the same bird). "Aqua Boogie" is about Sir Nose refusing to swim; even though it's pleasurable, he sees it as another form of dancing, something that interferes with his perpetual cool. "Ahh, let go of my leg," he says, almost screaming. "I hate water." "Aqua Boogie" went up to number one on the R&B chart and parked there for a month. "Psychoalphadiscobetabioaquadoloop" dwarfed "Promentalshitbackwashpsychosis." Was it the longest word ever in a hit song title? Not quite, since it's exactly the same length as "Supercalifragilisticexpialidocious," from *Mary Poppins*, and "Hyperbolicsyllabicsesquedalymistic," from Isaac Hayes. Great minds think alike, and think along.

★

Musically, *Motor Booty Affair* was an extension of *Funkentelechy vs. the Placebo Syndrome*: funk as we had designed and refined it, but with an even greater sense of its own status as entertainment. Richard "Kush" Griffith and Junie did some of the arrangements, and they took them to the edge of what was acceptable for pop music. We had cabaret styles, Vegas-type arrangements. We had fanfares, like we were announcing a horse race. Junie had done some of that when he was with the Ohio Players, but on *Motor Booty Affair* he ran wild with it. That kind of thing might have sounded corny in another environment, but we were already so far out there that we weren't interested in coming back. Other bands kept their distance from anything that smacked of pure entertainment: they wanted to be serious, or spiritual, or Afro-cultural. In some cases, they even worried that we were making a mockery of what black pop music was becoming, somehow risking its legitimacy. "Man," they said, "don't mess it up." But we weren't messing anything up. We were moving into territory that I associated mainly with the Beatles. Even though it was more than a decade old at that point, I was still fucked up from *Sgt. Pepper's Lonely Hearts Club Band*. It had so many styles, from avant-garde rock and roll to song craft that was almost like Rodgers and Hammerstein, that it became a style all its own. *Motor Booty Affair* is, for me, our Beatles peak: it's the most ambitious record, the most layered, the one that's most ripe for rediscovery.

That feeling extends beyond the music. We had always known that there was a strong visual element to the record: it says so right on it, "A Motion Picture Underwater." And Overton went all-out with his illustration, starting with the way he incorporated little butts into the capital letters on the title: the M, the B, and the A. And he drew an incredible inside piece, a full gatefold mural of the world he had imagined. To this day, it's one of my favorite moments in the history of P-Funk art. Everything about that album was fun. Everyone fell into the concept willingly, enthusiastically. Maybe the Beatles analogy needs a little fine-tuning. Maybe it's not just that the record was ambitious sonically, or that it was stylistically diverse, but that it had a sense of humor that extended over the whole project, a kind of comic self-awareness. And maybe, then, in Beatle-speak, it's not our *Sgt. Pepper's*, but our *Yellow Submarine*. For me, that movie changed the game completely, as much as any Beatles record. It was a perfect monument of nonsense, a way to take grown-up topics and statements and play them off as kid stuff. There's a monster in that movie that starts to suck fish out of the sea, and then it sucks up the entire sea floor, and then it sucks itself up. That's the kind of creature that populates *Motor Booty Affair*, too: a playful darkness. For that record, we all lived in our own Yellow Submarine.

One Nation came out in September, and *Motor Booty* followed in November. That meant that we had to promote with Warners first, though that was a less-than-ideal situation. Warners was dealing with lots of shit stacked in layers. Someone over there had gotten it in their head that we were going to unite a bunch of groups, take over black music, and then make a run at the pop charts. But we had no interest in uniting Sly and Chaka and Cameo and the rest. If I was going to try new things, it would be with newer, younger acts. I wasn't going to fuck with people who had already established themselves. Their fear may not have been rational, but it was real, and the result was that they didn't promote as inventively or as energetically as Neil. He promoted the fuck out of the radio to get a hit, and they were content just to trail along behind, drafting in the wake he was creating.

Neil sent us to Europe to work *Motor Booty Affair*. Our first stop was London, and early on in that trip someone arranged for us to take a tour of the House of Lords. I went, listened to the tour guide, tried to take it all in, and toward the end of the trip ducked into the bathroom to do some coke. While I was snorting it up, the toilet flushed, and a lord walked out of the stall. He had his wig in his hand. He looked me up and down and said, finally, "I'm sure you're not the first." I was scared then a motherfucker. I didn't know what to say. Plus, it was hard to say anything—my mouth was frozen from the blow. So I resorted to Logic. Logic was this little stuffed animal I carried with me everywhere. When I got in situations that were too sticky to slide out of, I let Logic do the talking. I held him up and the guy actually started talking to him.

About a week later, I was at a club getting drunk with the two promotions guys who had been assigned to me: Lothar, a German guy, and Mike, a Jewish American. They were trying to one-up each other by telling the grossest concentration-camp jokes they could think of. I didn't think it was funny at all. It was some tedious shit. I collected my stuff and headed back to the hotel. It's good I did: they got drunker and drunker, got in a fight at the club, and ended up stumbling up to my room and stealing my minibar. When we were checking out, the hotel clerk ran his finger over the bill. "Mr. Lothar," he said. "It seems like you had quite a night." They had thrown my minibar out of the window, and then thrown their own. When they got clear enough of their hangover, they told me the good news: that while they were in the club, they heard "One Nation Under a Groove," and that the place was going crazy for it. Here we were, promoting Parliament, and our Funkadelic record was taking off under our noses.

After London, "One Nation" was rocket propelled. When we got to Luxembourg it was number one already, and the same thing happened in Germany. It went all around the world, taking over, and we followed it.

And so that was the end of Anti-Touring. From the start, we knew that the *Motor Booty* stage show was going to be a motherfucker. We were fully into the Broadway mentality. We had fish costumes for everyone in the band. We had giant, brightly colored coral. There was even a thought early on of putting a tank of water on the stage and performing behind it, though we decided on something more theatrical and simpler: fans laying flat and crepe paper blowing up like seaweed. Nene suggested building huge dolphin statues and suspending them over the crowd; he even had some friends in Mexico make them out of cement. As nervous as I had been during the Mothership tour when the little ship was out over the audience, I definitely wasn't putting no motherfucking five-hundred-pound dolphin above people's heads.

The Motor Booty Tour was scheduled to open at Madison Square Garden at the beginning of 1979, but somebody filed the wrong paper or made the wrong call, and the trucks with all the equipment got sent ahead to Milwaukee. We arrived at the Garden to find that we had no props. Many of the band members wanted to cancel, and some of them even went ahead to Milwaukee, but canceling was one of my hang-ups: when people paid to see us, I thought, we had to deliver. We had the Brides with us, along with some of Bootsy's musicians, and we cobbled together a group that could play the *Motor Booty* material. I was scared to death about how the crowd would react. We had tiny little amps that couldn't communicate the power of the band. We had promised water and couldn't deliver it. I made opening remarks to the crowd: "Most people wouldn't perform under these circumstances but we're going to perform anyway," I said. "The only water's going to be if you sweat. If you want your money back, ask." It ended up being one of the best shows we ever did. Only seven people asked for refunds.

The tour became a monster. In Washington, D.C., we were the headliners at RFK Stadium for a bill that included a bunch of go-go bands. People in D.C. love their go-go, and they stretched out their sets. The whole show was supposed to be finished by 9:30 P.M., but it was already 10:30 by the time Bootsy went on. He played a tighter set than usual, but we didn't take the stage until eleven. There were curfew laws in effect, union restrictions, and we were told in no uncertain terms that it would cost $10,000 every thirty minutes. Tiger Flower, Darryll and Carol, were freaking out. They had dreams of boats and houses and cars, and as it got closer to overtime it became clearer that they were going to have to pay penalties. "George has to go on," Archie said. "He's the headliner." They said that it was either Parliament-Funkadelic or Bootsy, but that it couldn't be both. Archie kept insisting, and Tiger Flower stormed out.

A few minutes later, Archie got a call from our booking agent at the time, David Libert. He was frantic. "Archie," he said. "George can't go on. They have me in a van with a gun to my head. I do believe that they're going to kill me."

Archie laughed. "David," he said. "These people aren't killers." There were some people he would have worried about, but Tiger Flower weren't among them. "Besides," Archie said, "if George doesn't go on, there's going to be a riot, and who knows how many people will be killed or hurt then."

We went on. Penalties were assessed. As a result of the penalties, Tiger Flower didn't pay the sound company, which meant that the next night, at the Richmond Coliseum, the sound company stiffed us. They didn't show up with our equipment. We didn't panic. We banded together with the other groups on the bill—L.T.D. and the Bar-Kays and Evelyn "Champagne" King—took everyone's equipment, and built a sound wall. Nobody thought that it would work, and everyone was afraid to try. Finally, Evelyn stepped up. She was the youngest of the bunch. "Show got to go on," she said. We all played with that sound wall, and it worked perfectly. At the show, we had a huge One Nation flag, big enough to cover a portion of the football field, and it wasn't until we were packing up after the show that we noticed that the flag had disappeared. It must have taken thirty people to carry it off, but we haven't seen it since.

That year was like ten years all in one: it was heady and dizzying and liberating. Along with the main records, we were putting out extra records at a clip: the Brides, Parlet, Bootsy, a second record from the Horny Horns. Bernie Worrell's solo record, *All the Woo in the World*, came out right around then, too, and that ended up being one of my favorite P-Funk side projects. It had one set band and an excellent sound, very tight, very artsy-fartsy. This was also one of the rare times that Bernie came forward into the spotlight. He majored in accompanying in music school and that's what he does best, and what he does most. He'll step up behind you and make you sound like the best thing in the world. But *All the Woo in the World* proved that there was also magic when he was at the center of things.

The new wave of side projects brought us in contact with a whole new crop of artists and musicians. The Parlet and Horny Horns records featured artwork by Ronald Edwards, who went by the name Stozo the Clown. Stozo was like a junior Overton; when we played Constitution Hall in Washington, D.C., he used to come up to us and show pictures he had drawn of me, Sly Stone, and James Brown. And we acquired another P-Funk guitar hero: Blackbyrd McKnight. Blackbyrd was an old friend of Archie's. He used to jam with Archie's college band in Archie's garage, and he had gone on to play with Herbie Hancock's band, the Headhunters. As we were putting the Brides together, he came to us as a lead player, and we quickly brought him into the main P-Funk fold. From the start, he brought an incredible mix of professionalism and invention; he was one of the most profound guitar players we had ever worked with, almost at the level of Eddie Hazel. Eddie had so much more feeling than anyone else, but Blackbyrd was versatile in ways that you had to see and hear to believe. He could just pick up a guitar and play a classical piece note-for-note without studying sheet music. That meant that we could try things with him that we wouldn't have even bothered trying before. We had so many ideas about where P-Funk might go. We were going to do records where the artists were our lawyers, records where the roadies played and sang. They were all citizens of the nation we were founding, and the sky wasn't even the limit. We had been in space.

★

There were some sad notes, of course. At times reality descended. Glen Goins had left, along with Jerome Brailey, to start a band called Quazar. They recorded an album for Arista, but before the record could come out, Glen passed. He had Hodgkin's disease, had been sick in fact as long as we had known him. When he first got with us, they told him he only had two or three months to live. He ended up surviving another three years. Tiki Fulwood also passed, from stomach cancer. We were all young men then—I wasn't yet forty—so to lose friends and bandmates to illness wasn't anything that made sense.

Another source of pain seemed like a pleasure at first. Near the end of the year, I was doing coke with a limo driver, a girl, and she turned to me and said, "You've got to try this." Right there in her hand was a freebase pipe. I took it. I tried it. The first motherfucking hit off the pipe, I thought I had found acid again. It was so good and powerful that it was like busting a nut. When that first high finally passed, I knew I had to have it again, as soon as I could. What I didn't know at the time—what I couldn't have known—is how long I would spend trying to find my way back to that initial surge of good feeling, and what the cost would be.

NEVER MISSIN' A BEAT

One Nation Under a Groove created a new idea for the next Funkadelic record, Uncle Jam Wants You. We had toyed with a kind of new funk patriotism, and we took that one step further, along with bringing some of the Afrocentric elements of the music into the light. For the first time since America Eats Its Young, we didn't use a piece of Pedro's art for the cover. Instead, there's a photo that shows me sitting in a wicker chair, in a parody of the famous Huey Newton portrait. Some people read the image as threatening, or paramilitary, but they were only looking at the surface. I was never a huge fan of the Black Power movement. I admired their aims, but I was more about dogs than dogma. I wasn't likely to get into a shootout with Black Panthers and Simba Wachanga, and I sure as shit wasn't going to get caught in the crossfire. Just as disconcerting, though, were the White Panthers. They were a presence in Detroit in the late sixties and early seventies. I supported the general idea of John Sinclair's freedom, but his followers made a habit of going around to black men and saying, "Hey, brother, are you on our side?" This sounded strange to me, like words that were losing aim as they traveled. They weren't brothers in blackness. Were they brothers in humanity? If so, why were they doing something strange with the word, moving it into this space where it sounded like SDS-type shit? In my mind, the message was always snarled when you had people pointing at a power structure and condemning it as they went about installing themselves at the head of a new one. I was more strategically naïve, trying to get to the best of times through the jest of times. Military icons and symbols had been considered a central part of revolution, but to me they were also a central part of comedy, and that's how I ended up there in the Huey Newton chair, sitting in the middle of a Funkadelic cover with the One Nation flag and two Parliament props, the Bop Gun and the flashlight.

None of this meant that we weren't trying for some kind of revolution, only that the revolution we had in mind was peaceful, hedonistic, and prone to winking at itself in the mirror. A record can overturn just by turning, can bring about revolution just by revolving. At its heart, *Uncle Jam Wants You* was a recruitment poster for music that was fighting for its life; we were trying to keep dance music alive without submitting entirely to disco. "(Not Just) Knee Deep," the central track on that record, was made with an eye toward trying to identify and isolate the essence of P-Funk. There are sections in there where we stripped down the twenty-four tracks on the mix to one or two, pulled down everything but a few voices. That was a test, for us, and then for audiences: Could P-Funk be identified from a single second on a single song? My argument was that it could. Songs had DNA, which went all the way back to *Clones of Dr. Funkenstein*. Even if you only had a tiny particle, the rest of the sound was implied. Other songs on the album were reinforcements, in the mock-military sense: "Uncle Jam," "Field Maneuvers," "Foot Soldiers (Star Spangled Funky)." If *One Nation Under a Groove* had been our Declaration of Independence, this demonstrated our willingness to defend that independence.

As it turned out, we were on war footing, at least where Warner Bros. was concerned. We knew that "(Not Just) Knee Deep" would be a huge single, but it became apparent from the jump that Warners wasn't going to work the record hard at radio. That meant that we had to do it ourselves, and we took it to jocks like the Electrifying Mojo, who loved it. All of a sudden the song was all over the airwaves in Detroit, and not just in Detroit: in Richmond, and Los Angeles, and other places, too, spreading across the map like it'd been spilled on it. And still Warners was unhappy. I remember getting ready to go onstage and the Warner Bros. promotion man was right next to me, yelling in my ear: "It's not going to go pop!" There I was, about to step out in front of forty thousand people, with the song hitting in a half dozen cities, and he wanted to talk about what the record wasn't going to do.

"Knee Deep" was only the center. Everything was whirling around us. The more funk bands we put out, the more other labels and other producers tried to create funk bands that sounded like us. That was all well and good—it was the sincerest form of flattery—but in fact we were going for something even more visionary. We were thinking in terms of shelf space. I remember conversations we had back then about getting funk separated from soul and R&B in the record store. Our concept was to break it out as a separate category and then fill that category.

In that climate, as we tried to break categories and make categories, the record label's primary interest seemed to be to limit our reach. They didn't want another Motown springing up, and P-Funk was the leading candidate to cause that kind of trouble.

There was a precedent for this kind of thinking. Back in the early seventies, the major labels had realized that the vast majority of their profit was coming from black music, and the Columbia Records Group had commissioned the Harvard Business School to do a study and figure out why all those profits were flowing to companies like Motown. That study circulated for years. It became the playbook for putting the freeze on black-music companies. Warners' moves in those late years of Funkadelic smelled like the Harvard Study.

Sometimes the Parliament-Funkadelic relationship felt like a seesaw, with the rise of one band coinciding with the decline of the other. Parliament had been riding high from *Mothership Connection* to *Motor Booty Affair*, at which point Funkadelic sprang up with *One Nation Under a Groove*. I was getting six or seven hundred thousand dollars as an advance for each Parliament album, comparable to what pop records were getting and more than most soul records. Even so, as we started work on our next one, I started to feel the tide receding. It was how the system worked. The record business operated on a principle of planned obsolescence. The same was true in other businesses. A suit is cool until it's not. A pair of shoes is cool until it's not. That's how Western capitalism has always worked. Consumers get trained to think that the thing they possess doesn't meet their needs anymore—even if your car is driving like a dream, you'll run over every pothole in the world just to bust an axle and get yourself a new one. The only remedy is a new possession. In the record world, for a little while, that means a new album from your favorite band, but soon enough it means a new band.

The album that emerged from that thinking was *Gloryhallastoopid (or Pin the Tale on the Funky)*, a long title but one that made perfect sense. We were glad and a little surprised to still be around. How could we still be a dominant force in funk music? At the same time, we knew it couldn't last forever, and we wanted to be in control of the wind-down the same way we had been in charge of the windup. Pinning the tale, or the tail, was a way of beginning to end the story. And in true Parliament fashion, the story we told wasn't just about the band, but about the whole universe. The prologue summed it up.

Quarks, gluons, red giants, white dwarfs, big bang
There are eight billion tales in the naked universe

It's the outer-space version of the old joke that opinions are like assholes, because everyone has one, and we went back to cosmology and astronomy again and again. *Gloryhallastoopid* was our Carl Sagan record, with songs like "The Big Bang Theory" (a dense weave of brass, guitar, and synthesizers) and "Theme from the Black Hole" (which brought back Sir Nose). We were returning to the beginning of time, trying to figure out how existence (and funk) might have started in the first place. Our concerns weren't all mental and philosophical, of course. "Party People" was a James Brown update: instead of getting on the good foot, we talked about foot funk. "May We Bang You?" has a triple meaning: science, sex, and music. And "Theme from the Black Hole" was all about the relationship between astronomy and ass. As the lyrics said, "a tale is nothing but a long booty," and the song opened with "a toast to the booty," then later shifted into a toast to the boogie: "Bottoms up." The sound was heavy on horns and synthesizers, and much of the new energy, as always, came from new blood: Michael "Clip" Payne, who had started out working with Norman Whitfield at Motown and had been with us since *Motor Booty Affair*, took on an expanded role in the band, singing and playing keyboards.

The set of songs was so coherent that we imagined it as a stage play called *Popsicle Stick*. We actually performed it at the Apollo Theater, the landmark institution in Harlem, which was in jeopardy of being closed down at the time. Artists pitched in, and for our part we played a three-week stand to help the place stay open. Those shows were billed as "George Clinton's Production of *Popsicle Stick*," and I only came onstage in major cities. Mostly, I was back in Detroit with Sly, getting deeper into studio production. The songs were not only theatrical, but were reflecting what was happening in the movies, the same way that *Mothership Connection* had paralleled *Star Wars*. A few weeks after *Gloryhallastoopid* came out, Disney released a science-fiction movie called *The Black Hole* and it starred, among other actors, Joseph Bottoms. Black hole, bottoms up.

In addition to probing the mysteries of the universe, *Gloryhallastoopid* illustrated one of the strangest phenomena in our own little world, which was the way Overton Loyd's illustrations had of angering people. Overton drew caricatures of everyone in the band, and while some people loved what he did, others couldn't stand seeing themselves in his funhouse mirror. Roger Troutman, a keyboardist and songwriter who had been a childhood friend of Bootsy's and joined us around that time, was violently angry at the way Overton made him look: cute, but with big eyebrows and a little devilish. Philippé Wynne tore his up. On *Gloryhallastoopid*, Overton drew the cover art, and to pay off the pun of the subtitle, he created a donkey character. We divided responsibilities, though, assigning the inside art to Pedro Bell, and in the course of making his Pedro puns, he lettered in something about the "Stone Shitty Band," which was a takeoff on Rick James's Stone City Band. Rick put two and two together, somehow got five, and became convinced that the donkey on the cover was supposed to be him. I told him the donkey was too pretty to be him. It was clean.

Within a year, *Gloryhallastoopid* turned true: the tale got pinned. In 1977, Neil had sold half of Casablanca to Polygram Records, and they would buy him out entirely in 1980. From the start, Polygram wasn't happy about the way Neil spent money. To say that he didn't run it like a bottom-line business was an understatement. He put nearly every penny of profit back into promotion, from stunts to parties to whatever else came to mind. On top of that, there was the matter of his sales figures. He pressed so many copies of each record and shipped so many that on the books it looked like he was selling a billion records. But somehow most of those records ended up coming back to him; people liked to say that Neil shipped gold and returned platinum. It was a good system for the Casablanca artists—we benefited from the inflated sales figures and from his lavish promotions—but it wasn't as good for a corporation in for 50 percent. The tension between the label and the corporation escalated. Polygram sent out one accountant to check Neil's numbers, but within a couple weeks he had been turned: he was driving around town in a Porsche with a coke spoon around his neck, and he didn't seem too concerned about Casablanca's finances. The second guy was German, and he hung in there long enough to find evidence that

Neil had cooked the books. What was funny was that the only group that was truly in the black was Parliament. Even though he was spending tons of money to showcase us and promote us, the expenditure was minimal compared to what he was spending on acts like Donna Summer and Kiss. At any rate, after this German guy discovered proof of Neil's creative accounting, Polygram decided to shut down Casablanca's West Coast office and ship everything to New York by truck. The truck never made it. Somewhere in Ohio, it caught fire and all the records burned.

Neil took the cash from the sale and started Boardwalk Records, which tried to set up a similar roster: rock and roll acts like Joan Jett, funk bands like the Ohio Players (relatively late in their career), pop groups like Get Wet. Except for Joan Jett, none of them reached the heights of the big Casablanca artists. During the Casablanca-to-Boardwalk transition, Neil had wanted us to come over with him to Boardwalk, though I didn't learn about his desire for fifteen years. I'm not sure we would have gone, but it would have been nice to be able to factor that into our decision. And what was our decision? It was complicated. When Neil left Casablanca, we raised the possibility that we would leave, too, and take our masters with us. Casablanca said that they wanted us to stay, and that to prove their loyalty they would give us an imprint of our own, a label under the Casablanca banner we'd use to release P-Funk material. We called it Choza Negra, which translates as "black shack": we were the little house out back behind the white house, which is what Casablanca meant. We had several projects in mind, including a record for Bernie Worrell and one for my son Tracey. The deal was complicated. We got control over masters, artwork, and publishing, but Polygram claimed that we still owed them a debt from past records, and to offset that, we gave them a portion of our publishing rights as a collateral loan.

The negotiations were successful, but they also occurred under a cloud of bad feeling. We weren't happy that Neil was gone. The label wasn't happy with what we had asked for in the wake of his departure. And all the black acts in the company had been placed under the control of one executive, Bill Heywood, who had a grudge against us; he had been the man in charge of the Ohio Players when they were Mercury's big act, and his acts were constantly stymied and prevented from climbing the charts by P-Funk's records. There was one incident during that time that captures the flavor of the negotiations. Archie Ivy and Nene were in with Casablanca, explaining how Neil's departure meant that we were free to go unless they got better terms for Parliament. One of the guys from Casablanca started banging on the table. "How can you complain?" he said. "We just signed a deal for your boy's soundtrack work!" They didn't know what he was saying—and, as it turned out, neither did he. Casablanca had signed a deal with a composer named George S. Clinton, who had scored some films.

As a result of all of these issues, the first Parliament record to come out under the Casablanca/Choza Negra banner, *Trombipulation*, wasn't aggressively backed by the label. It's a shame because that record had a real good concept. Rather than go back to the beginning of the universe, we decided to go back to the beginning of our own universe, to transport Parliament to the time of the Parliaments. It was still P-Funk, but it was P-Funk with doo-wop in mind: there's a song on there called "New Doo Review" that comes right out and makes the argument that funk is the "new doo."

But if going back to Plainfield in our minds meant going back to doo-wop, it also meant something just as important: going back to the barbershop. "New Doo Review" split the difference: *doo* was doo-wop and also hairdo.

For that record's cover, we didn't use one of Overton's illustrations. We had something else in mind: a photo that would show me in ancient Egypt, rising up among the pyramids and the Sphinx. But it wasn't me as I looked in 1980. It was a version of me equipped with an elephant's trunk—the nose beyond Sir Nose, the organ that was filled with funk rather than devoid of it—and an incredible wave in my hair. That was a demanding photo shoot, to say the least. For the trunk of funk, we went to one of the dudes who put extension dicks on people, and he built us a special prosthetic to fit over my nose. That shit was on so tight you could have picked me up by it.

I had my hair done, and done right, by a guy I knew named June, a barber from Newark. He was the fucking best there was. He hadn't done that kind of wave for twenty years, and he conked the shit out of it and made just a beautiful work of art there on the top of my head. That cover photo isn't treated at all. That's how my hair looked.

Trombipulation was the flagship of another big idea, which was to start cross-promoting our records with real-life hair products. The same time it came out, Bootsy put out *Ultra Wave*, and we went to Johnson & Johnson and tried to sell them on a campaign. That was a blunder, as it turned out, because we didn't have the kind of backing we had when Neil was running Casablanca. The corporations we were working with after Neil wanted things to be done a certain way, through certain channels, and the record label didn't support our right to swim in open ocean. Things felt more locked up and constricting than they had in years. Bootsy brought some incredible tracks to those sessions, and songs like "Let's Play House" were high-end examples of late Parliament, filled with horns, horniness, and humor. But I could feel the ice freezing.

★

Around Christmas of 1979, midway between *Gloryhallastoopid* and *Trombipulation*, I bought a farm. There was a guy we all knew named Richard who provided things for rock stars. People with money wanted toys, and he was a kind of personal shopper. When he asked me what I wanted, I thought about it for a while, and told him that mainly I was interested in weed and blow. He laughed at me. "You have plenty of that," he said, "and plenty of money to get more. Think higher." He thought higher for me. He bought some paintings by Salvador Dalí, a letter Mick Jagger had sent that included handwritten lyrics, a William Burroughs manuscript. None of those were bad things, but none were perfect fits. Finally I sat down and really thought about it. I had been working straight for a decade, living mostly on the road. If I paused and took a measure of things, what did I want? "I know," I told Richard. "I want a farm and some land with a lake on it." I was born a country boy. I grew up running around in fields and fishing in creeks. As much as I had grown to love Detroit and Los Angeles, I loved being outside in nature, where there was peace and privacy. Richard went right out and found three or four properties in the country outside of Detroit, including one where they didn't have a lake but were willing to build one. Monies changed hands, and just like that I was a gentleman farmer.

The first day I was on my new farm, I sat in the main house

and walked around the place. It was just what I had expected, and within hours I was already hearing new kinds of sounds—or maybe it was the absence of certain old kinds of sounds. Either way, I was sure that it would be a place where I could recharge. Later that day, I wandered into the barn, which had everything you need to run a farm and also everything you would need to build a highway. The guy who had owned it had been contracted to build the interstate, and the house had been partly built with leftover materials from that job. But what caught my attention was a book sitting on top of a wooden box, facedown. I went over and turned the book so I could read the title. It was a history of Roswell, New Mexico, which had supposedly been the site of a UFO sighting in 1947, and an analysis of the government conspiracy to cover it up. Since I had been a little kid, I was always interested in the possibility of alien life. I was absolutely certain that man wasn't alone in the universe. How could we be? To think that Earth was the only planet with life was the height of arrogance. The stories I invented for P-Funk—Star Child, Dr. Funkenstein, the landing of the Mothership—were my way of dealing with these questions. The Roswell book in the barn was like the book about clones in the Dallas airport train, another message being sent directly to me. Even in the country, in the middle of peaceful nothing, my obsessions were finding me.

That same winter, I reconnected with Sly Stone. Nene had brought him around in the fall before I went out to the farm. He had met Sly through Bootsy; they were doing a short film for a single from *Bootsy? Player of the Year*, "Roto-Rooter," up on Hollywood Boulevard, and Nene had taken footage of them in a limo.

A few weeks later, in New York, a bunch of us were supposed to go to an event commemorating Martin Luther King Jr., but we couldn't make it, and instead we ended up at a small party over at Jessica Cleaves's house. Nene showed up with Sly, who Jessica knew from back in the early days, when she was lead singer of Friends of Distinction. Whenever Sly and I had met before, it had been in passing, or backstage during a tour. Even when we had been on the road together, I hadn't really sat down and talked with him for any extended period of time, man to man, friend to friend. In New York I had time, and we hit it off immediately: we had similar interests but different worldviews, similar skills but different histories. We had everything to talk about, from music to politics to drugs to the strange, distorted-field psychology of stardom. Sly had been on top of the world when I was just coming up—he was an idol and an icon, one of the brightest lights not just in pop music but in the world—but the seventies had belonged to P-Funk and other artists, and Sly had fallen off slightly. Or rather, the market had receded from him, though he was just as brilliant as ever. If anything, he lacked momentum, and the confidence to think that he'd find his way again. He knew that the world had taken him down a peg, and it preoccupied him. During that party, Sly asked me a question. "Man," he said. "Who in your circle is going to rib me for not being a big star anymore?"

"I don't know many people who think like that," I said. In fact, I could only think of one, my ex-partner Liz Bishop. "She'll say something for sure," I said. "You can bet the fucking house on that." The only other one I could think of, maybe, was Nene, and I suspected that Sly already knew that. At the end of the party, I told Sly to come see me in Michigan anytime he wanted.

The holidays came and went. I moved out to the farm. And

then Sly came out to the farm. He was always in one bind or another in those days: at that time, I think he was on the run from a dealer up in Connecticut, and I had even heard that he'd been kidnapped for a time. I told him he could stay with me as long as he wanted. He ended up staying a year. We'd fish in the morning, then get high, have some lunch, then continue with the party. We were wrecked half the time at least. But we were also recording, and the shit we were getting down on tape was crazy. Sly could be sitting there doing nothing and then open his eyes and shock you with a lyric so brilliant that it was obvious no one had ever thought of it before. I hadn't made records with him before. I was impressed and humbled all at once. He was the strangest mix of personalities I had ever seen: funny as fuck on one hand, careless and wild but meticulous on the other, a badass when it came to arranging and producing.

He also made a prophet out of me, a little bit. A few days after Sly showed up, Liz came in and saw him standing there. "Mister Sylvester Stewart," she said. "Who's on top now? I remember when you were a big deal."

"That's got to be your ex-wife," Sly said. Then he turned to Liz. "Was I cute?" he said. He had a twinkle in his eye when he said it, so you could see the star that used to be there, and also see how the man who was remembering stardom suspected that it was all a big joke.

One afternoon, the weather was too nice to sit inside, so Sly and I got into the car and went for a drive. After about five minutes, Sly had an idea. "Let's go get David," he said. David was David Ruffin, who had been the lead singer for the Temptations. David was home, and he got into the car. As soon as we started driving again, Sly had another idea. "Let's go score," he said. Off we went to the dope man's house.

Just before we got there, I asked Sly if he had any cash on him. He didn't. He turned and looked at David, who shrugged. It's not an uncommon occurrence to show up at a drug dealer's house without cash, which is why it's important to establish credit. When we pulled up in front of the house, we sent Sly inside to try to arrange things. He had the slickest rap, the tongue with the most silver in it. We saw Sly talking to the dealer and then they motioned for us to come up the walk. "Credit's fine," the dope man said. "I'll set you up. Just give me a minute because I'm busy."

We sat outside on the stoop, watching the nice weather go by. Or rather, two of us did. David sprung up and started pacing. "What's wrong?" I said.

"Waiting's wrong," he said. "Doesn't this shit bother you, man?" he said.

"He said a minute," Sly said. "Just stay calm."

"Fuck that," David said. "Why do you let motherfuckers treat you like that?" David paced faster and faster in front of the house. His forehead was so wrinkled you couldn't have ironed that shit flat. I started to ride him a little. "What do you want?" I said. "You want him to put the shit on Temptations rush?" He mumbled about going in and strong-arming the guy, or getting in the car and driving away, but he did neither. He wanted. Eventually he calmed down, and eventually we were served.

That was only one of hundreds of scores, but I think about it often. What ultimately saved David that day—what saved us all through that time, maybe—was desperation. It's ironic, but it's true. Crack ruled you in part because it cost too much money. And it put you in a jungle where you were either top cat or you were prey or you were one of the thousands of animals going about its business, not especially visible, not especially troublesome. That's where we were at the time: we were all three begging, and we weren't worth anyone's trouble. Pretty soon after that, David had a comeback with Hall and Oates. They made a record with him and Eddie Kendricks, *Live at the Apollo*, and it was a big hit, a major part of how the eighties rediscovered classic Motown. That's what did him in. When he had money again, he was a target. He died about a decade later, after reuniting the Temptations and touring the world, and though some reports claimed it was an overdose, there were too many suspicious circumstances hovering nearby: there was missing money, people who weren't willing to talk.

Another time, Sly and I were visiting a dealer who could sing you every song from every album Sly had ever made. Whenever we bought from him, he was over the moon that he was selling to his idol. One day, light-pocketed as usual, Sly resorted to barter. "Man," he said to the dealer. "I'll tell you what I'll do. I don't have any cash on me, but let me give you a copy of the album I'm working on." The guy was beside himself with joy. He took that tape like it was a religious artifact and put it in a special desk drawer. I don't think he had any intention of listening to it. That would have been too much for him. Just to have it in there, heating up the place, was enough.

We got the drugs and left. About a block from the house, Sly told me that it was a blank tape. I bagged up. I couldn't believe it. "Yep," he said. "Blank. Nothing on it whatsoever. It's just some fucking tape I found in the studio."

The next time we went to score, I thought Sly was going to tell the guy, but he didn't. Instead he asked if his album was being taken care of, and even told the guy he could listen to it, but in a way that made sure that wouldn't happen. Sly kept the guy going like that for a week or two, and finally I felt so bad that I had to cop to it. I waited until Sly was out of the room and turned to the guy quickly. "You know there's shit on that tape," I said.

"What do you mean?" he said. "The music isn't any good?" He looked devastated.

"No," I said. "I mean there's nothing on the tape at all. It's blank."

The expression on his face was like a kid who was told there was no Santa Claus, but even worse: there was no Christmas at all. Even when I promised that we'd pay him for the dope, all he could do was nod numbly. When he recovered enough to speak, he told me that he wasn't even mad at Sly. His reaction was more like admiration. "Come on," he said. "How can you be mad at *that* motherfucker?"

Once, Sly and I were playing a show, and when we went on-stage, Tom Joyner came and stole our pipes. When we came back afterward, he was standing there holding the pipes upside down, draining them, which is a crackhead sin. Years later, on his radio show, Tom would clown about me when I got busted, or lost a court case, though he never seemed to mention any of the stories that involved him. Another time, I had to send Sly to get Bootsy from the hotel. We were playing the Capital Centre,

and Roger opened up. About twenty minutes before his set was
scheduled to end, we looked around: no Bootsy. Someone told us
that he had left for the hotel and wasn't coming back. He meant
to punish Roger—someone, probably Nene, had put some fric-
tion between Roger and Bootsy—but he was punishing us all.
Sly volunteered to go get Bootsy. He went to the hotel, knocked
on the door, and started wheedling. "Bootsy, man," he said,
"you made me promise that I wasn't going to fuck up in front
of George. I'm coming to get you, man. You have to be a good
example for me." Bootsy was up on the bed with the pillow in
his mouth to keep from laughing. "Come on, Bootsy," Sly said.
"I've played these hotel rooms before. Nobody comes to see you.
When somebody does, you need to answer the door. Come on,
man." Bootsy was on the verge of busting, but he couldn't come
out. Finally, Sly knew he was up against it. He came back and
told us that at least he had tried. He played his set, and he was
excellent. That night, he even gave himself an extra reward for
trying to coax Bootsy back—he came out of the Mothership. He
emerged and walked down to the bottom of the steps, and people
were applauding like crazy. And then, about ten seconds later,
they started applauding even louder. He was proud. He thought
the applause was for him. What he didn't see was that I was right
behind him, buck naked.

Sly was the most perceptive person I had ever met. He remembered everything about everyone, put you immediately in the
Sly file. But a normal conversation with him was more like an
interrogation. If you told him you grew up in Kentucky, he'd ask
you about the horse races, and if you answered too slowly, or

too specifically, or with too much of an interest in the way he was hearing your answer, he'd know that he had caught you in a lie. Once we were hanging out with Henry Mayer, the young guy who we sent around to radio stations for Parliament. "Hey, Limp," Sly said, "didn't it use to be the other leg?" Henry had always walked a little crooked, but Sly had the idea that he was putting his limp on, maybe not faking it entirely but exaggerating, and damned if it wasn't true that Henry had switched legs somewhere along the way.

Lots of people tried to be like Sly. Take Rick James: more than half of the shit he did was in direct imitation. But there were only two people who were capable of that kind of cool: Miles Davis and Sly. I didn't know Miles as well, but watching Sly was a strange experience, both educational and disorienting. To me, crazy is a prerequisite for greatness. But it doesn't have to be actual craziness. I play crazy, when in reality, I'm pretty close to sane. Sly wasn't playing. He believed in his own abilities, but he also believed in his own legend. And while he was a real nice guy in most ways, he wouldn't hesitate to misuse you when it came to money and drugs. Of course, he was so ahead of the game that he wouldn't try to trick you. He'd come right out and ask you if he could misuse you. If he wanted money so he could make a drug buy—maybe he wanted to impress a dealer or a girlfriend—he had a way of asking. He'd say, "Can I star?" If you gave him the money, you had to make peace with the idea that you might never see it again. Giving money to Sly wasn't a loan. You had to come back at him the same way he came at you. I'd say to him, "That was fine, but I will be starring in the show next week." That would make him laugh. He loved people who knew how to get theirs.

One afternoon we were at the airport and we heard a voice calling Sly: "Mr. Sylvester Stewart?" We looked down and saw this lady in a wheelchair, her arms all bent and folded by some kind of palsy. "You were very good last night," she said to Sly. "Very good." Sly almost never let his guard down, but this time he was in a great mood from the show—he had done an extended version of "Stand!" where everybody got up and everybody got down. He leaned in to kiss the lady. Just then she snatched back, all curled up, and said, "About time you got your shit together." Sly didn't know what to do. He wasn't usually at a loss for words. He stopped in midair, leaning over her. "Hey," he said. "Hey, hey." His voice was suddenly really heavy, resounding like he was back onstage. "Fuck you," he said, "you wheel-kneed bitch." There were about twenty people standing there, some from the band and some not, who heard the whole thing. Everybody ran in every direction because they couldn't laugh right there. They ran like roaches when the light comes on. The lady just sat there, looking stunned, stars around her head like in the cartoons.

But the lady wasn't wrong about Sly needing to get his shit together, especially when it came to playing live. Many times, Sly didn't have performances that really connected with the crowd, and sometimes he would refuse to come out at all. In fact, all you had to do was tell him to do something, and that was an iron-clad guarantee that he'd do the opposite. The only way you were going to get him out there was to kill him. I felt nearly the opposite: when the Motor Booty Tour had threatened to derail in that first show in Madison Square Garden, I had taken a skeleton crew out there and hoped that bare bones would be enough. Sly used to tweak me for being so conscientious. "George has those little ones," he would say. What he meant was that I survived in the business by understanding other people's behaviors and motives, and by knowing that they were part of a larger picture. Sly got so mad sometimes that he wanted to kill someone, but I considered the consequences. "You can't be mad at the kid in the mailroom," I said, "because one day he might end up running the company." And I didn't redirect my frustration wrong: if a promoter was being unreasonable, I didn't take it out on the audience. Sly admired me for it. He wished he could keep a cool head. He just couldn't. Like Miles, though, he was in a special zone, in rare air. They were so good at what they did that the bad shit didn't count. They got a pass.

Sly and I were different when it came to drugs, too. I have a big drug reputation, and some of it is earned, but in other ways I've always been a punk user. I was the same way as a kid. Other kids were thugs for real, but if a group of us went to rob a store, I made sure to leave before anyone wearing a uniform appeared. I couldn't get caught up in that shit or else my father would whip my ass. Plus, when I thought about it, I realized that I didn't have to really rob the place. I just had to be there to be seen with the people who were going to rob it. Drugs were the same way. I got high but I tried never to get strung out. I wanted to go to bed at a time that made sense, so that I could work the next day. And I hated the idea of using down to the bone and then jonesing for more. Sly operated at the other extreme. He would party until everything was gone and then use tactics to resupply himself. One night, out on tour somewhere, he slipped a note under my door. It was written in his handwriting, which was beautiful. He wrote like he was addressing wedding invitations. "Knock knock," it said, "put a rock in a sock and sock it to me, doc. Signed, co-junkie for the funk." Everything that motherfucker wrote was like a song lyric. Later on, while he was in a battle with his label, paranoid about people trying to get new songs from him, I told him I was just going to publish his dope notes.

YOU CAN WALK A MILE IN MY SHOES, BUT YOU CAN'T DANCE A STEP IN MY FEET

Warners was trimming the sails on Funkadelic. Polygram was putting Parliament in dry dock. But we had an idea for a new flagship: a label of our own, overseen by me and by Archie Ivy, which we'd call Uncle Jam Records. It made perfect sense. We had proven with *Funkentelechy vs. the Placebo Syndrome* and *One Nation Under a Groove* that we could deliver hits, but we had also proven with the Brides and Parlet and especially Bootsy that we could oversee other acts.

From the start, we had an Uncle Jam roster in mind. We had Philippé Wynne, who had been with Bootsy way back in the Pacemakers days. He had gotten famous as the lead singer for the Spinners and had been one of the main singers on "(Not Just) Knee Deep." I knew that Philippé had a solo record in him. We had Roger Troutman, who had played around Cincinnati and Dayton before joining up with Funkadelic. We had Jessica Cleaves, who had sung with us for years and was ready for her close-up. And we had Bootsy, sort of.

In the late seventies, Bootsy had encountered a speed bump

regarding his use of the Rubber Band name. There was a little folk act called Rubber Band somewhere in California, and the guy who ran that band sent a letter to Warner Bros. It wasn't a combative letter. He was a Bootsy fan. He was just looking for a little payout for consideration, five hundred dollars, a thousand tops. It seemed like a painless solution and I recommended that Bootsy just pay him. But Warner Bros. copped an attitude and refused to pay. The case went before a judge, who upped the settlement to five thousand. Even then, Warners kept going. They looked right at the judge and said, "We're Warner Bros. We can pay that standing on our head." The judge looked right back at him and said, "Oh yeah? Try five hundred thousand and get back on your feet." Just like that, Warners was out a half million dollars. The ruling stipulated that the label couldn't take the payment out of Bootsy's royalties, but they did it anyway. We did Sweat Band sessions when the Rubber Band was hanging in the balance, but it snapped back into place predictably, and he went on to record a few more records for Warners.

Armed with our artists, we sent our lawyer, Ina Meibach, and our managers, Leber and Krebs, to get a deal, and they came back with an offer from CBS. The plan called for four albums through Uncle Jam, with an advance of a quarter million for each. It was good money, especially since many of the tracks that would make up the albums were already under way, though I had friends who were wary. Some of them wondered why we needed to expand that way. Others worried that the Uncle Jam deal was part of a plan to topple P-Funk, that these additional albums were intended to overload the circuit and short us out. As I was getting ready to sign the deal, that occurred to me, too. I was already committed to something like seventeen other albums: releases from Parliament and Funkadelic, of course, Bootsy's records, projects with the Brides and Parlet, the Horny Horns, a solo album with Eddie Hazel, and more. I had help, of course. Tracey, my son, was an incredibly prolific lyric writer. I had production and arrangement wizards like Junie and also Ron Dunbar, who had overseen the Brides. I was sure we could do it.

As we were signing, I was told that Leber and Krebs were planning, with Ina's knowledge, to overpay themselves out of the advance. Nene flipped out. He said that they were robbing me blind. He got loud on Ina about how she was ripping us all off. He may have been a little rough, but there was truth to what he was saying: that was just how things were done in the record business. Ina also represented the Who, and whenever their manager, Kit Lambert, was in New York, she would lock up her office early, because Kit had a habit of coming around unannounced, and she didn't want him looking at any paperwork. Entertainment lawyers had a habit of being half in the shade, and Nene, at least at that point, wasn't having any of it. We severed our ties with both Ina and Leber and Krebs. When Ina left, it was with a warning to Nene: "You can say anything you want to me," she said, "but don't ever talk like that in front of the artist."

The bad feeling from their departure lifted quickly. Archie, Nene, and I were now running a record label, and we went to seal the deal with Walter Yetnikoff, the head of CBS, and Dick Asher, who had been brought over from Polygram to be CBS's deputy president. We were wearing the military outfits we used on the Anti-Tour and for *Uncle Jam Wants You*, and at one point during the meeting, Dick Asher leaned over and said, "Don't sew those stripes on too tight." I didn't get a definitive interpretation of his remark, but I took it to mean that we needed to watch our backs, that we shouldn't get too big for our britches. No one was safe in the record business. (It also seemed that Asher was taking a shot at Yetnikoff, who he would later feud with over using independent promoters. Yetnikoff would win that feud, and Asher would be out within a few years.) I laughed it off at the time. I saw only one goal, which was to make new music, and I had enough confidence in myself and the people around me that I was sure it going to be a Motown for real.

Uncle Jam got rolling. We released the Sweat Band record. We released Philippé Wynne's solo record, *Wynne Jammin'*. Third up was Roger Troutman. We were already familiar with Roger, not just because he had worked with Funkadelic, but because he and his family band, Zapp, were signed to Warner Bros. In 1979, they were working on their debut for Warners, which included a song called "Funky Bounce." Someone—maybe Roger himself, maybe Bootsy, who was working with them, brought me the track. I didn't love it. I didn't hear where it was going. One section, though, really appealed to me. I thought that if I isolated that and then had Roger add his trademark talk-box vocals and organ, it could really be something. I looped the section, called Roger, and told him that I had made a new song. He wasn't thrilled, but I had some leverage—I was trying to finalize his Uncle Jam solo deal—so he went along with it. That song became "More Bounce to the Ounce," which was a monster hit. People loved the same groove I loved. I made sure that Roger and Bootsy were listed as producers, not from altruism but from strategy. I couldn't afford to pay them what I thought they were worth, but both of them were extremely creative, and they deserved some real money. Making them producers was one way to make that happen.

After "More Bounce to the Ounce," we started right in on Roger's solo album. The song I thought would be the single was a cover, Roger style, of "I Heard It Through the Grapevine," and there was another strong track called "So Ruff, So Tough." Of all those early Uncle Jam records, Roger's record was the one that I thought had the most commercial potential. Roger seemed to think so, too. A few weeks before the album was scheduled to come out, Roger told me that he wanted to make a gesture of his appreciation: he wanted to give me $10,000, and to do it onstage. Sly thought something smelled funny. "Suits don't be doing nothing like that," he said. "There's got to be another reason." Sly called Roger and his band "Suits" because of how they dressed, and he was skeptical about an onstage payout because the whole Zapp crew had a reputation for being extremely cheap. They had an old bus and some of the guys in the bus had to double as bus drivers. When they weren't recording, they took jobs as roofers. "They ain't just going to give you no ten thousand," Sly said. I wasn't sure he was right, but it was Sly talking, so I didn't take the money.

The release date drew closer. One night, I got a frantic phone call from someone at United Sound studio. "Roger's masters aren't here," they said. He had come in and said that he needed to take them out so that he could "add horns in Ohio," and the studio released the tapes to him. They shouldn't have—he didn't own them—but our stuff was fairly loose. We were running crosstown regularly; it wasn't that odd for masters to go from one studio to another. I called around until I located them: they were over at Warner Bros., where Roger himself had taken them. He was planning to put them out with Warners. In short order,

Warner Bros. released the album, and it was the exact same album that we had intended for Uncle Jam. It had the same title, *The Many Facets of Roger*. It had the same cover design. "I Heard It Through the Grapevine" went out as the single, and it was a big hit, like I thought it would be. It just wasn't a hit for Uncle Jam. Bob Krasnow came over to talk to me in Los Angeles; I was staying at the Beverly Comstock. "You're a label now," he said. "This is just business." I raised hell and expected CBS to do the same. But they didn't fight very hard, which made it clear that the backing I thought we had was more a figment of my imagination than a reality.

When Roger's tapes mysteriously disappeared from United Sound, other things began to come apart at the seams as well. When we turned in the new Funkadelic album to Warner Bros.— it included the tracks that I had been working on with Sly—I got an advance, but found that it didn't go as far as it used to, both because we were doing so much recording and because the drugs were getting more expensive. Out there in Los Angeles, working on sessions, trying to piece together various projects, I suddenly felt stranded, without any real source of support.

One of the projects was a record that had started out as something for my younger brother Jimmy Giles. We had created a band for him called Jimmy G. and the Tackheads, and we were starting to get songs lined up. One of them, "Hydraulic Pump," was a standout. Philippé Wynne sang on it, and after him we got other vocalists aboard, too: Sly, Bobby Womack. With the three of them, it seemed larger than a Jimmy G. and the Tackheads record. I called Armen Boladian and proposed to him that we start a new label for the express purpose of releasing "Hydraulic Pump." We decided to call it Hump Records, and he agreed to pay $90,000 for the song. While I thought of the deal with Armen as only a stopgap, Nene loved the idea that we had found a new source of funds. "He's a water hole," he told Archie. "Why just take this one little thing?"

Deciding who to trust was complicated by the fact that I was high nearly all the time. One night, Sly and I drove out and sat in the car in front of a Denny's for an hour or so, waiting for a dealer. Sly prepared all the equipment and utensils so we would be ready to smoke the crack as soon as we took delivery. When the coke came, he made a rock and took a hit. Meanwhile, the people in Denny's had been watching us sitting there for so long that their suspicions were aroused. Someone made a call, and as we drove out of the lot, the police met us coming in. The car was so cloudy from crack smoke that they couldn't really see in, but we saw them clear as day. I broke the pipe and put the remaining drugs in my mouth. When the windows went down they recognized us, and they sat us on the curb and mocked us: "If it isn't Sly Stone and Dr. Funkenstein." They went through the car, found nothing, but managed to get an old fragment of pipe from Sly's trunk. It was enough to hold us overnight. The next morning, a friend of Sly's came down and got us out. Jail wasn't pleasant. It never was. But what was worse was the sense of being on the slide, with gravity increasing. I don't like stories where people melodramatically announce that they have hit bottom, as if that somehow suspends or justifies the rest of the choices that they have to make, as if it erases the other characters and the very idea of consequence. On the other hand, I don't know how else to explain that day and the days that followed, when I was marooned in the wake of turning in new material, when I was watching Uncle Jam come down around my ears, when I was scrambling to make a little bit of money so I could make more music.

I didn't necessarily want P-Funk to be all about me. At times I wished that others would step in and pick up the slack. But that wasn't happening. Starting in the early seventies, maybe around *America Eats Its Young*, I had tried to set up a system where everyone was capable of creating records. All the people working with me trusted me and I trusted them to work with one another. The part where I earned their trust seemed to work out, more or less. I stayed optimistic. I dreamed up things that happened: as my friend Ronnie said, people saw some money come out of a bank and turn into a Mothership, and that process had some magic in it. On the other hand, as it turned out, people had trouble trusting each other. That was something I didn't understand. If you're going to learn anything, it's that you have to work with other people. You can't always ensure that your creativity is in working order, and people can differ on their opinions of a song. But damn, the basic shit that's required is that you get along. Every time a band member started working as an arranger or a producer, I took him on a fishing trip and talked through the process. There was a kind of manual of what to do and what not to do. Working well with others was at the head of the to-do list. But the lesson had trouble sinking in. Instead, people who had every reason to be close collaborators kept their distance from one another; Junie and Bootsy lived right near each other, practically grew up together, and they never thought of working together. Roger used to call me every night to tell me what was happening in this session and that one, rather than talking to those other musicians directly. The result was that communication between the acts was poor, and fault lines started to open up. There wasn't a quake yet, but there was the possibility of one.

In the midst of all that chaos, another Funkadelic record came out. The funny thing was that I had nothing to do with it. Fuzzy, Calvin, and Grady did. They had left the band numerous times before. Grady usually came back, but the other two stayed away. Finally, Grady left for good, too. The concept of the band had moved beyond them, at least in their minds. They didn't feel there was room for the Parliaments in the P-Funk world. They created their own band on the side, hooked up with a producer named Jerry Goldstein (who had been a singer in the sixties band the Strangeloves), and cooked up the idea that they were still Funkadelic, that the three of them somehow had rights to the name. And then they went and released an album called *Connections and Disconnections*, which came out in Europe in 1980 and then in the United States in 1981. How can you go and release an album by a band with the same name as a band still signed to a major label? It seemed patently absurd. But I knew what they were trying to do. I understood the impulse to create your own work. I never saw too much or heard too much about their record, but what little I heard made me think that it was neither good nor as bad as people said it was. When I was asked about it by reporters or by other bands, I played it off. As a kid, I never liked to see the artists that I liked fighting among each other. That kind of backstage drama wasn't useful for fans. Also, there wasn't interpersonal animosity. When we ran into each other on the road, or back in Detroit, the vibe was always pretty okay. They were guys I had known forever, since we were kids. Grudge didn't come into it. In the whole messy business, only one thing bothered me: when they gave interviews as me. Those interviews were more sins of omission: reporters would call, thinking they were talking to me, and Fuzzy or Grady or Calvin would ignore the misunderstanding and just let the interview run. When the piece came out and someone clarified, the papers called them back and said, "Oh, I thought you were George," and they would just laugh or shrug. Eventually, the courts got around to dealing with the case, and they determined that the three of them didn't have any claim to the name. The actual ruling was stylish: in the judge's words, "There is no partnership in the ownership of the Mothership." Over the years they've kept rereleasing that record, and in 1998 they joined forces with Ray Davis, who was sick at the time with throat cancer, to put out an album under the name Original P.

When we came back to Detroit after Roger's defection, there was a cloud of stink around us. Ronnie Ford told me that it was difficult to find musicians to work with us, that people kept their distance. Maybe there was a whisper campaign, or maybe people had had their fill. Internally, there was just as much dysfunction. Personality issues with Nene were intensifying.

From the first time I met him, when he came in to set up the P-Funk documentary, he was a relentlessly strategic person. He would interview me and scrutinize my beliefs. He tried to find out if I was into religion, which philosophies I endorsed. It could have been honest curiosity but it didn't feel that way. At one point, he gave me a copy of Machiavelli's *The Prince*, which seemed to be a way of hiding behind a clear announcement of his own intentions. When he negotiated contracts for us—and there were plenty to negotiate, at all levels—he would march into of-

P-Funk was full of cartoon characters, from Sir Nose
to Star Child. Here's an Overton Loyd cartoon of
a man who's anything but a cartoon: my longtime
confidant and manager Archie Ivy.

Promoting *One Nation Under a Groove* with Archie Ivy
at a Los Angeles radio station.

Enlisting in Uncle Jam's Army was more painless (and funkier) than enlisting in Uncle Sam's Army.

Another Overtoon: Sir Nose, refusing as always.

New doo review: Philippé Wynne, Bootsy Collins, me,
and Maceo Parker in 1980.

You shouldn't-nuf bit, fish: hung up and hanging on the line.

32

Taking a break on the set of the "Atomic Dog" video.

33

Smelling the stank: just offstage in Washington, feeling how funky the band is.

Sons of the P: Me with my sons Darryl and Tracey.

Doing some paperwork in the office.

Funk Rock: with the great comedian Chris Rock.

Office meeting: With Sly Stone, dressed for work.

Let's play house: standing in front of my childhood home
in Chase City, Virginia.

Rainbow hair, mirrored glasses, and an endless crowd.

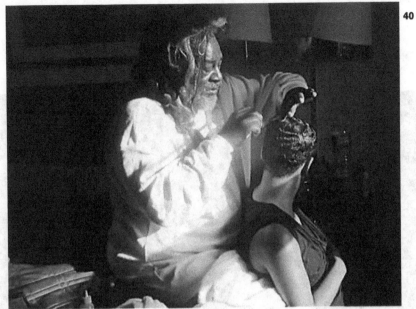

Doing hair is like riding a bike: once you learn how,
you never forget.

In the studio with Sly Stone.

Dr. Dr. Funkenstein: receiving an honorary degree
from the Berklee College of Music in Boston.

The Smithsonian has its own spaceship, just like P-Funk.

A cat in a hat.

Taking it to the stage at Lupo's Heartbreak Hotel in
Providence, Rhode Island.

The past surprises the present: posing with the spectacular
mechanical ad for *Motor Booty Affair*, many years after the fact.

The new Funkadelic album, *Shake the Gate*, with cover art by Pedro Bell. For a taste of the album, including a free download of the title song, "Brothas Be, Yo Like George, Ain't That Funkin' Kinda Hard on You?," just scan the book cover with your smartphone or visit www.BrothasBeLikeGeorge.com.

fices, stand right in front of desks where nice people were trying to do their work, and be unnecessarily abusive. His attitude was never healthy, never forgiving, never straightforward. Once, we were riding along the highway in the bus and there was a billboard advertising some hip ministry that showed a picture of Jesus with a rock-star hairdo. "Wow," I said. "He looks like one of the Bee Gees." Nene got upset with me, but not on Jesus's behalf. He looked kind of like that, too, and he seemed to take it personally. "Are you comparing yourself with Jesus?" I said. I was just joking, but that only made him angrier. I forgot about the incident right after it happened, but about a week later, in a hotel, Nene got the Bible from the desk, said, "You think I care about this?" and flung it against the wall. I just walked away from that one. "I'm not standing next to you," I said.

The Bible wasn't his only prop. In his early years with us, Nene never bought us drugs; he steered clear of that aspect of the business. But then once, he was traveling to Argentina and asked for some money to bring back coke. He wanted $30,000. Everyone thought that was strange, and I agreed, but I was also relieved that he was finally asking for something. He came back with six kilos of coke, which is an ungodly amount, and brought one kilo over to my house. I broke it open. It was a motherfucking mountain of powder. I had all these puppets at my place, marionettes of Mickey Mouse and Minnie Mouse hanging from the ceiling, and I liked to play little games with them, stuff money in their hands. Mickey had two thousand. Minnie had the same. Nene noticed the puppets and blew his top. "Disney will have you lynched for that," he said. "You can't do that!" But it didn't stop him from bringing in more drugs, getting better and better at surfacing with them. He brought around something called "pasta," which was cocaine melted into a kind of paste: I think maybe they treated it with airplane fuel, or kerosene, which soaked into the coke itself. It was brown and nasty and had everyone at everyone else's throat, because when you used it, it didn't give you more than a little buzz, which was irritating as shit. We knew some people at the University of Michigan, and we found a kid there who got us a scientist who could turn it back into powder. But for six months there, it was all pasta.

By 1980, there was a division in the P-Funk world between the people who could put up with Nene and those who couldn't. Jessica Cleaves couldn't stand him. Boogie kept his distance; Catfish, too. Ronnie Ford, who started coming out on the road with us in 1979, later told me that it was evident to him that something was awry. He didn't feel comfortable saying anything because he was fairly new to the P-Funk family, but he had been a barber for years, and he knew personalities. He had met every kind of motherfucker there was, and he bristled at Nene. Nene even clashed a few times with Sly. The two of them were arguing one day, and Nene said, "My man is Archie." Sly paused for a little while, gave one of those slow-burn looks, and then said, "What is this, who-loves-Archie-the-most week?"

His talent for rubbing people the wrong way extended beyond the band. We used to go to an El Salvadoran nightclub on Sunset Boulevard where the Cubans hung out. They would put on one Cuban song, and all those motherfuckers sitting there would start crying like babies. Lots of them were Bay of Pigs guys, and I learned some inside information from them. You know how you can tell if somebody was really at the Bay of Pigs invasion? Ask, "What happened to Milton's drawers?" When they all got locked up in Cuba, somebody stole Milton's drawers. If they don't know what you're saying, they weren't there. All of those guys owed Nene a favor, but all of them hated him. "This guy here," they'd say. "He got my mother out of Cuba and my brother of out jail. And while I'll do anything in the world for Archie, I won't do shit for Nene." There was one guy named Jorge who used to sit there quiet. Nene got him to smoke coke all night long and he had a heart attack. He was almost dead. Nene went to see him in the hospital with a crazy therapy: he took towels from the rack and stuffed them in Jorge's gown to make titties. He put a wig on Jorge's head and then did his lips with lipstick. "My love," Nene said, "you cannot die on me." Jorge said that right there and then he made a pledge to himself: "I'm going to live so I can kill this motherfucker."

As manipulative as Nene was, he was still effective, which is why I was slow to harden against him. Plus, I saw the way he tweaked authority—my style was different, but the aim was sometimes the same—and how people were infatuated by his aggressiveness and daring. David Carradine was one of his best friends, and the two of them would set up a meal, get all the food on the table, and then pee on it. I wouldn't have done that, but I understood the idea of disrupting something so traditional. Every time my suspicions about Nene began to mount, I weighed my misgivings against the fact that he was clearly helping with our business relationships. He was a fixer, a clarifier. He spoke frankly to managers and lawyers who were robbing us blind, and the next thing you knew, they were gone. In that sense, at least, I trusted him. Plus, it was vital to send him around with Archie on his visits to labels. Archie was fairly young and he wasn't yet sophisticated in business matters. He hadn't yet mastered the rhythm of a board meeting: when to lay low, when to speak up, when to charge in with a demand. Nene was a master at those kinds of things.

The record that I turned in just before Sly and I were busted outside of Denny's, *Electric Spanking of War Babies*, came out in August of 1981, and it wasn't exactly what I wanted. The recording process had been long and spread out—I did some sessions with Sly, some with Junie, some with Bootsy, some with Ron Dunbar—and as we wrapped it up, I realized that I hadn't been in any shape to bring things into proper focus. The sound on the record was too thin, without that trademark United Sound power. There are some arrangements that are too busy. I'm not sold on the way the tracks were sequenced.

It's a shame, because I love that album. I love the title. I love the concept. *Electric Spanking of War Babies* was an extension of the line drawn from *Uncle Jam Wants You* to *One Nation Under a Groove*, in the sense that it examined the darker side of patriotism: the idea was that governments promote their own agenda through mass media, which was electronically manipulating and beating up the brains of the Baby Boomers. The bomb was dropped on Japan. They were flattened. Over the next decades they advanced so much. I wondered if maybe some of their abilities had been enhanced by the bomb, or if some defense mechanism was triggered that had strengthened them. I knew we were being bombarded by technology and radiation, these threats of nuclear power. This was at the height of the Cold War, when every James Bond movie found him fighting over missiles. What if the bomb was, in small doses, a solution? I put a party song down, with lyrics like "You can walk a mile in my shoes, but you can't dance a step in my feet," and then I got to the more complicated issues: Vietnam, LSD, the moon landing, computers.

We imagined a government in partnership with big business, which is something that has since happened for real with Clear Channel. These days, try to find a radio station that isn't rigidly formatted to maximize corporate profit. At that time, at the beginning of the Reagan era, there was a movement toward deregulation of industries, and that meant antitrust laws and other safeguards to prevent companies from acquiring total control were weakening. The new deregulated mass media could be controlled by whoever put the most money on their side of the scale.

The other major song on that record is "Funk Gets Stronger," which exists in two versions, one produced by Sly and the other by Sly and Bootsy. Both of them have serious grooves, and the longer one, which we called the "Killer Millimeter Longer" version, has some of Sly's most poetic lyrics.

"Funk Gets Stronger" was our way of reminding people that we could take a punch. It presented the antidote to the electric spanking, the pure and powerful force that could stop the deception from happening.

Other songs explored different types of deception. Nancy Reagan's Just Say No to drugs campaign didn't start until a little later, but that idea was something you could already feel in the culture. That was, for me, a major misstep in social management. As far as I was concerned, anytime you made something taboo, that increased its value. Human intelligence, when denied something, will immediately ask why. That goes right back to the Garden of

Eden. As a form of social management, a war on drugs is a terrible strategy, ineffective and self-defeating. Nancy Reagan was probably sincere in her motives when she promoted Just Say No, but she had to know somewhere deep down that it didn't work.

Another form of control that was beginning to bubble up at the time was oversensitivity in sexual matters. Prudishness seemed like another terrible strategy, especially since it usually went hand in hand with media using sex as a false shock tactic. Cue "Icka Prick":

> *Icka prick and iron pussy*
> *Yucka fuck and muscle cunt*

Almost every song on *Electric Spanking of War Babies* dealt with those same central issues, though they approached them from various angles. There's a track called "Brettino's Bounce" named for the kid of the percussionist Larry Fratangelo. It was an instrumental with various world rhythms all mixed in together: African drums, Bahamian junkanoo. Even that was connected to the main theme: there was a beat, a rhythm, that communicated as effectively as a television or radio. That was the original mass media.

If we hadn't felt like we were on good terms with Warner Bros. for *Uncle Jam, Electric Spanking of War Babies* made it clear that we were on even shakier ground. The record was abandoned by the label. They only pressed ninety thousand copies, and that was in the wake of two consecutive platinum albums. I saw that they really didn't want it to happen.

Since the lyrics talked overtly about social control, it made sense for Pedro to draw one of his man/machine covers, and he did a piece with an H. R. Giger feel, a portrait of a woman who was using a kind of military-industrial-complex sex toy. We were told that we got letters of protest about it, which wasn't anything new. We had gotten a few letters of protest on every album since the beginning. Every artist does. But this time, the record company acted on it, and every time they pressed more copies, they switched that cover art for inside art. This dance over the cover—it wasn't censorship, exactly, but it was control—felt like spillover from the last few years. They still seemed upset about the unexpected way that "One Nation Under a Groove" had blown up and nervous about what we might do if we regrouped and started a new label.

At the time, it was hard to see the whole chessboard. When you're fucked up on crack, you function from behind a thickening smoke screen. Whenever I had an inkling that something was amiss, I discounted it by 60 percent at least. I figured that more than half of what I was thinking was coming directly from the drugs and the paranoia. But sometimes when you say the sky is falling, it actually is. Warner Bros. wasn't there for Funkadelic. Casablanca didn't exist in the same way it had, for Parliament or anyone else. Uncle Jam Records had been like Howard Hughes's *Spruce Goose*, which had flown for a second and then returned to earth. As we went out on the road with a series of concerts we called the World's Greatest Funk Tour, I started to realize that we were not just touring behind *Electric Spanking of War Babies*, but behind the entire decade. *Funkadelic*, our debut, came out in March of 1970. *Electric Spanking of War Babies* had been released in August of 1981. Between Parliament, Funkadelic, and all our spinoff acts, there were almost forty albums in all. You could stack them and the pile would be too high to get your hands—or your head—around. In late 1981, after a final show in Detroit, I suspended operations for both Parliament and Funkadelic.

THE DOG THAT CHASES ITS
TAIL WILL BE DIZZY

Getting high laid me low. I'm not especially judgmental about drugs, but I can't ignore the fact that they interfered with my ability to do what needed to be done. The record companies had done their best to put the brakes on P-Funk, and I was fucked up enough to let it happen. At a time when I needed the best advice and counsel, I had Nene Montes. I couldn't get rid of him, because he was my lifeline as the ship was sinking. All of a sudden, it was impossible to line up work. It was like rolling the clock back fifteen years, back to the mid-sixties, when I was just getting in good with Mr. Wingate at Golden World.

At the worst down-and-out point, a man named Ted Currier brought an idea to Nene. Ted, who was heading up the black-music division for Capitol Records, had a band he wanted me and Bootsy to produce: they were called Xavier, and they came from Dayton, Ohio. They wanted us to create a single for Xavier, though under slightly unconventional conditions—we would be monitored closely, because people weren't sure that we could deliver. We wrote a straight funk record called "Work That Sucker to Death" that turned into a big hit for Capitol (and, years later, was featured prominently on the Sonic the Hedgehog video game). It was a Xavier single in name only: you can hear me call out to Bootsy right in the middle of the song. It was P-Funk through and through, with P-Funk percussion, P-Funk guitar, P-Funk chants, and P-Funk energy. We just flipped that shit right around. It was easy. I knew we still had our fingers on the pulse.

Within a few months, the success of "Work That Sucker to Death" led to a solo deal for me with Capitol. Nene was instrumental in getting the deal, but as always, his style set the tone for my relationship with the label. He ran the shit out of both Capitol and Currier, raising so much hell in my name that no one wanted to deal with him. Sly still had his antennae up around him, and he wasn't too fond of Ted Currier, either. One time, we were riding in a car and Ted was sucking up to Sly. Sly hated that. Once he figured out that you were buttering him up, he'd misuse you to death. Flattery was his weakness, and he was always on guard against it. After that, Sly just drifted away, there in the car. He pretended to be so high that he nodded out so that no one would talk to him. I learned to do the same thing from him. When you go out in public like that, acting stoned and dizzy, people leave you alone. They think you're a crazy motherfucker, and they respect your right not to participate in their reality. In that car, at that time, reality wasn't cutting it. We were all talking about music, and someone mentioned Miles Davis. "Who is that?" Ted said. We all laughed until it was clear that he wasn't joking: the head of Capitol's black-music division didn't know who Miles Davis was. After we all got out of the car, Sly turned to me. "Man," he said, "that motherfucker's full of shit."

That may have been true, but I had to be signed, and so I signed with Capitol for four albums. As usual, I had tracks ready to go. I was recording with two different production groups. One was led by Junie Morrison, or rather, it consisted of Junie and me, trading ideas, polishing up tracks. The material I did with Junie was an extension of the songs we had recorded for *One Nation Under a Groove* and *Electric Spanking of War Babies*, though with even more decoration and sound effects—the eighties were all about bright colors, the neons of new wave. There were songs like "Pot Sharing Tots" (a pure pop ballad about a love affair between two toddlers) and "One Fun at a Time" (an ode to monogamy), along with "Computer Games," which became the title song of that first solo album. "Computer Games" was a door to the future, even if it was an unhinged door: it was a diamond-hard dance song narrated partly by Mother Funkenstein that devolved (or evolved, depending on how evolved you were) into a surreal, cartoonish list of boasts about how I could out-Woody a pecker, out-banana a split, out-toilet a seat, and so on.

Junie and I had gotten so comfortable working together that we didn't even really need to be in the same place. He would go in, do his work, and leave. I was mostly in a hotel getting high, and I got out when I could get out and came to the studio and added my part. When I wasn't working with Junie, I was cutting tracks with Garry Shider and David Spradley, not just for *Computer Games* but for a second album that was growing from the seed of the "Hydraulic Pump" single I had put out on Hump Records. That second record wouldn't be credited to me as a solo album—it was a group album I had decided to credit to the P-Funk All Stars, which was just Funkadelic by a different name. Those two projects sprung up simultaneously, which was a kind of throwback to the Parliament-Funkadelic days—I had two distinct styles that I could go to, depending on the material. The difference was that I wasn't necessarily looking to make albums that had a single tone.

So maybe one day I'd concentrate more on work I was doing with Junie, but the next day David and Garry would do something that fit better with the solo album, and I'd rearrange the set. That's what happened with "Loopzilla," which was a kind of medley song that David, Garry, and I imagined as the sound of a radio station running through snippets of other songs: "Dancing in the Streets," "I Can't Help Myself (Sugar Pie, Honey Bunch)," Zapp's "More Bounce to the Ounce," and even recent late-period Funkadelic hits like "One Nation Under a Groove" and "(Not Just) Knee Deep." "Loopzilla" was originally the end of another song called "Pumpin' It Up," but while "Pumpin' It Up" ended up on the P-Funk All Stars record, I saved "Loopzilla" for the solo project.

Working with Garry and David was a different experience from collaborating with Junie—they were a team rather than a solitary producer, so their work had more of a social component, with more conversation and more fellowship. That meant, oddly enough, that there was a greater chance that I'd feel left out if I came by and saw them working. One night I came in to find that they had done up a new track, just the basic music. I was fucked up something major, nearly out of dope, starting to get paranoid that they might be moving ahead without me. Can you be left off your own solo album? That's crack for you. Anxiety focused me, and I shifted over to a supervisory tone, told them to play me what they were making. "I'll just put some vocals on here," I said, trying to sound businesslike. At that point it was mainly just a dragging percussion sound, without the keyboard melody, and I just started right in with a freestyle, making things up as I went. The vocals stayed spoken rather than sung because I didn't know what key the thing was in.

As with "Computer Games," the lyrics were a free-associative stream of puns and phrases.

> *Yeah, this is a story of a famous dog*
> *For the dog that chases its tail will be busy*

The spontaneity of the lyrics didn't mean that they weren't considered. Dogs had a long history in soul music, stretching back to that great string of Rufus Thomas singles in the early sixties: "The Dog," "Walking the Dog," "Can Your Monkey Do the Dog," "Somebody Stole My Dog." I was thinking about how those combined comedy and soul, but also how they connected to other common phrases. Treat him like a dog. Dog day afternoon. It's a dog's life. What did those sayings mean, exactly? That men had instincts that couldn't be suppressed? That failure was an inevitable part of the equation? Most of the hard-luck cartoon characters were dogs. They were hangdog. They were underdogs. I settled on "Atomic Dog" because it was a Reagan-era idea, something for the Cold War. I wrote a song about human behavior as animal behavior: "Why must I chase the cat?" could have been about pussy, drugs, or money, but no matter which of those you picked, it was still about the unthinking, relentless instinct to pursue. "Atomic Dog" was rooted in cartoons, too, though not as aggressively as "Computer Games": only Huckleberry Hound made a second appearance. And then, of course, there was a chant, the kind of thing that would spread out across a crowd and keep on moving until it filled an auditorium:

> *Bow-wow-wow-yippie-yo-yippie-ay*
> *Bow-wow-yippie-yo-yippie-ay*

It was the catchiest thing I had made since the glory days of Parliament, and just as I was finishing it up, I got bad news from the past. Neil Bogart had died, not even forty years old, from cancer. People said he had lymphoma, but they said other things, too, and there was talk that he was taking quaaludes in large amounts right up until the end. I don't know. I wasn't with him. I can't say if fast living caught up with him or if he was still going so fast that he ran into something immovable. But his death reminded me what it was like to have a collaborator on the business side who understood our creative vision.

When *Computer Games* came out in November 1982, Capitol picked "Loopzilla" for the first single. We played a few small club dates to promote the record, and then, after the New Year, Capitol sent me over to England for a series of promotional appearances. At that time I was in Miami, living in a hotel, mostly staying inside and getting high. The day I went to England I got my hair done in a little shop in Coconut Grove. The girl did it up in braids and put beads on them. Those braids pulled the skin on my head back; the effect was like a face-lift. When I look at those pictures now I laugh because I know how tired and strung out I was, but I look real fresh. Over in England, I appeared on *Top of the Pops* with Grandmaster Flash. I was technically promoting "Loopzilla," but all anyone wanted to talk about was "Atomic Dog." That's when I realized that the song had blown up.

I went right back to Miami to get a group together for the tour. It was a full house: we had Eddie, Blackbyrd, and Michael on guitar; Bernie and Junie on keyboards; Dennis Chambers and

Rodney "Skeet" Curtis on bass. We had Boogie and Ron Ford, Garry Shider and the full horn section, even Bootsy and Catfish for some of the shows. Maceo was the bandleader, and that let us do a kind of greatest-hits set. "Atomic Dog" was going to have bite along with its bark. A few days before the tour, Nene took us to the house of a guy he knew somewhere in Miami. There were so many keys of coke you couldn't get in the front door. Once you were inside, you had to slide around the edges of rooms. I got so paranoid being around this much drugs. There was an Italian guy there with a Spanish accent, which didn't make much sense, but he was nice enough, and he kept saying how happy he was to meet me. "George," he said. "Take whatever you want." I was scared as shit to be there. I was ready to run and they were laughing at me. I grabbed a handful of powder and when I got home I made a big crack rock from it.

That rock became my good-luck charm. The success of "Atomic Dog" rattled me a little. I liked knowing that I could succeed, but the spotlight was a little blinding. I didn't want to fuck things up. To settle myself down, I vowed that I was going to go everywhere on tour with that crack rock, but that I wasn't going to smoke it. I wasn't going to kick drugs, but I pledged not to break that specific rock for the duration of the tour.

I got through one day with the rock intact, and then a second day. By the third or fourth day, I started to think that maybe I really could go the whole six weeks. At that point, the "Atomic Dog" rock became an ego fix all its own. I'd play marbles with it, or show it around, proud that I wasn't going to give in. Other people would come by and look at it like they were staring at the Hope Diamond. "You haven't broken that?" they'd say. If I wanted anything, I would buy half a gram of coke and snort it. And if there was a girl who wanted crack, I would buy some for her. "If you care about that rock," I'd say, "you don't really like me."

The rock presided over a great tour. We played everything from early Funkadelic and mid-period Parliament right up through the *Computer Games* material. And the band was versatile and powerful. It was like a fusion band. The rhythm section, Dennis and Skeet together, could make everything go so fast. They were always trying to run Blackbyrd off the stage, and he was the last person in the world you could run off of a stage. The Atomic Dog Tour took us across the country, from New York to Cleveland to Detroit to Long Beach. After the last show in Los Angeles, I went to my room at the Renaissance Inn to celebrate the end of the Tour—and by celebrate, I mean smoke the rock. I had been holding the whole time, six weeks without crack, and now the rock and I were going to pat each other on the back.

I prepared all the equipment, and then sat on the bed buck naked with my legs folded in full lotus position. As I got ready to light the pipe, I could feel my heart and my mind racing. All junkies have rituals, trivial things they do to make them think that they're in control of the experience rather than the drugs being in charge, and one of mine was to take some toilet paper and wad it up in my nostrils so that I wouldn't get too excited and blow the flame out with my nose. I took a hit and was getting ready to blow out the flame when the toilet paper caught on fire. I dropped the pipe and heard it pop on the floor next to the bed. Then I took my finger, covered one nostril, and blew my nose so hard that the flaming toilet paper shot out across the room. It hit the drapes and that shit just went up in flames. It seemed like it was covered in gasoline. I was still in full lotus, legs numb, but I rolled out of the bed and snatched down the drapes. That left nothing on the window, and right across the way I saw an office building with three secretaries looking out over their desks. I ducked down behind the air conditioner so they wouldn't see me naked.

So there I was, down on the floor, beating the drapes, trying to put out the fire, when the smoke alarm went off. Now I didn't care if the secretaries saw me. I grabbed a chair and reached up to the smoke alarm to take the battery out, but as soon as I touched the alarm the noise stopped. I got down off the chair, and it started again. Paranoia started to set in. I started to feel like I was being watched; I started to see the whole scene from outside of my body. I sat on the bed stock-still, certain someone was coming to arrest me. When no one came, I swept everything into the desk drawer and called downstairs to the desk. "I was smoking a cigarette and the alarm went off," I said. She told me it was okay but she was laughing like somebody had told her a hell of a joke. I put on my pants and went downstairs past the desk. Nobody said anything, and it was only then that the paranoia started to recede. When the maid came in the morning, I gave her seventy-five dollars to get everything fixed.

As it turned out, Los Angeles wasn't the final stop. The promoters added one more show in San Francisco, and that night somebody gave me some shit that was bad news. I don't know if it was poisoned or laced with dust, if something was really wrong with it or if I wasn't right for it at the time, but I really crashed. I got deathly ill, which was a real rarity for me. Most health problems I solved with prune juice: fever, blister, whatever. My constitution was strong. Not that time: I was ruined on crack and having trouble recovering. As soon as the tour ended, I went up north in California to Crescent City to fish, and had myself a kind of retreat. At that time, in that cabin, I started putting the crack in joints and in a wooden pipe, and that way I was able to smoke for the next three years without incident.

"Atomic Dog" put me back on the map. We filmed a video, and it won several awards, even though MTV wouldn't show it—this was before March of 1983, when Michael Jackson's "Billie Jean" video broke the network's color line. The song was on the radio wherever I went, blasting out of boom boxes, store windows. Kids were quoting it back to me.

Funnily enough, Bootsy had an "Atomic Dog" of his own that same year. I hadn't worked with him very much since *Sweat Band* and *Ultra Wave* both came out in 1980. When P-Funk dissolved, he went his own way to tend to the solo career that he had been thinking about for a few years anyway. In 1982 he released a record called *The One Giveth, The Count Taketh Away* that didn't do much on the charts, or for that matter, creatively; I did only one song, "Shine-O-Myte." In the wake of that album, though, he put out a song called "Body Slam," which was basically a remix of "Countracula," one of the songs from the record. A DJ worked it up for him and they did it right. It was futuristic and danceable, kind of like the records Malcolm McLaren was making—it made sense to me that they ended up working together later. The bass was huge and elastic, and there were some funny horn arrangements in there, too. To see "Atomic Dog" and "Body Slam" meet on the chart reminded me of when "Flash Light" had stepped aside for "Bootzilla" back in 1977. It felt like a reunion. Bootsy had been one of my most valuable collaborators through the highest heights of P-Funk, and whenever I heard one of his records, especially after "Body Slam," I had mixed feelings, some nostalgia, some regret, and plenty of itchy trigger finger. He always had good tracks at the root of his records, and I always wished that I could have gotten to them. Without the extra ingredients of P-Funk—the idiosyncrasy, the community, Bernie's keyboards or my lyrics—he reverted to something more conservative, James Brown grooves like "Philmore." He never faltered in setting up a great foundation, but he didn't always know where to take it from there.

"Atomic Dog" was so huge that it brought along other records in its path. The first was *Urban Dancefloor Guerillas*, which was what we called the P-Funk All Stars record that grew out of "Hydraulic Pump." There was another pet song that Garry and David and I finished up as a kind of sequel to "Atomic Dog" called "Copy Cat." There was a great track called "Generator Pop" with shuddering bass and screeching guitar. But Garry and David weren't the only producers on the album. Sly had worked with me on "Hydraulic Pump," and he also coproduced "Catch a Keeper," which was a holdover from *Electric Spanking of War Babies*. There's "One of Those Summers," a beautiful ballad I did with Junie Morrison. There's "Pumpin' It Up," which sounds almost like electronic music until Eddie Hazel uncorks a solo. And so many great vocalists sing on that album: Philippé Wynne, Bobby Womack, Lynn Mabry, Sheila Horne. If *Urban Dancefloor Guerillas* had come out as a Funkadelic record, it would have been a perfect comeback.

For the cover, we had an embroidered jacket made, put it on a young woman who was the daughter of one of the promotions guys, and then took a picture of her standing on a boat. The record was released on Uncle Jam, of all labels. I had assumed it would come out on Hump, like the single, but Nene took the record back to CBS without asking anyone and submitted it to fulfill the terms of the Uncle Jam deal. It replaced the Jessica Cleaves record, which was never delivered, and that was the four-album history of Uncle Jam Records. I was sad then that the Jessica album didn't come out, and I'm still sad. She was a great soul diva, mainstream enough to be a big chart artist but with enough of the P-Funk character to really stand apart. That's a beautiful record that deserved release then. I hope it gets released in its original form eventually.

Urban Dancefloor Guerillas came out at the exact same time as my second Capitol solo album, *You Shouldn't-Nuf Bit Fish*. In the most superficial way, it was a sequel to *Motor Booty Affair*—or, at the very least, a chance for me to use the leftover fishing puns I had collected for that record. Again, I worked with both the Junie camp and the Garry and David camp, along with other collaborators like Michael Hampton and Bootsy. The first song on the record, "Nubian Nut," was credited as a cowrite with Fela Kuti, because we took a section out of a song of his called "Mister Follow Follow." I loved Fela and everything he did. He was like Bob Marley but without any of the naïveté—he practiced realpolitik through and through.

The rest of the songs were dance songs, more or less, though they were also little morality plays. "Quickie" starts out with rock guitar and a sharp electronic drum and goes on to look at the proper sexual protocol when it's the woman who wants the one-night stand.

Another song, "Last Dance," was a complementary scene piece, the story of a guy trying to pick up a girl in a club and failing because he was a "psychedelic wallflower." The main idea is that you should always try, because you never know when you'll succeed ("Maybe she'll get funky with you"), and in the background, there's a vocal re-creation of the chorus of David Bowie's "Let's Dance." We filmed a video for that song, filled with brightly colored 1980s backgrounds. The director had the concept, based on what he thought MTV might want. I would have been into something more avant-garde or comic. Visually, I was more influenced by the animation of Monty Python and the Beatles, and I always imagined doing something like what Peter Gabriel did for "Sledgehammer." But the times called for a certain style.

Though it was only my second album with Capitol, the label was already acting like Warner Bros. had in the waning days of Funkadelic. Promotions men started having strange ideas about how to put a record out into the world. They picked "Nubian Nut" as the single, which was clearly the wrong choice for the market we were trying to crack: "Quickie" would have lit up the ghetto first, and then the pop stations would have come and found us. Selecting "Nubian Nut" was a form of chasing pop success, and that was like chasing your tail.

Toward the end of mixing *You Shouldn't-Nuf Bit Fish* I was in Miami, staying at the Sheraton Four Ambassadors. At that time it was part hotel, part residence, and Stephanie and I would go down there for a week, fish, work, fish some more. One day we came home from the boat and I had an ounce of cocaine in my pocket. The second we came into the hotel, I noticed that the lobby was all lit up, and that among the normal staff there were a few strange men. They were clearly government agents, and of a high order. You could see the Petrocelli suits and earpieces. And then I remembered: the week before, one of the guys at the hotel had told me that the vice president, George H. W. Bush, was coming to the hotel for a presentation. They closed in on us the second we came through the door, not just the men in suits but the dogs who were with them. The guy at the desk waved to the agent. "That's the Clintons," he said. "They're all right." Two of the men walked us to the elevator, and a lady agent and a dog stepped in with us. I was scared to death. I was sure we'd be busted. All the way up, I tried to be friendly, made small talk with the agents. We got off at our floor and as I hurried into the room, I saw a cop stationed at one end of the hall and another cop at the other end. When I called downstairs to ask, the guy at the desk told me not to worry. "Just stay out of their way," he said. "Everything will be fine."

We started some work on a track, and all of a sudden a huge helicopter rushed past the window, decorated with the presidential seal. I turned on the television and found them setting up for a speech on one of the news channels. I followed it in real time in my head as it happened on screen. Bush would land on top of the hotel, take the elevator down to the lobby, and come to the podium. Sure enough, in two minutes, he was there. The speech he gave that day was one of the keynote events for the Reagan administration's Zero Tolerance policy toward drugs. If they discovered any drugs, even a seed and a stem, they could confiscate boats and cars. They could freeze your assets. And there I was, twenty floors above him, doing lines of the coke that had been hidden in my pocket as I came through the lobby. I'm sure I wasn't the only one.

★

Strangely, the Bush helicopter wasn't my only run-in with the U.S. government that year. The Uncle Jam lawsuit, which had started back in 1981 when Roger Troutman had taken his masters from United Sound and left CBS Records for Warner Bros., had been clarified to some degree. We had come into possession of a letter written by Bob Krasnow, an executive from Warner Bros. Back when Zapp's first singles were out, Krasnow had gone to see the band in concert, and he had noticed that everything was about Roger. All the energy onstage revolved around him. Even though Warner Bros. had Zapp tied up, Krasnow felt that he had been tricked, and we found a letter by Krasnow in which he said, in no uncertain terms, that he had to move fast in getting money to Roger and signing him above and beyond his Uncle Jam commitments, which were probably sealed by handshake deal only—if you can believe it, that's how we did our business.

Just as we were getting ready to take this letter to court, along with other documents, the case took another crazy turn. William Westmoreland, the American general who had been in charge of American military operations in Vietnam, filed a libel suit against the CBS television network—Westmoreland claimed that CBS, in the course of preparing a special, had lied about the way Westmoreland had estimated Vietcong troop strength. With *Westmoreland v. CBS* looming, Pierre Leval, the judge for that trial, cleared the rest of his calendar—a calendar that included us. What that meant was a quick, unsatisfying ruling, a summary judgment that determined that, on the merits of the case, it didn't look like we would win. We could have appealed, but one of our legal philosophies, promoted by Nene, was that we never took legal representation on a contingency basis. And so the result was that many questions remained unanswered: how exactly Roger had moved from point to point, who (if anyone) in our camp had known about it, why CBS Records hadn't fought harder to punish Warner Bros. for taking Roger's album away from them.

As confusing as the Roger case was, it was only the beginning of a series of legal tangles. When I had dismissed Leber and Krebs as managers, our office had drafted a letter explaining how we no longer needed their services. In that letter, we had included a line about how if we owed them any money, we'd be happy to discuss it. It was just a formality, language designed for politeness in the hopes of bringing things to an amicable close, but that line hung me. In legal terms, it gave them an opening to take us to court, which they did, asking for just south of $300,000. And when the court looked at the language, they saw it as a tacit acknowledgment that we owed them money. It wasn't a tremendous amount of money—somewhere around $250,000—but the P-Funk organization was at a point where cash flow wasn't great. We had offices in Detroit and Los Angeles. We had studios open all the time. There was plenty of money coming in, but plenty more going out. But how a cash-flow issue turned into a bankruptcy was beyond me. We had plenty of assets and no debts. I could have walked right into BMI and gotten a loan staked against my catalog.

Still, the people I had around me, the people I trusted with managing my affairs, advised me to go to the hearing. Nene and Howard Hertz, a lawyer who was working with us, went with me to get representation, and Armen even paid for those lawyers, who included Bob Hertzberg and Mike Ryan. I went with my team to the hearing, and nobody showed up on the other side except for Leber and Krebs and their attorney, Stanley Kramer. There were claims connected to that bankruptcy that suggested that I owed money to record labels as a result of unrecouped advances. So where were the labels? Why hadn't they at least hired local counsel? We went through a series of questions about my assets and debts. One of the central questions turned on the copyrights, and whether I had transferred them to Armen. This was an important issue for any court trying to figure things out. If the copyrights had been transferred more than a year earlier, then they officially resided with Armen. If they had been transferred less than a year earlier, then they were still considered part of my assets. But the fact was that I had never transferred them. They were still owned by Polygram, because of the deal we had struck with Casablanca. I said, quite clearly, that I hadn't transferred anything to Armen or Nene or anyone else. How could I? The line of questioning continued. At one point it was so redundant that the judge dozed off a bit. The lawyer seemed skeptical. He wondered where all the money from our biggest mid-seventies hits had gone. "What happened to the Mothership?" he said. "It just flew away?"

"Don't they all?" I said. Everybody laughed and it woke the judge up. When I left that hearing, as far as I knew, it was over. But the proceeding kept going for almost two more years without my knowledge. In the years since, several times, we've gone back to Detroit and tried to look more closely at the full set of claims and the actual final judgment, and we can't find it.

My third Capitol solo record, *Some of My Best Jokes Are Friends*, came out in the summer of 1985, and though it wasn't technically a concept album, I wanted to look a little more aggressively at the way that music was changing. I stayed on top of shit by talking to the younger people. We called those kids and their tastes "bubblegum," and I watched them closely, kept an open mind for everything, whether it was Duran Duran or Howard Jones or Animotion. Lots of bands had good grooves of a certain flavor. As it turned out, many of those acts were copying us, or at least their idea of us, so we copied them back and watched how that weird feedback loop turned out. That record was a strange one in other ways, because I mixed it with Nene.

One of the brightest of the new wave lights, Thomas Dolby, appeared on that record, playing keyboards. He came to our attention through the label; he was on Capitol, too. He came to Miami at one point and we went deep-sea fishing. We were after amberjack, which is the fish of choice when you want to give a tourist an exciting fishing experience; they bite and take the line straight to the bottom when they hit. They were heavy and strong, so I got him an electronic reel to help him bring them in. Thomas was one of several younger musicians who contributed to the record. I wrote the title track with Doug Wimbish, who had been the house bassist at Sugar Hill Records and later went on to play with Living Colour. And I did a song called "Bangladesh" with my son Tracey Lewis. Tracey, who recorded as Trey Lewd, was like an even more cracked version of Junie. What was strange about Tracey was that I hadn't been a part of his life for years. He had worked all around in the record industry as a young kid, done some sessions with Sidney Barnes, who had been my partner in the early days at Jobete. When Tracey finally came to me, he was fifteen, and he was on the wild then, into everything all at once. But I could tell that he was brilliant, that he saw everything from such strange angles. I loved how his mind worked when he wrote lyrics, how he found his way to the least expected combinations of ideas. We hadn't grown up together, but when we got together, it was like we had always been that way.

★

Tommy Silverman, who founded Tommy Boy Records, started doing a music conference he called the New Music Seminar, and in 1984 he invited me to speak. It was a great lineup; I would be on a panel alongside Madonna, who had just made her first record, and James Brown. Before the event I tried to be smart and told James to give me eighteen splits. He did it before I could even get the words out of my mouth. Then he came back at me and told me to give him two splits; I busted my nut even before the first.

The seminar came at an interesting time in the music industry, just after the birth of MTV, right in the midst of the corporate record world of the eighties, and the panelists were articulate and interesting about how pop music needed to rethink its aims to appeal to younger audiences. After the event, this kid came up to me and introduced himself. He had read an interview with me where I said that I thought some of the new wave acts, including Thomas Dolby, were at the vanguard of funk. In the interview, I had said that if history was any indication, some white group from Europe would end up being the Led Zeppelin of funk—the same way that Page and Plant had co-opted blues, some British group would redeploy funk and make it the planet's preferred music. This kid objected to my analysis. He told me that it didn't have to be that way, not if I would produce his band's record. His name was Anthony, he said, and his group was called the Red Hot Chili Peppers. I shook his hand and told him that when he and his guys were ready, they should come out to my farm. About two months later, there was a knock on the door.

The Peppers were a California band, but they were comfortable in Michigan—Anthony's family was from Lansing, which was only about fifty miles from where I lived. We rehearsed, wrote songs, and did preproduction. I took them into the hood to one of my friends' studios, one of those places where music was recorded by day and drugs were sold by night. Then they went home and came back about two months later for more recording. In the meantime, I had checked up on them, and they checked out; my son Tracey, who was out in L.A., knew about the growing funk scene, bands like Fishbone, and the Peppers were in the same circles. They had a following, and they had musicianship, and they had charisma. I started to think that maybe Anthony was right, that they could be the group to bring funk to the masses. I figured that the labels were itching to get a white group to take the music truly mainstream. They couldn't do it as long as we were still in the lead. Partly it was because we wouldn't let them change the word *funk*. There was constant pressure to do so. Even some of the P-Funk band members were embarrassed by it. It kept them definitively black. And they saw other bands, whether it was Earth Wind & Fire or the Gap Band or whoever, moving subtly away from it into pop or rock or that unlabeled crossover space. The Peppers had a unique ability to stay funk and rejuvenate the genre.

They brought me some songs, and we wrote some more. They also had the idea that they would pick one big song from the past to do on each record. On their first record, they did a Hank Williams song, "Why Don't You Love Me." On the records they did after they worked with me, they tried Bob Dylan's "Subterranean

Homesick Blues" and Stevie Wonder's "Higher Ground." On the record I did with them, *Freaky Styley*, they covered Sly's "If You Want Me to Stay." It was instructive and then some. When we started, Anthony could not sing at all. He could chant and he could shout. He was a vocalist for sure. But if you do a song like "If You Want Me to Stay," you're going to be able to sing by the time you finish learning that shit. It was an education for me, too: I would have never tried to sing that song until I tried to analyze it for him. Producing the Peppers, and other young bands, put me back in touch with music from earlier decades as more than a fan.

The Peppers, because they were young and white, could get away with a political directness that wouldn't have worked for an older soul or funk band. At that point in my career, trying to re-fashion myself as a radio artist, I was very leery of saying some of the shit he was saying. I could have done it when I was younger, in the earliest days of Funkadelic, but it was a different time then. I was a little older. I was charting. I had formal responsibilities to bandmates and fans. My days of direct political speech were over.

The Peppers also gave me a new perspective on drugs. The same thing that had happened to black stars with freebase and crack was happening to white rock stars with heroin. Seattle was the epicenter of that problem, but it went up and down the West Coast, from Layne Staley to Bradley Nowell to Kurt Cobain, of course. I saw that white groups were going to get pinned by her-oin, and I told the Peppers to watch out. They didn't. When they were with me, they were dabbling and more. We had to take one of them at one point and put ice on his nuts to keep him from dying. I saw them tiptoeing up right to the edge of what a body could bear. And then they went over: Hillel Slovak, their original guitarist, ended up overdosing in 1988.

But I loved the Peppers. I had a great time with them. It was like in the early seventies, when we would bring new young guys into Funkadelic and feed off their energy. I was definitely a kind of mentor or teacher or father figure. I told them all the experiences I had and then let them draw their own conclusions. I made the same jokes that we had made in the barbershop back in Jersey. When they eventually cleaned up their act, they were just as addicted to straight living as they had been to smack. They went way past clean. We saw them again in Germany in the mid-nineties, and they were on a major health-food kick, all kinds of juices and tofus and whey. It was the same way with the Beastie Boys. When they were with us on tour, then they were wild as hell, and then later they had Buddhist monks touring with them. But like the Peppers, they reversed race in the best way: they had real skills and they used their platform to do interesting things. They were the cream of the crop.

While we were working on *Freaky Styley*, the Peppers and I went to see Aretha Franklin play a show. The preproduction guy in the studio had a big white Rolls-Royce, so Flea and Anthony Kiedis and I packed in and we went to the concert hall. We were just clowning, being high and shit, and we ran into Aretha's sister Carolyn before the show. "I'm not sitting with you," Carolyn said, "because I know you're going to act like a fool, and Aretha's going to come down here and kick someone's ass. I don't want to be in the line of fire."

In 1985, the bankruptcy cloud spread: my assets were tied up in court, and it looked like I was in danger of losing my farm. I went to Armen and the two of us came up with a strategy to save the place. I let him administer all the songs that were still available. He could go and get anything I had coming. In return, he would pay off the farm, and he could keep an extra $100,000 for himself in the process.

Things were also shifting in my relationship with Nene. A few years before, I had started a project with my younger brother Jimmy Giles. The band was called Jimmy G. and the Tackheads, and the album, *Federation of Tackheads*, was shelved several times before it was finally released. Nene had received a $200,000 advance for the Tackheads record, and everyone was waiting on him to release the money. Jimmy asked, and asked again, and eventually Nene sent him $2,500. Then he went radio silent again. He couldn't be easily reached down in Florida and people were getting agitated. Then a few weeks later, more small payments showed up for people in the band: maybe Blackbyrd got a few thousand, maybe Andre Foxxe did. Whatever the case, it was clear that most of the money was stuck with Nene. When I called him to see why it wasn't happening faster, he acted like I was causing a problem, though he also sent me a few thousand, either from guilt or to quiet me down. By the time the money finally started to appear, I was furious, not really talking to him anymore. I knew things had to change.

One day, Bob Young, who was head of business affairs at Capitol, called us and said that Nene was coming around the office looking for money; some of the payments from the Capitol albums were supposed to go through Tercer Mundo, the company that Nene and Archie had set up. Bob knew that we were uncomfortable with Nene, and he had an idea. "I think," he said, "that I have some way that I can get rid of him for good." Bob suggested that we buy Nene out for $70,000 and move everything from

Tercer Mundo into another company, which we called EGMITT; it stood for "Everybody's Gonna Make It This Time." We went down to the Capitol Records office, me and Archie and Stephanie, and officially severed ties with Nene. He wasn't happy, but he didn't object. He was at a point where he needed the money. But he couldn't resist one last play. Rather than just sign Tercer Mundo over to me, he insisted on signing it over to Archie under the theory that it needed to be protected from me. Archie, of course, signed it right over to me. We were finished with Tercer Mundo and, as far as we knew, finished with Nene.

I have a soft spot for the last solo record I made for Capitol, *R&B Skeletons in the Closet*. That's the record that brought me new musicians like Amp Fiddler and Steve Washington, who helped me do amazing things. Most people want to do records cleanly for radio, and sometimes that works brilliantly. It worked with Neil Bogart for Parliament. But as a solo artist, especially after the freedom I earned with "Atomic Dog," I was always thinking along more radical lines. I wanted to make music that most people might not fully understand at first, but that they'd come back to the year after that, or a decade later. Art outlasts charts. Amp was a jazz musician, and he helped create some of these extended pieces on the record, sort of like Bernie had done a decade before. There's a multipart composition called "Mix-Master Suite" that picks up where "Loopzilla" had left off. In my mind, it was more in keeping with musique concrète composers, a way of using samples and interpolations to design a new type of classical music. Ten years after the record came out, it was working in a well-established mode, and maybe then it was more easily digestible.

There were some great moments on that record. One of the singles, "Hey Good Lookin'," had backup vocals by Vanessa Williams, who had been crowned the first black Miss America and then forced to resign in the wake of a nude-photo scandal. Another single, "Do Fries Go with That Shake?" charted higher than any other solo single except for "Atomic Dog." *R&B Skeletons in the Closet* was also my first attempt to deal directly with hip-hop. I had been aware of it since just after *Uncle Jam Wants You*, especially in the New York area, where kids would come out with their boom boxes and start rapping over background music. It was connected to Jamaican toasting a little bit, and to the dozens, which was the comic playground insult game kids had played as long as I could remember. I liked the energy of rappers, the way they combined musical simplicity and intricate wordplay, and I liked the idea that a turntable was an instrument. The minute they got an Anvil case, they were musicians.

It was also a lifeline for funk. Music kept changing, year after year, and if you didn't embrace change, change would just turn its back on you. As rap grew into hip-hop, another element came into play, which was building your new song on an existing foundation, and sampling soul and funk. Hip-hop gave us a chance to get back in the game. Where else are you going to hear your own music? On a K-Tel compilation? It didn't hurt that early rap grew right out of P-Funk. One of the earliest songs I can remember, "Funk You Up," was by a girl group called the Sequence, which included Cheryl Cook, Gwendolyn Chisolm, and the future solo star Angie Stone. They were like the sister act to the Sugar Hill Gang. They didn't sample the song outright but replayed a section of it, which meant that rights had to be secured through publishing channels. I didn't understand that fully at the time, though. No one did, really, except maybe Armen. He was already designing ways of collecting on our publishing whenever a section of a P-Funk song was incorporated into someone else's work, even if the sample (and thus the master) was never used.

Financially, rap would turn out to be a major factor, but I was focused more on the creative aspects of the genre. And they were a mixed bag. After that first surge of creativity, I heard mostly average hip-hop acts. They were competent but not spectacular. Every once in a while, though, the genre would throw out a genius and I would perk up. The first time I can remember that clearly was in 1987, when someone played me Eric B. & Rakim's "Follow the Leader." I had heard lots of rappers by that point, but that fucking record stopped me absolutely dead in my tracks. It was a what-the-fuck moment. The lyrics on that record, with that cool flow, sounded just like the Five Percent Muslims I had heard preaching years before in New York. When they chant, they add knowledge. Rakim had that cadence down perfectly. And his words had meaning for days: they were street, poetic, witty, wise. When I heard that record, I felt like I hadn't done anything in the music business. Damn, I thought. I have to start all over again. It was a feeling I loved, like a boxer coming out of retirement. There was excitement at the tips of my fingers.

The other hip-hop group that had me from the start was Public Enemy. When I heard "Bring the Noise," I knew that they understood the way that sound could either organize upward into music or dissolve into chaos, and how both of them were parts of the same continuum. When you admit what you're making is noise, you're halfway there. They had the vocals and the sonics: they said it right off the bat, with "Bass, how low can you go?" In P-Funk, we were always tuning our guitars down or setting up Bernie's synthesizers to get the deepest vibrations possible. They had the ideas. "Can I tell them that I really never had a gun?" was top-level thinking about the ways that criminals get created, how society needs to identify enemies so it can protect its idea of itself. And they had some of the same sensibilities that made P-Funk work. They had concept albums and affiliated acts. Most important, they had a sense of how to treat their own product so that they were taken seriously without being taken too seriously. Chuck D was the chief information distributor, but Flavor Flav put a check on things with comedy. Some of the people in their circle didn't understand at first how things were supposed to work. Professor Griff spoke out of turn, which he had the right to do, but he did it without the proper balance, without the proper coordination with Chuck and Flav, and that disrupted the group's carefully organized structure. The grace note with Public Enemy is that I had something to do with their name. For years, I didn't know that it was my voice saying "Public Enemy" on their record. They had sampled from "Undisco Kidd" and slowed the vocals down.

The thing I admired most about Public Enemy was that they figured out how to be outspoken in corporate America, which was nothing easy. When John Lennon said that the Beatles were bigger than Jesus, he got in trouble, and he was John Lennon. I understood what he meant, but that's not the lesson I took from the controversy. Lennon's remarks taught me that everything significant has to be leavened with comedy. When I'm asked about something serious, I try to make jokes because deep down, I know that I don't know what the fuck I'm talking about. I don't mean that I'm wrong about everything, or that there's nothing I'm right about. I mean it as a matter of philosophy. How can I be so presumptuous as to say something definitively bad or definitively good about somebody? If there's a controversy already in place, I'll sometimes weigh in, but I try to be clear that it's just my opinion. It's clear to me fairly quickly that there are at least two sides to most questions, and that the other one is just as valid as yours. That's why tolerance is the only thing that really makes sense. Take sexual orientation. I know what I prefer for me. It hurts me when I poop, so I can't imagine anything going up in my ass. I don't even like to hold my own dick when I pee. But what do I know? Anything in the world can be sexy to a person. I've seen motherfuckers fuck radiators. I'll fuck a gay girl if she lets me. And so if I'm ever asked seriously about gay rights, I tell people exactly what I would tell my kids and my grandkids. Do what you want in life. Do what you are. If you talk to me, I'm not going to put you down. I'm going to help you become you. Over the years, we've played with musicians who were straight, and we've played with musicians who were gay. Why should I care? I don't give a fuck who he's fucking. Can he drum?

RHYTHM AND RHYME, RHYTHM AND RHYME, RHYTHM AND MOTHERFUCKING RHYME

There were only a few stars who carried the torch for raw funk in the mid-eighties, and the baddest of them all was Prince. He knew P-Funk in and out, and he was trying some of the same tricks we had. He believed in the two-band balance, though he did his own take on it, setting the Revolution up against the Time. He wrote and produced for outside acts like the Family, Sheila E., Jill Jones, and more. And his Camille character, a sped-up voice that was one of his alter egos, had more than a little Star Child in it. Prince had been hip to us since the early days. He was the perfect age. In the late seventies, when he was getting ready to debut as an artist, he had brought his first record to his label, which happened to be Warner Bros. During their meetings, they played him *Ahh . . . The Name Is Bootsy, Baby*, and it stopped him cold. He didn't even want to go forward. He took his own record back home and worked on it for eight more months. Mo Ostin from Warner Bros. told me that he had been talking to Prince once and that Prince had given me a compliment: he said I was up there with Elvis and James Brown.

In the early eighties, the feeling was mutual, especially after records like *Dirty Mind* and *1999*. I heard his songs everywhere but more than that, I listened into the middle of them and heard a rock or new wave update of some of the same things we were doing in Funkadelic: *1999* especially, with the sped-up and slowed-down voices, the mix of commercial singles and out-there experiments, even the cover art. Then he exploded with *Purple Rain*. He was such a talented songwriter, especially when it came to absorbing other people's styles and making them into something distinctive. Like Stevie Wonder, he wrote songs that were instant standards. "Purple Rain" would have played straight as a country song, or a folk song. But unlike Stevie Wonder, he didn't like people to cover his material. I didn't get that. I thought he didn't understand what publishing was for. It's to stick a flag in a song and claim it so that when someone else works with it, you get paid.

After *Purple Rain* he could do anything he wanted, and one of the things he wanted to do to was run his own label. Warner Bros. set him up with Paisley Park, which was named after a song on his *Around the World in a Day* album. We had overlapping communities; our late-seventies bootlegger, Billy Sparks, had ended up in the *Purple Rain* movie, and the Electrifying Mojo, who was a P-Funk obsessive, became one of Prince's important early supporters. I called him and started a conversation that led to a record deal. When I signed to Paisley Park, I split the money between myself, Archie, my lawyers, the IRS, and Armen. Armen got almost half, in fact, in repayment for fronting me the money that had saved my farm from foreclosure.

For my first Paisley Park album, *The Cinderella Theory*, I worked with many of the same musicians who had been with me during the Capitol years: Blackbyrd McKnight, David Spradley,

Amp Fiddler. The sound wasn't radically different from those records, though the production was glossier. The lead single was "Why Should I Dog You Out?" which grew out of some work I had done with a British group named Well Red. The song I made with them, "Get Lucky," had a funky lick but was a dance track. I decided to bring it over to make a new song. The lyrics were built from a goofy "dog you out" chant we were doing onstage at the end of extended live versions of "Atomic Dog"; we name-checked famous dogs in pop-culture history: Goofy, Snoopy, Marmaduke, and even Spuds MacKenzie, who was huge at the time. I wish I had mixed it at United Sound, because it didn't come out with the bottom as strong as it should have, especially on cassette releases.

That album was positioned as something expansive, because people thought that signing to Prince's label would open up two generations of funk to each other, but in some ways it was a very claustrophobic record. The biggest songs on there were, at some level, about the elevating power of music, but they were also about the various kinds of prisons and limits that surround people everywhere they go. "Airbound" had a drug subtext, especially in the chorus: "We gone, we gone, we gone, we gone / Never to ever come down." And "Tweakin'" was about drugs, too, but also about urban culture and the way that music functioned as a kind of inner-city news network. Both Chuck D and Flavor Flav from Public Enemy appeared on that song, and Flav had one of the most memorable lines: "George will tell you, 'Hold my jammy while I go P.'" Other tracks came together the way they had in the old days, with a mix of new compositions, in-studio jam sessions, and reupholstered versions of old songs. There's a cover of Harry Belafonte's "The Banana Boat Song" that was born when Bootsy came up with a funky track and I just threw the first thing on top of it that popped into my head. "There I Go Again" is almost a ballad, with me, Belita Woods, and Joe "Pep" Harris from the old Motown psychedelic soul group the Undisputed Truth. The album also dipped into Bahamian junkanoo rhythms. A few years earlier, I had been asked down to the Bahamas to see if I could help figure out a way of making junkanoo as popular as reggae. That seemed unlikely—reggae came from a bigger island that was more capable of creating international stars, and it had a more developed political agenda—but I liked the junkanoo sound.

When I visited Minneapolis to work on *Cinderella Theory*, Prince came by the studio to say hi, but he kept his distance, tried to give me the right conditions to get work done. The most one-on-one contact I had with him was late at night. I'd be at the hotel by myself getting high, and he'd call me and ask me to come over to his house. I'd go over there and we'd talk: I was always interested in conspiracies, big international ones like the Trilateral Commission, or multiple governments banding together to conceal the evidence of alien landings. There's a book that conspiracy theorists love called *Behold a Pale Horse*, by Milton William Cooper, and I used to read it to Prince out loud, more silly-serious than straightforwardly earnest. I believed in conspiracies, but they condition you not to believe in anything—it's probably more accurate to say that I believed in the idea of conspiracies, in the idea that nothing was as it seemed and that strings were always being pulled behind the scenes by unseen hands. Prince listened, sometimes asked questions, sometimes joked. I don't know for sure what he thought about the book. For the most part, I didn't do drugs right in front of him. I wanted to be respectful. When I had to smoke, I took the pipe into the bathroom and did my business there. Prince has always claimed that he didn't do any drugs, and I never saw him do any, but he must have at least done coffee, because I don't know any other motherfucker who could go to sleep at five thirty in the morning and be back at eight daisy fresh.

★

The title song of that album, "The Cinderella Theory," quoted from the melody of "Oh, I," a Funkadelic song from *Electric Spanking of War Babies*. It also connected back to the themes of that record. Some people took the title as a comment on the fact that we were signed to Paisley Park—someday my Prince will come—and that was partly true. In the fairy tale, Cinderella comes out of the ball, loses her shoe, and the prince goes to find her. In my version, she was out skinny-dipping and she left her bathing suit on a tree; the prince went from girl to girl trying to match it. But the song also flips the story and wonders, briefly, if Cinderella wants to be found by the authorities—what's the prince if not an authority?

I was trying not to be stupid about it, not to be too straightforward. I didn't want to lean on the idea so hard that it fell over. But I knew that the system scrutinized entertainers, that they kept tabs on us, that in some cases they loaded up artists with drugs (sniff, sniff, sniffin') so that they couldn't interrogate the system and change it. That song was so slick. Sly wanted to cut it; he loved the counterpoint and the rhythm. But Sly was heading in his own direction in those days, which was always a deeply strange direction. A few years earlier, he had been in the studio working on a new record and all of a sudden a voice came in and said something. He assumed it was an engineer speaking to him through the mic, so he answered, but there was no one there. A few seconds later, he heard it again. He thought he was tripping but he was too hardcore to admit that he was paranoid. As it turned out, he was working with one of those outboard pieces of gear that just regurgitates the sound that you put into it, and he had accidentally put a sound on the machine. Every sixty seconds or so, it would resurface, and Sly would think it was a voice talking to him. Even when he figured it out, he was still jumpy, and he called the whole sensation "Eek-A-Boo," which was his private slang for being scared by the ghost in the machine. He recorded a song about it, "Eek-Ah-Bo-Static Automatic," which ended up on the soundtrack to the *Soul Man* movie.

Another time, he blew up his house in Bel Air. Someone was doing drugs there and they left the ether open. The fumes are like wavy cartoon lines; they find fire and then the fire follows the fumes back to the source and explodes. When it's going critical, you can hear it go up in a whistle. Sly was back in a corner of his house, in a bathroom, and the ether had drifted from the kitchen. When he lit the pipe, it blew up the part of the house he was in— it was an addition, and it separated from the rest of the structure. When the smoke cleared, the bathroom had fallen clean off. He was standing on the edge of the house as cars drove by. He was standing on a ledge about six inches wide, with the door heading into the kitchen right next to him. He slid back into the house, closed the door, and stayed like that for more than a year.

When I wasn't in Minneapolis recording *Cinderella Theory*, I was spending much of my time in Los Angeles, and part of the time I was hanging around the fringes of the movie business. In 1988 I did a cameo in a movie called *The Night Before*, which was one of the first starring roles for Keanu Reeves. I lost a twenty-thousand-dollar check on the set and one of Keanu's boys found it. The year after that, I moved deeper into the movies. I cowrote the theme song for *Howard the Duck* and also produced a record by a band that grew out of the film world—or rather, a band that pretended it didn't exactly grow out of the film world. Otis Day and the Knights were an R&B band famous for their appearance in the movie *Animal House*, where they played a frat party and did a frenetic version of the Isley Brothers' "Shout." They were beloved and successful. The only problem is that they weren't real. But in the wake of their movie, they started taking on the feel of a real band. DeWayne Jessie, the actor who played Otis Day in the movie, could sing (though in the movie they had him lip-synch over vocals by Lloyd Williams), and he had been touring the Knights around the country as an actual band. MCA Records decided to reverse-engineer them as a real recording act. Jheryl Busby, the president of MCA, came to me to oversee the project, and I got the P-Funk team together and assembled a set of songs for them: not just "Shout!" and other oldies like "Shama Lama Ding Dong," but also a few early Parliament and Funkadelic songs, "Testify," "You and Your Folks," "I Can Feel the Ice Melting." As we were producing the Otis Day and the Knights album, we gave MCA a record called *Our Gang Funky*, which was a compilation with some of the newer artists we were working with: Cadillac Heights, BabyFatt, Maxi Muff. *Our Gang Funky* wasn't a huge record, but it started a trend that I'd revisit later, when P-Funk went through a collection and re-collection phase with the Family Series.

★

One evening in Los Angeles, Archie Ivy and I drove away from a coke dealer's house up onto the 405 expressway, took the exit to head home, and saw flashing police lights in our rearview mirror. The cop who walked up to our window said that Archie's headlights weren't on, which wasn't true. More than that, it wasn't possible: you couldn't even start his car without the lights coming on. The cops searched the car like they knew what they were looking for, though they didn't find it—I stuffed the paper with the drugs down into my pants. But the paper was open, and as I walked around, everything leaked out: coke, paper, all of it. When we got down to the jailhouse, the police somehow managed to produce the same amount of cocaine that had leaked out through the bottom of my pant leg.

From jail, we called Nene's daughter. We hadn't seen him in a while—it had been a year or two since we'd spoken—but we knew that he could pull some strings in Los Angeles. He and one of his guys got there before anyone even knew. It was under an hour. And there he was just like old times, standing out in front, smacking the news people.

I probably shouldn't have called him. We needed to get out of jail, but there was an unintended consequence, which was that Nene was back in my life. Almost immediately, he started in on me about a bank in Panama that he had a stake in, and how he wanted me to invest with him. I resisted. If nothing else, I had learned that. But then he went back to playing dirty pool. We were out one night, and he leaned over to me and said, "Your problem is that you won't tell Stephanie about your bitches." He had some nerve, because he was seeing people on the side, too. "I'm glad you're into hippieism and freedom," I said. "Everybody's free to do whatever they do, right?" He said right. "Well,"

I said, "can your girlfriend have her other man in here and fuck him in front of you?" I wanted to provoke him.

That night, I went straight back home and told Stephanie about all the people I had been messing with. I wasn't proud of it or defiant or anything. It was a fact of life for musicians, and something that had been happening for decades, but I was going to be damned if I let Nene control what happened. Stephanie took the news in stride. She was angry at me for having girls on the side, but she was angrier at him for bringing up the issue the way he did, that kind of crypto-blackmail shit. We ended up getting married, Steph and I, in Toledo in 1990. Nene was mad about it— he didn't like anything that was outside of his sense of control. The next time, he was frustrated to hear that we had gotten married, and he said so. She came right back at him: "Don't you ever call me and tell on George. That's not going to work." Nene did the same thing to Archie Ivy, spread word that he wasn't treating his wife right. Or he'd call Ronnie, get him upset, and then call me and say that Ronnie was freaking out without quite mentioning who had lit the fuse in the first place. And if he was talking to me about them, you can be damn sure he was talking to them about me. That's how Nene was back in the seventies and how he was in the nineties, and it only took a bit for the present to fall in line with the past.

★

Hip-hop came in waves, and just as I was certain that I had understood the first and the second and the third, the fourth came along, and this time it was personal. The debut album by the rap group De La Soul, *3 Feet High and Rising*, was released in 1989, and it immediately became a huge hit. One of its biggest singles,

"Me Myself and I," was built solidly on a sample of "(Not Just) Knee Deep." I loved the group's attitude and their music, and I was pleased with the way they dealt with the sample, too. The record was out, using our music. To head off a lawsuit and also, to some degree, to do the right thing, their record label, Tommy Boy, paid us $100,000 to use it. At the time, we didn't know if that money was being paid as a result of masters or publishing. There were no rules worked out yet, no real understanding of how samples were supposed to be accounted.

A few other rap acts ponied up with money, too. Digital Underground paid for "Let's Play House," which was the basis for "Humpty Dance." X-Clan paid for using "One Nation Under a Groove" in their song "Earth Bound." In those cases, the process worked the way it should have worked. De La Soul also put the song out as a twelve-inch, and one side was basically just our original song. Still, in the Wild West of hip-hop, this seemed like it was okay.

We were just figuring out how to work the new system, but Armen was a full chess move ahead. Because he was getting regular earnings statements and we saw only occasional summaries, he had time to strategize. For him, the strategy involved more lawsuits. He filed suit against Public Enemy. Terminator X, the DJ for Public Enemy, had used a sample of the *Trombipulation* song "Body Language" on his solo album *Valley of the Jeep Beats*. The suit was for the outrageous sum of $3 million. Armen's executive assistant, Jane Peterer, went on MTV explaining that they were suing on my behalf, which wasn't the case. In fact, I had to go back on the channel myself with Chuck D and Flavor Flav and say that as far as I was concerned, there was no problem using the sample. It led to the claim being dropped.

Nene came right back with a flurry of his own litigation. He threatened to sue every record company, along with Armen, on behalf of a group he called the Association of Parliament-Funkadelic. The group, which Nene assembled, consisted of a bunch of guys who had worked in our office. They weren't musicians or songwriters. But Nene's move was another false front designed to make it look like someone else other than Armen—in this case, him—was acting on my behalf. I guess he figured that in court people would look at four black guys sitting together and assume that they were seeing P-Funk.

With cooler heads, we could have worked out a nice system, scaled to sales. If an artist sampled us and didn't sell very many records, that artist wouldn't have to pay us very much. But if an artist sampled us and sold between half a million and a million records, the cost would be fifty thousand; if sales exceeded a million, the price would go up to a hundred thousand. That's just a broad sketch of what I had in mind. I'm sure there were even more nuanced ways to charge, and I would have been receptive to them, too. What I wasn't receptive to was tying everything up in court, in red tape and malice. That fucks it up for everyone, because then you're talking about five hundred different cases involving thousands of songs. It's litigation, and it's a docket, and it's a judge taking a panel of jurors and playing both records, the hip-hop song and the original, and asking if they can recognize one song in the other. If the jury couldn't, the case was thrown out, no matter how egregious the borrowing was. And if they could, then there was a byzantine settlement process with no transparency. Artists couldn't tell how much money was changing hands. Everything was obscured by a legal fog. At around that same time, Archie and I went to Warner Bros. to try to collect money from MC Hammer's record "Turn This Mutha Out," which basically lifted "Give Up the Funk (Tear the Roof off the Sucker)" wholesale. In the process of investigating that record, we discovered that Warners claimed to have our catalog, and that Armen was claiming the publishing for the *Mothership Connection* songs, and in fact everything: every Parliament, every Funkadelic, everywhere my name appeared. When we looked into it further, Warners got nervous. They said they would have to get back to us. When they finally called Archie back, they were belligerent and unhelpful. But the paper trail, or whatever of the paper trail we could find, seemed to suggest that Warner Music had acquired our catalog by buying Chappell Publishing, which included Polygram, which also included Rick's Music. (The Chappell catalog also included "Happy Birthday to You.") But based on various provisions in our contract, Polygram had no authority to sell our catalog. And when we asked Polygram how it was sold, they said they had acquired my power of attorney and transferred those copyrights to the label, who later sold them to Warners. Strange doings, strange days.

The album that really upped the ante on the sampling question was Dr. Dre's *The Chronic*, which took over the world in 1992; its biggest songs, its main singles, were powered by P-Funk. More specifically, they were fueled by a certain type of P-Funk sample. There was a scatter plot of P-Funk samples in hip-hop; they differed by region. The East Coast had more interest in the early Funkadelic records. Rakim sampled "No Head, No Backstage Pass." Public Enemy sampled "Undisco Kidd." But East Coast producers cut and sliced and rearranged, while West Coast groups tended to take them wholesale. Dr. Dre went right for the biggest Parliament hits, the ones with the fat synthesizer and horn lines that could hold up an entire song. "Let Me Ride" took "Mothership Connection" almost wholesale, and in the video there's even a scene of Dre being invited to a Parliament concert.

I knew Dre all the way back from N.W.A, though that was a group I wasn't sure about. They acted hard, but the ghetto out there is like our suburbs. I couldn't believe that the police went crazy when they said "fuck tha police." That wouldn't have been a big deal back in New York. As it turned out, that controversy was the best thing that ever happened to them. It got them noticed by the FBI, put them on magazine covers. When they came to Detroit the police department came and lined up, out of uniform. They had five hundred officers there. The police actually asked me to go talk to the group, as a kind of ambassador, to see if I could get them to forgo playing "Fuck tha Police." Dre was scared as hell. Cube didn't want to be talked into any shit. The D.O.C. was there, with his scratchy voice, saying that N.W.A was going to do whatever the fuck they wanted. They ended up not playing it.

In the wake of *The Chronic*, other West Coast artists started to build their sound on our samples. Snoop Dogg's *Doggystyle* came out the next year, Warren G's "Regulate" the year after that. I did a duet with Ice Cube on his own version of "Bop Gun," which was on his *Lethal Injection* album. That's how P-Funk fathered G-Funk. It also fathered another round of Armen's sue-and-settle strategy. If the hip-hop song got too close to anything in the P-Funk back catalog, Armen would sue, and the artists would settle just to keep from going to court. He also started to design a legal strategy based on the principle of interpolation. Under this theory, a hip-hop artist not only couldn't sample a record, but couldn't even have someone come in and play any part of the song: the bass line, the horn line. If a West Coast rapper had a keyboardist in who played a keyboard figure that was similar to something in "Flash Light," Armen felt justified suing them. This was a foolish way of approaching things, and it had a chilling effect, not only because Armen sued over everything, but because he wasn't honest when it came to disclosing settlements. Nene opposed Armen, but Nene wasn't being honest about what he owned, either, and the two of them started warring in court about who controlled the catalog.

Meanwhile I tried to settle things the only way I knew, which was through music, and in 1993 I released a three-disc set called *Sample Some of Disc, Sample Some of DAT.* The record had hundreds of keyboard figures, horn parts, guitar riffs, and drum breaks, all taken from P-Funk records. It was basically a sampling kit that bypassed publishing fees. If you let us know that you wanted to use one of the samples, we'd charge you for it according to a scale we had worked out. Armen was infuriated by this, because it was threatening his revenue stream, and he tried to get *Sample Some of Disc, Sample Some of DAT* treated the same way as any hip-hop record, arguing that it was basically an anthology of unauthorized samples. We weren't the only band to do that: Prince released a set later called the New Funk Sampling Series that had the same idea.

All in all, I have mixed feelings about the way that hip-hop affected P-Funk. It brought P-Funk's music back into the public eye and ear. There's no doubt about that. But it also put a price tag on everything again, which meant that the people who had a vested interest in ripping me off were back in strength. The new money coming in over hip-hop was like blood in the water for sharks. And every time I hired a lawyer to look into it, that same lawyer ended up on the other side, waving back at me. Could I have kept the train on the rails if it wasn't for the drugs? I'm not sure. Plenty of stone-cold-sober people get ripped off, too.

To this day, the record companies haven't paid me fairly. But the problem isn't a rapper problem. They're artists, and I love their work, whether it's Ice Cube or Humpty or Too $hort or EPMD or Public Enemy. When there are artists who have remained true to the P-Funk philosophy, I love them even more. Early on, I told Snoop Dogg he was the pick of the litter, and he used that phrase until he became Snoop Lion (though he's still doggin' and lyin'). I love artists like Mystikal, for the way he updated Joe Tex and used those second-line New Orleans rhythms. And, of course, Eminem was a star from the word go. He wrote like Smokey Robinson, with hooks and metaphors and real ideas that were sharpened and elevated by his obsession with structure. All of the rappers know that I never came after them personally and that I never will. Artists aren't allowed the luxury of fighting with each other. The lawyers and record executives fight over you and around you, for their own reasons. Those people went to school to beat you for your shit.

Two of my favorite records from the extended P-Funk family came out during that period: Trey Lewd's *Drop the Line* and Bernie Worrell's *Blacktronic Science*. Trey Lewd was my son Tracey Lewis, whose mother was my old writing partner Vivian Lewis, and *Drop the Line* was a perfect encapsulation of his aesthetic: funky, danceable, a little raunchy, and funny as a motherfucker. I cowrote a song called "Rooster," and there are also collaborations between Tracey and "Clip" Payne ("Wipe of the Week"), Tracey and Andre Williams ("Duck and Cover"), and Tracey and Cecil Womack Jr. ("I'll Be Good to You"). One of my favorite songs was a collaboration between Tracey and Amp Fiddler, a dirty nursery rhyme called "Yank My Doodle." Warners released the record but supported it weakly at best, which wasn't especially surprising at that point. Because of it, Tracey got a reputation as a musician's musician, which is usually a way of saying that you're brilliant but you have some hitch that prevents you from reaching a larger audience. Prince was crazy about Tracey from a writing point of view, but I think that there was a sense that Tracey, at that point, was too much to handle as a human being: wild, bursting with ideas, impossible to regulate.

Blacktronic Science was also filled with great material: songs like "Time Was (Events in the Elsewhere)" and "Dissinfordollars" had monster grooves and philosophical lyrics. And the method was sound: Bernie kept the spirit of old Parliament alive by playing classical keyboard over funky beats. But the record also illustrated how things had shifted since the seventies. Bernie was operating more or less as a jazz musician, on a jazz label (Gramavision put that record out), and to my ear, it didn't have enough bottom. It didn't sound like United Sound. It should have been a proper Parliament record, for purposes of heft.

At right around the same time, I started another anthology project: the Family Series, five volumes of rarities and outtakes. The first, which came out in 1992, was called *Go Fer Yer Funk*; the second, *Plush Funk*, came out later that same year; and we went all the way on through *A Fifth of Funk* the following year. Those records let me highlight some of the odds and ends that didn't make it onto records over the years: songs like "Funkin' for My Mama's Rent" by Gary Fabulous and Black Slack, "These Feets Are Made for Dancing" by Ron Dunbar, "I Really Envy the Sunshine" by

Jessica Cleaves, along with tracks by the Brides of Funkenstein, Junie Morrison, and Sly Stone. The Family Series records are uneven, but in the best way, moving from artist to artist, tone to tone, similar only in that they are all presided over by the funk.

★

Because of the legal snarls, things were getting harder, especially on the financial front. There was music everywhere but at times money got too tight to mention, not just for me but for everyone around me. Ronnie Ford, who had been my best friend from when we were kids, had come to Detroit to be a barber and ended up working with P-Funk on a number of songs. He wrote "Wizard of Finance" from the *Funkentelechy vs. the Placebo Syndrome* album. At some point in the early nineties, Ronnie had decided that he had given too much of his life to drugs and bad living, and he and his wife, Lydia, left Detroit for work in California. But the job that had been promised to him somehow got unpromised once they arrived, and Ron and Lydia and their kids ended up homeless. Homelessness meant street living at first, and then it meant spending every night in a motel that wouldn't even let them leave their stuff there for days on end—they'd have to check out every day and then check back in when Ron showed up with the money he earned from collecting cans. The poorest people pay the most for things, relatively, because they have no credit, no collateral, and no leverage. During that period, Ronnie went to Armen to see if there was any money floating around. Armen wouldn't even give him fifty dollars, even though songs Ronnie had worked on had found their way into some of the West Coast rap, N.W.A and Snoop Dogg. So Ronnie and Lydia were right there in Los Angeles, listening to their songs go by them in passing cars. Even worse, Armen sent out word that he had given me the money to give to Ronnie, which made me look like the bad guy. Even when Ronnie ended up getting a little money out of Armen, maybe two thousand, I advised him not to cash the check. When you cash a check from Armen, you're agreeing to some other shit, like giving up your rights to the song for the rest of your life. Nothing that comes from him comes without strings.

These hard times came during a period when lots of the Funk-adelic family were in the woods, not just as a result of financial crises, but addiction, disease, or other problems. Some of them never got out of the woods. Eddie Hazel died in 1992. Drinking got him. Drink is the most dangerous, in the final analysis. Many of the guys who developed heroin problems kicked it only to go back into the bottle, which is always the endgame.

Old friends, old problems, old ways, but sometimes new wrinkles in the fabric. In April of 1993, I inducted Sly Stone into the Rock and Roll Hall of Fame. Sly and I hadn't been talking much, but the organizers assumed that he would most likely show up to the induction if I was there, and that he probably wouldn't show under any other circumstance. He wasn't someone you set your clock by. The day of the ceremony, I came for sound check, and people were buzzing about Sly. The rest of the Family Stone was there, but all everyone wanted to know was whether Sly would really appear. As it turns out, he was there already, hiding out in the kitchen, though only two of us knew that, me and his mother, Alpha. Everyone else was speculating, maybe even making side bets. Clive Davis couldn't talk about anything else. He wanted to see Sly so badly because Sly had been his favorite person back in the early days. He missed him. When the ceremony started, I gave some introductory remarks, and then Freddie Stone stepped up to the microphone. He assumed, like everyone else, that Sly wasn't there. Just as Freddie started speaking, Sly came out from under the curtain right behind us. He looked up at me. "Hi," he said. "Those mothers thought I wasn't going to show." Even though Sly didn't perform with the band, it was a great night. Eddie Vedder inducted the Doors. And Cream was inducted, which was a kind of brain twist: I got to watch two of my most important influences and think about the way that I had built Funkadelic on the intersection between their two bands. Jimi Hendrix had it right when he said that Cream was quitting just as everybody else was getting started. I also got to watch how a band acted when they put old rivalries and infighting behind them. A few weeks before the Rock and Roll Hall of Fame ceremony, I was on my way up to the Apollo Theater to give an award to Lisa Lisa, and I saw Bernie Worrell walking with Jack Bruce. I came up right behind them and heard Jack bitching about the induction, and how hard it was going to be to see Eric Clapton and Ginger Baker again, and how they didn't have any goodwill left. I stepped into their conversation and told Jack that it wouldn't take them any more than twenty-five minutes to patch things up. The night of the induction, Jack was sitting right near me, and he leaned back and told me that it had only taken fifteen. I'm sure that after that they went right back to being at each other's throats, but for that one moment, you have to let bands be family again.

★

As soon as I signed to do *Cinderella Theory* with Paisley Park, I knew that I wanted to do a second album with the label, too. And the second time around, I wanted more Prince. During the first record, he had been so respectful—maybe a little too respectful.

I understood why. Of all the people who had tried to help save P-Funk along the way, of all the people who had taken it upon themselves to help reupholster us for a new generation, Prince behaved the way I would have behaved if I had been entrusted with a comeback record by Sly Stone, say. I wouldn't have interfered. I wouldn't have presumed to know what the fuck he was doing. I would have been very reluctant to tell him what to do. But as we worked on the album, I was thinking that if there was anyone I wanted to have input, it was him. He had such a broad understanding of music, of the intersection between rock and pop and funk. I encouraged him to work with me: I told him, "I'll send you the tapes, you P on them, and send them back to me," and after *Cinderella Theory*, we collaborated on one song for *Graffiti Bridge* called "We Can Funk"—I performed it in the movie—and maybe that made him a little more receptive to the idea of working with us. Whether it was him directly or his intermediaries, he was much more of a presence the second time around. He weighed in on things. He added textures and colors where he previously hadn't. We even had a proper collaboration on "The Big Pump," a funk-celebrates-funk song in the tradition of "Pumpin' It Up."

As luck would have it, Prince was in a strange position with Warner Bros. in 1993. The second Paisley Park record, *Hey Man . . . Smell My Finger*, came out at a time when Prince was squarely in the corporate crosshairs. He had started down a dangerous road with his second movie, *Under the Cherry Moon*, which the company assumed would be a straightforward commercial success like *Purple Rain*. But *Under the Cherry Moon* was a black-and-white romance in the style of old studio films, not an autobiographical rock opera with a half hour of killer live footage. Prince further alienated the company by killing off the main character, Christopher Tracy, at the end of the movie. These kinds of unorthodox creative decisions hurt the sales of *Parade*, the soundtrack for *Cherry Moon*, even though one of the songs on the album, "Kiss," was among his biggest and best hits. He had gone on with Warner Bros. after that and made them plenty of money with albums like *Sign O' the Times* and *LoveSexy*. You would have thought they could have gotten over their petulance and resentment. But by the time we were doing the second record with him, the relationship had cooled to the point where the R&B promotions man didn't even come to the premiere of *Graffiti Bridge*. When I asked them why, they got sarcastic with me. "We have more records to be worked," they said.

The lead single, which was also one of the last songs we did, was "Paint the White House Black," a topical record that played off the fact that there was a President Clinton in the Oval Office (not to mention folding in a little joke about Casablanca and Choza Negra). When Bill Clinton first emerged onto the national political scene, people used to ask me if I was related to him—I don't know if they were joking or if they hadn't seen pictures of him (or, maybe, of me), but they asked anyway. And then, after his election, there was this idea that because he was a southerner who came from a modest background and seemed to have a sense of social justice, he was America's first black president. That pointed back to *Chocolate City* and Mayor Gibson in Newark, and it opened up into the idea of "Paint the White House Black." At the beginning of the song, Dr. Dre makes a fake phone call. "What's boppin'?" he says. "Could I speak to the president? Yeah, just tell him he was smokin' last night at the club. You know what I'm saying? What? He don't inhale? Well, I know I got the wrong motherfuckin' house."

There's a raft of rappers on that song: Ice Cube, Public Enemy, Yo-Yo, Kam, MC Breed. Getting them all together in one place was important at that time, which was right in the middle of the East Coast/West Coast rivalry. The song updates "Chocolate City" but also "One Nation Under a Groove"; the idea was that unity had to come from the people, not from the government.

> *And let the love shine from the right house*
> *Be it the black, red, or white house*

Another song, "Rhythm and Rhyme," had the same dense lyrical style, though it was more overtly a tribute to hip-hop acts like Eric B. & Rakim—metaphor stacked on metaphor, tight turns in the verses, a chorus that was like a steel band tight around the whole song. I was so energized by what I heard from the best rappers. I felt like I was back in the late fifties or early sixties, in awe of Frankie Lymon and Smokey Robinson again.

> *Therefore, this rap rendition in tradition of competition*
> *Mace the motherfucker before the first emission*

That whole record hit hard, and was overtly political in parts. "Martial Law" has a version of an old jailhouse toast from the fifties—"Cracking a bottle of champagne, they exchanged lyrical gratifications verbalized in the form of a toast"—performed by Louie Kabbabie, and goes on to talk about the hypocrisy of law enforcement and music ownership.

The songs sounded young, angry, reenergized, partly because I had fully absorbed that first wave of hip-hop and partly because I was working with producers who were right in the moment. I did both "Paint the White House Black" and "Martial Law" with Kerry Gordy, Berry's son, who I had known since he was a baby. When I was with his mother, Ray, at Jobete in New York, she would go off to hang with her boyfriend, Eddie Singleton, and she'd leave the kids in the office with us. And "Hollywood," which was a satire of West Coast entertainment life, I did with Dallas Austin. I knew Dallas through Joyce Irby, who I had recorded with years before. She showed up at a session, just a little girl with a bass in her hand, no case. We did a song called "Fenderella," which ended up being her nickname—a funkier Cinderella. She went on to sing in the band Klymaxx, and then to collaborate with Dallas. That's how he came to my attention. We worked on "Hollywood" in his new studio in Atlanta, which had been Bobby Brown's building, and the place was like the barbershop had been back in Plainfield, and then some: there were so many young kids hanging around there, artists at the beginnings of their careers like Usher, Busta Rhymes, Outkast, the ABC crew, Too $hort, Goodie Mob. They were sitting around like kindergartners, learning from me but teaching me, also. Too $hort knew so much about Funkadelic that he gave me an education. He played every album I ever did, including ones I had forgotten. And I picked up new production techniques, too: I was still recording with real drums—I could sample them after they were played, but it wasn't until Atlanta that I learned how to build them straight out of the drum machine. Within a few years, that Atlanta scene blew up. It seemed like everyone who was there became famous. When I first heard about TLC, they sounded cool, but it took me a bit to realize that they were the little girls who used to come around Dallas's place.

Hey Man . . . Smell My Finger was a hot record. People loved its texture and its message. But support was lacking from the label. Over the years I've seen a variety of ways in which companies help records succeed or fail to do so. In this case, they deliberately stepped away from it. I can only speculate on their reasons. Maybe it was related to their lack of patience with Prince. Maybe they were breaking in new radio people. Maybe they honestly just didn't see how they could succeed with it. But when we sensed that they weren't working with us, we went over their heads and started dealing straight with the programmers and jocks. Berry Gordy, Kerry's father, caught wind of it and told us not to do that anymore. His theory, being Berry, was that you can't anger the company. He thought it would only make things worse. In retrospect, he was right. It's a shame, because we had a video for "Martial Law" all ready to go. It had been directed by Reginald and Warrington Hudlin, who I had worked with on their movie *House Party* (I played the DJ at a fraternity reunion). The very next year, the Hudlins did a pilot for HBO, a black take on *The Twilight Zone* called *Cosmic Slop*. One of the segments was an adaptation of a short story by Derrick Bell, who was the first tenured African-American law professor at Harvard, called "The Space Traders." The idea of it was that aliens came to Earth and agreed to solve all the planet's problems—they would give us infinitely renewable energy, pay off the debt, leave a Utopia when they went—if they could take all the black people in America back to their planet. The spaceships that Bell imagined were "huge vessels, the size of aircraft carriers," sort of anti-Motherships.

There were big-screen developments to go along with the small-screen ones: after *Hey Man . . . Smell My Finger*, we appeared in an *Animal House*–type movie called *PCU*—it stood for

Port Chester University, but also for political correctness and the way that early-nineties thinking was getting in the way of fun. A version of P-Funk appeared in the movie as the band that saves one of the fraternity houses. We played a cover of Prince's "Erotic City" (on the studio version, it was me and Belita Woods performing the song) and a new song called "Stomp."

The British band Well Red, who I had collaborated with back in the mid-eighties, sent word to me that another British rock band, Primal Scream, were big P-Funk fans and wanted to work with me. They came to Detroit and I met Bobby Gillespie, their lead singer and songwriter. I liked their sound. They had absorbed lots of American music, the same way that British rockers had back in the sixties: they could do southern rock, swamp rock, all kinds of blues variations. I recorded a song with them called "Give Out but Don't Give Up" that became the title track for their album. While I was working with them, I was reading the music papers, like usual, and I saw an ad for four Funkadelic rereleases: *Hardcore Jollies*, *One Nation Under a Groove*, *Uncle Jam Wants You*, and *Electric Spanking of War Babies*. They were the Warner Bros. albums, spanning from 1976 to 1981, but for some reason they were coming out on Priority Records. Why weren't they still in the Warner vaults? I called Nene, who was surprised to hear that I was surprised; he said he had taken control of the masters on my behalf, under the auspices of his company, Tercer Mundo. The more he reminded me of that transfer, the less I remembered it. I felt that he was being dishonest, and Armen did, too. They started to fight about the ownership of the masters.

Looking back, it's clear that I didn't give the matter the right amount of attention or scrutiny. Some of my energy was taken up by my excitement over *Hey Man . . . Smell My Finger*, and then by my frustration over the way that Warner Bros. had failed to properly promote the record. Some of my energy was consumed by crack, and all the tweaking behaviors that junkies like to do—worrying when I'd get my next fix or what calamity would befall me if I didn't. When I was able to sit down and think about the circumstances surrounding the albums that were rereleased on Priority, the picture was all blurry and folded. It was true that the masters had been with me since our settlement with Warners regarding the last days of Funkadelic. But they had just been sitting there, gathering dust. I couldn't get a real label to give us a real deal with acceptable terms. So how did this happen? Eventually, I learned additional information that seemed to clarify matters. What Priority had in fact used was not the masters, but a digital tape of the records that was spirited out of Warner Bros. by the wife of a former employee. Some of them may have even been sourced from vinyl. If you listen to the Priority rereleases, you can hear that the right track is too loud.

I called Shep Gordon, a manager who had worked with Alice Cooper and then with us. Shep was one of the true legends in the business; everyone respected him for his honesty, generosity, and clearheadedness. Years later, Mike Myers would make a documentary about him called *Supermensch*. When I called Shep, I laid it all out for him—the way that Uncle Jam had collapsed, the bankruptcy hearing, my growing fear that I was up against more than a decade of deceit, paperwork pasted on top of paperwork, and possibly a two-flank assault by both Nene and Armen, pretending to be enemies when they were in fact colluding to take control of my music. Shep sighed and said that he didn't see any way out. Even if I was right, he didn't know how I was going to fight it.

★

In the midst of that period, I started work on a new album, *Dope Dogs*. I had listened to lots of hip-hop by that point, and certain styles in particular impressed me. I loved the Bomb Squad and the work that they were doing with Public Enemy, so I started to do my own version of the same thing, sampling older P-Funk records. I tried not to use the most obvious samples—other people had mined the ore right out of them—so for the most part, I drew from outtakes, rarities, or live tracks. I produced that album myself, in the most labor-intensive way possible. I took a loop of three or four seconds and ran it from the beginning of the song to the end, after which I muted the parts of the loop I didn't want to use. I knew there were more sophisticated ways of handling the source material—the Bomb Squad actually cut songs into pieces surgically and put them in the precise places that they wanted for maximum impact, sometimes even changing the original in the process—but I didn't have the skills to do that, or, for that matter, the interest. I was more like an old Disney animator who couldn't get his head around what Pixar was doing. I needed to work by hand. Like hand-drawn animation, there's something compelling about that technique. After that album was released, hip-hop kids started coming up to me saying, "Who made that beat for you?"

Once I had the loops, I brought Blackbyrd McKnight in to play over them, and then put Bernie on the organ. Blackbyrd was still in Detroit with us at the time, living on his own farm. Others came in and did the same thing, the present paying its respects to the past. I made sure that album was a complete account of family, not just the P-Funk family but my actual family. My son Shawn is on the record, along with my daughter Barbarella and her daughter Tonysha. My son Tracey, of course, had plenty to do with it, and his kids contributed vocals: his son Trafael and his little girl Patavian, both of whom Stephanie and I were raising at the time. They may not have been clones of Dr. Funkenstein, but they had his DNA.

More so than any album since the golden years of Parliament, *Dope Dogs* orbited tightly around a set of ideas. For that one, I sat down and thought hard. It started out with a simple curiosity sparked by a news story I saw about what happened to drug dogs when they retired from the police force or the DEA. They were cast aside and basically left to die. I started asking myself questions about the life that those dogs were forced to live. In the process of being trained to look for drugs, they had to sniff for drugs, which means that they got a habit. When they were finished, they were strung out and incapable of doing anything else. It was the existence of an addict. Then I started to look into other uses and misuses of dogs, and I was struck by how many of them were related to drugs in some way. Drug dealers always had pit bulls with them for protection. In Michigan, there were university labs where they experimented on animals: dogs with rods to their heads being used for everything from behavior modification to cosmetics testing. Whereas on past records, I had written traditional verses and traditional choruses, on *Dope Dogs* I just wrote and wrote until stream-of-consciousness puns turned into rivers. The result was probably the densest set of lyrics I had ever produced. In "Just Say Ding (Databoy)," I imagined the life of a lab dog.

Just say ding-dong and I'm sprung.
I spring every time a bell is rung.
I'm not a ding-a-ling, I'm not a ding-dong.
Mine is another story.
Told of a goddamn laboratory.
Biological, illogical.
Where's the logic in a rod
That's lodged in your head till you're dead.

"U.S. Custom Coast Guard Dope Dog," which functioned as a kind of title track, tied together various strands of thought that had been alive in P-Funk since the seventies: government conspiracy, selective prosecution, why society insists on punishing basic animal behaviors.

U.S. Custom Coast Guard dope dog
Keen sense of smell, trackin' the telltale trails of cartels,
Dope boats, big dope
Never a gram or o.z., kilo too low-key.
Gotta be tons of P-blow, bales of lumbo
When other dogs sniff at other dogs' tails,
He can track the profits from a dope sale straight to the stank
account.

That song took me back to the day in the Sheraton when I saw George H. W. Bush's helicopter landing so that he could deliver the Zero Tolerance speech, and took me back even further than that, to *Electric Spanking of War Babies*, and its ideas of how media controlled the culture.

There are party songs, too, but they party across history: "All Sons of Bitches" quotes, or samples from "Atomic Dog" and "One Nation Under a Groove," not to mention Sly and the Family Stone's "Stand." There's also a callback to "Paint the White House Black," but the song's really about the human party, how we're all sons of bitches no matter what our racial background, political beliefs, or national affiliation.

> *If the dogs in the world unite to get the riches*
> *The silly may really pay sons of bitches*
> *Can paint the White House black like the president requested*
> *I voted for that son of a bitch I suggested*
> *Just think of the type of the shit that we could piss on then my*
> *   friend*
> *I got a list of the top ten*
> *The Great Wall of China*
> *Woof!*
> *North and South Carolina*

Beneath the rush of lyrics, there was something more personal at stake. I forced myself to consider the possibility that all the catastrophic things that had been happening to me financially might be less a matter of dominoes falling than one of dominoes pushed. I had started off with an inkling that Nene was creeping, but when the Funkadelic masters had migrated mysteriously over to Priority, the ink spread until it blackened the water. And the stress of it all was getting to me. I had let myself get so tired that even if I saw the enemy clearly, I didn't have enough energy to war to that.

At risk of being taken down, taken apart, and taken away, I went back to the only powerful place I knew: funk. There was something big in there for me, an overarching idea about how a man who is on his last legs can renew himself through the creative process. That's when I started thinking back to Star Child, reviving the idea that artists came from somewhere else, that they were not of this earth. People who make art are the bringers of the dawn, the children of light. It was just an idea at first, a what-if to shake up the what-is, but it made too much sense. During the writing of that record, I cycled through all that shit, running my mouth, testing how good it felt. The first track, "Dog Star (Fly On)," was a close cousin to "Maggot Brain," with Blackbyrd paying (and playing) homage to the recently departed Eddie Hazel, along with an opening monologue about interplanetary matters:

> *So what is the real deal in this world?*
> *Once upon a shine, a long time aglow*
> *A beautiful bright star, as fine as any goddess*
> *She has long held the dominant position in the sky,*
> *And had been admired by all for her beauty.*
> *But lately, she felt unwell.*
> *Indeed it seemed as though her life was ebbing away.*
> *Failing and failing, she clung to any companion star she could find*
> *Only to discover that they, too, felt the deathly grip and were weakening.*

The weakness of the dying star eventually turns back into the strength of a reborn one. It's a creation story, a funk nativity: at the end of the song, a shepherd goes out to see the star's "resurging renewed existence, as quick as the sun behind her." There had been other times in my career where I was clowning, but this time I was Sirius.

IF ANYBODY GETS FUNKED
UP, IT'S GONNA BE YOU

The Priority rerelease of the four last Funkadelic records back in 1993 had been a shock, but it had only been the first shock. After a year or so with the records out, the label had profits, and they needed to know where to pay them. Since Nene had sold them the records, they assumed that the checks should be directed to him, but they were well aware of Armen's reputation for litigiousness. They asked a New York court to help them decide where the royalties should go. It was something called an interpleader, a civil procedure that allows a plaintiff—in this case Priority—to compel two or more other parties to settle a dispute. In the interpleader, Armen and Nene, who were already fighting in California court over ownership of my catalog—everything from licensing to distribution to publishing—each staked their claim to the copyrights, and each set out to prove that the other side had no valid argument. At one point, in New York, Nene's side deposed Armen and his executive assistant Jane Peterer. The results, which we heard about from Nene's side, were shocking— Jane admitted that Armen had been doing cut-and-paste tricks on contracts, which involved taking signatures from one place and transplanting them to a new location or even a new contract. The

New York judge found this behavior abominable. Nene assumed that this meant everything would come back to him. Instead, the New York judge simply ruled that Armen's claim was invalid and shipped the case back to California. The judge there, Judge Real, set up a Special Masters so that the songwriters could get paid while the case raged on. After a little more back-and-forth between Armen and Nene, Judge Real grew frustrated. It's too bad, he said, that Mr. Clinton isn't alive, or he could help us straighten this out. Armen and Nene had to sheepishly explain that I was, in fact, alive. The judge sent for me, but before I could get there, Armen and Nene settled. The settlement was sealed, so I don't know what really happened, even to this day, but one of the results was that the publishing for many P-Funk songs were transferred from Nene and his lawyers to Bridgeport, Armen's publishing company. And then it was back to business as usual: Armen could collect and not pay anyone. The songwriters never got what they were owed, though they could always go and get a few hundred from Armen if they were in dire straits—if they were willing to sign away more of their future.

About a year after that, Armen tried to evict me from my farm in Michigan. He had been collecting on my behalf, supposedly, ever since we had cut a deal in the mid-eighties. I had paid him $100,000 and asked him to save my farm for me. What he had done, it seemed, was pay off the farm, but also transfer the title to himself. I made a counterclaim to try to expose the illegal transfer of title. During that case, in Michigan, I looked into the paperwork from the 1984 bankruptcy hearing, and I really started to see the strategy behind creating the false impression that I was deep in debt, millions of dollars to Armen, Nene, and record companies, among others, when the truth was that it was more a matter of a slight cash-flow issue. Not only had the amount I owed Armen been grossly inflated on the paperwork—a few months before that hearing, he set my debts to him at around $200,000, only to appear in the paperwork at more like $600,000—but he had also claimed similar debts for his various companies, Bridgeport, Westbound, and Nine, raising the total to $2.4 million. For his part, Nene had claimed that I owed Polygram and Casablanca each $800,000, and Capitol about $1 million. None of the labels had shown up in 1984, partly because those fake debts were absurd. The Michigan judge wouldn't let me bring in the information from the previous case, or from the case that was in progress in Los Angeles, so we lost. We appealed. But out there in Washtenaw County, there were only three judges: the woman who had heard our case in the first place, her husband, and one other guy. When the appeal came up, somehow the same woman ended up hearing it, and we lost again. Years later, I was explaining the case to a lawyer, and he stopped my story cold. "A judge heard her own appeal?" he said. "Tell me that didn't happen." I had nothing to say to that, and he just shook his head.

I had credited *Dope Dogs* to the broadest possible version of the organization, Parliament-Funkadelic/P-Funk All Stars, but it was time to get everyone back together for real. As I started going through tapes for the next record, I found that I had enough tracks, and enough different kinds of tracks, to bring everyone together again—Bootsy, Bernie, Junie, Garry, the whole organization. The legal wounds that had been inflicted on all of us (some were self-inflicted, of course) might never heal entirely, but music was a way of starting us on the road back to health.

Bernie and Bootsy took the most effort. I had to pay them $40,000 each to participate. People around me thought it was a crazy waste of money, but as far as I was concerned, they were needed. A reunion without them was like a stool without enough legs. It wouldn't have stood. Musically, they proved my point almost immediately. "Sloppy Seconds," one of the songs they did, was just ridiculous, a new coin minted from an old mold. "New Spaceship" is the other reunion song, though that one wasn't wholly new but assembled from old pieces. Whatever we were doing, we were doing right. That DNA was still there. Those two songs became two of the pillars of the new record, which we called *The Awesome Power of a Fully Operational Mothership*, or *T.A.P.O.A.F.O.M.* (pronounced "tap-oh-a-foam"). I credited it to George Clinton and the P-Funk All Stars, but it was the full real deal.

Many P-Funk albums had themes; that's one of the ways we built our legacy. On this one, the theme was the idea of legacy itself. The same way that we reunited the musicians, we reunited the artists: the album art included contributions from Pedro, Overton, and Stozo. The songs continued on in that vein. "Fly Away" was a kind of title song, and it argued that funk will always be here, that it will survive beyond all doubt and time. "Hard as Steel" figures personal and musical persistence as a kind of virility:

She like it hard
Hard as a rock
Hard as steel and still getting harder

Cause shit's got a heavy metal hard-on
Pussy posse pumped to get the throb on
Eardrum bashin' sounds come crashin' down
From the dance band on the bandstand
To the dance floor encore
Hard up for more

Other songs, like "If Anybody Gets Funked Up (It's Gonna Be You)," looked at how creative renewal could help to push past issues with copyright and intellectual property—they were an extension of the things I had started to write about on *Dope Dogs*. We had been taken away from the root of what we were doing: more to the point, what we were doing had been pulled up from the root and taken away from us. We had to fight for what was ours, for what we made. We had to find our way back.

T.A.P.O.A.F.O.M. was the triumph that came after the moment of painful introspection. Of all the records from the period, it's the one that people most often talk about as a source of late ripening: they sit on it for years and suddenly it comes clear to them.

To celebrate the release of the album, we scheduled a big concert in New York: Central Park, July 4, 1996. We called it the Mothership Reconnection tour, not just because Bootsy and Bernie were back, but also because the show marked the return of the Mothership itself. The original ship had met a sad end. The team we had hired as promoters, Tiger Flower, had ended up with it, for a time storing it in Darryll Brooks's mother's garage in Clinton, Maryland, of all places. And then they had sold it off for parts: the motor went to this person, the elevator went to that person. It was the dumbest thing in the world to do to something historical like that. Since it had been twenty years since the original build, we decided to rectify the mistake: we got blueprints from Jules Fisher and paid for a new one to be built.

The Central Park appearance felt triumphant: we had played in New York over the years, in one configuration or another, but we hadn't made a real impact like that since we pulled down the original Parliament and Funkadelic. It was a complex triumph, though. On the day of the concert, it was a little rainy and foggy in Central Park, which gave the show a mysterious feeling. That only increased when we went out for sound check and saw a little remote helicopter with some kind of invisible guidance system flying around the stage. Everybody was joking that it was aliens and shit. And in the wake of the show, we started to receive conspiracy letters that said the same thing and more—that the show had been watched by extraterrestrials. Many of them centered on the fact that July 4 was the anniversary of the supposed alien landing in Roswell, New Mexico, back in the late forties; those fans tried to establish a connection between Roswell and the reappearance of the Mothership. I hadn't thought about Roswell in years, though when I did, the string of coincidences started to vibrate again. I remembered back in the late seventies, when I bought my Michigan farm and found the book about Area 51 in the barn. I remembered the original Roswell incident in 1947, seeing the newsreels before the Saturday movie in Chase City, Virginia. I remembered how the government was supposed to have transported the alien corpses to Wright Field, which was just near Dayton, Ohio, which was also the home of so many funk bands. Years before, Bootsy and I had been in Toronto, listening to the radio, and the DJs were clowning on a news report about an old maintenance man who claimed to have seen those bodies coming in to the airfield in Dayton. "I know what I seen," he said.

"You're not going to make no goddamn fool out of me." We did that impression for a while, saying, "You're not going to make no goddamn fool out of me" in that old janitor's voice. I wondered, not for the first time, if this web had a spider somewhere that was spinning it.

After Central Park, we took the reunited group, including Bernie and Bootsy, to play a series of shows in Europe. The feel wasn't quite the same as the New York concert, and it wasn't the same as it had been twenty years earlier. Both Bernie and Bootsy, understandably, expected to be reinstated as coleaders, or at the very least, members of my inner circle. They were accustomed to being stars. But I couldn't let them come back and immediately lord it over the musicians I had toured with since the Capitol years—I had been with that group for more than a decade at that point. That perception of stardom, of tiers of status, had a kind of nostalgia attached to it; it reminded me of how things had felt in 1978, as the Brides and Parlet started to take some of the shine away from the Rubber Band. This time, though, it was worse: everyone was older, so they were needier, and they had spent a decade protected and promoted by their own families, who didn't hesitate to criticize me when they thought I was setting up an unfavorable situation. And so, almost immediately, it became clear to me that the reunion would be short-lived.

Even if everyone had been calm and accepting of the terms of the reunion, it wouldn't have lasted. No sooner did word get out that the band was back together than Nene and Armen popped right up. They started making offers to people: they dangled some money for Garry to do a record, or Garry and Bernie to go off to a side project. It was their same divide-and-conquer strategy, and it sounded even more alarms. If they had just been interested in money, they would have kept quiet and let us reunite. But their actions seemed to suggest that they were more interested in a lack of communication, that what terrified them the most was the prospect that we would all start talking and comparing notes.

As the *T.A.P.O.A.F.O.M.* tour ran its course, even the Mothership seemed to get the idea that things weren't going to be the same. The second Mothership looked good, but it hadn't been fabricated with the same care as the first one, and the insides weren't engineered as well. There were glitches in the mechanism. When the smoke cleared, I was supposed to be right there on top of the stairs, emerging from the cabin. Sometimes, though, the elevator stopped before I got there. In one show, I just climbed out and walked to the front of the stage. "I don't need a ship anymore," I told the crowd. "I'll just walk."

T.A.P.O.A.F.O.M. didn't do much commercially, and I started to see that the record industry that we had grown up with, and grown up in, didn't exist anymore. For that record, the label—Sony 550—didn't even want to press any plastic, which had consequences for the music but also for the package in general. It had such a good cover, but we couldn't explore the story with inside art. Back at Casablanca, Neil would let us tell the story, no matter what the cost. It was also depressing to see how it was handled in internal accounting. The record started out in pop but was moved over to R&B, which was a sure sign of trouble—the budget got cut in half. It was also a time when labels were gobbling up new artists whose music was made by computer, not just hip-hop but new pop acts, because those acts cost considerably less.

The computer revolution was, for me, a mixed bag. As much

as computer production let record companies skimp on money, computer distribution and the birth of networked computing truly reset the game. Putting out songs via the Internet meant world reach. That was the first record of ours to be sold as a download. At first, I had no idea what that meant. I had so many of those early machines and so many young kids explaining it to me, and it still was gobbledygook. But once I understood what they were saying, it made more than perfect sense. I couldn't wait until the moment when people could come and download it straight from me rather than using the label as a middleman. For that matter, I wasn't worried about unauthorized downloading—it seemed like a solution to a problem rather than a problem. Neil used to give away up to fifty thousand records, loss leaders, to sweeten the pot and get people interested. Free downloads were a newer, faster, cheaper version of that. Ultimately, the number of people who download for free is going to be a fraction of the total, easily offset if you distribute correctly.

As *T.A.P.O.A.F.O.M.* was coming out, Capitol sent a young executive to me to propose a new greatest-hits record, with the twist being that it would face hip-hop head-on. I had always collaborated with rappers on songs and remixes, most visibly with Ice Cube on "Bop Gun," which was a reworking of "One Nation Under a Groove," and they wanted a whole record of this kind of thing: P-Funk paying tribute to the way that hip-hop had paid tribute to it. Most of that record was done in the studio by others: they had rappers and producers work on the original tracks. I worked on just a few of the tracks. I rerecorded "Flash Light" with Q-Tip, Ol' Dirty Bastard, and Busta Rhymes; I recorded a new version of "Star Child"; and I remixed "Knee Deep" with new contributions from Digital Underground, one of the rap acts that was most open about the way they extended the P-Funk tradition.

Just as our music was coming back for a second term, the actual Clinton administration was reupping as well: Bill Clinton beat Bob Dole to extend his presidency. We had played the Youth Ball for Clinton's first inauguration. It went off without much incident, except that the president happened to walk out onstage during "I Call My Baby Pussycat," or "Pussy," which was an unfortunate (or maybe prophetic) coincidence given what would happen a few years later with Monica Lewinsky. At that show, his security people locked up one of our roadies, Barry Fields. Barry was one of those old sixties revolutionaries who was always mumbling about how the system was locking us up by locking us down. He had a book that he carried around that claimed that both Clinton and the elder George Bush had been part of a plot to run huge amounts of cocaine into the U.S. through the Mena, Arkansas, airport. At the show with Bill Clinton, Barry turned to one of the Secret Service guys and said something about Mena. They held him backstage until after the show, at which time the Secret Service agents returned him to me. I didn't understand Barry; I asked him what he was thinking. "I was just saying that so that motherfucker would know that I knew," he said.

That summer, right around my birthday, we were playing in Atlanta as part of the festivities surrounding the Olympics, and Chelsea Clinton came to the show. Before we played, she came backstage, and she was so excited. "I can't believe it," she said. "All of my friends are going to be so jealous." We set up to take a picture, and at the last minute it occurred to me that maybe I should conceal the little crack pipe I was holding in my hand. I made a fist around it. It was hot as a motherfucker, burning my hand up, but it worked—the picture, without a crack pipe in sight, was in *People* magazine. As we walked out to the stage, Chelsea was joking with me about the birthday cake that my crew had bought. "Let's start a cake fight," she said. "Hey," I said, "don't you make no sudden moves." Security was all around us—armed security. That's not how I wanted things to end, shot at close range by a guy who thought he was protecting the First Daughter. Later that night, there was a disturbance in the crowd, a Muslim teenager talking loud about the government. One of the Secret Service agents came up to me and asked me about him, and I vouched for the kid—he was related to people we knew, and he was outspoken, but he wasn't any kind of threat. "Thanks," the agent said. "How's Barry Fields?" Barry Fields? I did a major double take before I realized it was the same Secret Service guy who had held Barry over his Mena comments. And while holding Barry may have been excessive, those guys had a nearly impossible job to do: they had to keep people safe, assess threats, and do the impossible, which was to prevent all trouble. As we were leaving, we heard a muffled thump. That turned out to be the bomb in Centennial Olympic Park. It didn't sound like much of anything at the time.

At the end of that year, I moved down to Tallahassee. I had no farm. I didn't have very much money. I set up a studio and kept recording, and the band kept touring. My main goal at that point, though, was to try to get control of my catalog back from Armen: he was collecting on Parliament and Funkadelic, on solo material, and also on all the hip-hop payments for sampling. I refiled the suit I had lost in Michigan. Right at the start of that lawsuit, I pulled my new lawyer aside. "Listen," I said, "I know they're going to offer you lots of money to back down. If they offer you five million, take it and give me a million and a half." As it turned out, he didn't do very much for us. We eventually lost the case, I believe largely because of a backdated document that claimed that I had signed the rights to all of my songs to Armen back in 1982. The document had already been discredited as part of the interpleader back in 1994, which led to the settlement of the California case, but it resurfaced in Florida. My lawyer didn't object strenuously to it, and in my opinion it cost us the case. The day we were supposed to be doing the appeal he was in Switzerland. We lost the appeal, too.

If you were a historian of deceit, you could trace the legal trouble back to 1980, when Roger Troutman had gone from Uncle Jam to Warner Bros. Roger's departure ended the dream of Uncle Jam Records, and thrust us into the first phase of a legal nightmare. That's why April of 1999 was so strange. In a neighborhood in northwest Dayton, Ohio, one morning, police found Roger shot several times in the midsection outside his recording studio. He died a few hours later in surgery. When police searched the area, they found Roger's brother, Larry, also dead, in a car that matched the description of one that had fled the scene of Roger's shooting. There was a gun next to Larry with bullets that matched those that had killed Roger. The killing was a mystery, but not much of a mystery: Roger had wanted to dissolve the business partnership, which would have left Larry broke, and Larry had panicked.

When I heard about Roger's death, I was shocked. I could not have seen it coming. That kind of thing, sudden violence from within the inner circle, is always a shock. But the more I thought about it, the more I had to admit that I could have predicted some trouble. Larry was Roger's biggest fan. He gave his brother so much unconditional approval. I always thought that's what kept Roger from being a real rock and roll star like Eddie or Black-byrd. The Troutmans, and Roger in particular, were very good performers, but they didn't realize how much it took to go further. He was always having his ego stroked close to home, and because of that he never got big in the broader world: never really tested his idea of himself creatively or financially, never did the coliseum circuit.

Money—the ways that it moved or failed to move, the way it blocked up good sense and severed blood ties—was at least partly responsible for Roger's death, but by that point, Roger had separated from the rest of us. I saw similar things happen closer to home, as other members of the P-Funk tribe died off and the problems with their underlying finances were exposed. When band members died, money supposed to go to their rightful heirs somehow went to other people claiming to be their wives. For example, Glen Goins's mother was improperly listed as his widow on copyright renewal forms after Glen died. And even these deceits are executed over monies that were a fraction of what they should have been. The total amounts left behind are paltry when they should have been a hundred or two hundred thousand dollars a year minimum. You're talking about millions of records sold, in four different formats (vinyl, cassette, CD, and download), and then beyond that all the licensing and sampling. All the P-Funk members would be able to set their families up for life, and not just me, Bootsy, and Bernie, but Eddie, Michael, Glen, Billy, Boogie, and the rest.

★

In July of 2001, I turned sixty, and a few months later Archie and I went up to New York to do some recording. We were in midtown, using some studio time that Bobby Brown had bought. He and Whitney Houston had finished up early and let me and Archie use the balance of their time, along with a hotel room across the street.

We never made it across the street. In the morning, after a long night of work, Archie and I turned on the news, and we couldn't turn it off. It was wall-to-wall with coverage of the planes crashing into the World Trade Center. The city was locked up frozen all day. A girl brought us food on a bicycle. Archie went down the street to try to buy a copy of *Behold a Pale Horse*, but thought better of it—what if his name ended up in a database as having purchased the book minutes after the towers fell?—and turned back around. Everything was eerie. I had the same feeling I had when John F. Kennedy was assassinated, or when Sam Cooke died, or even when Hendrix passed: it was a surreal, underwater sensation, with things slowed down so much that you couldn't even get a good look at them. After an event like that, it's always hard to know what to do with art. Do you sharpen its tip and try to point with precision at the inexplicable thing that has just happened? Do you try to take people's minds off of it? Do you just go ahead as you would have anyway, under the theory that if you go off course, the terrorists have won? And there was another feeling, too—that I was being watched over by some kind of force. There had been so many major historical events that I had missed by a day or less. I had been in the air going to a concert during the San Francisco earthquake: the rest of the band was already on the ground. That kind of thing had been happening for years. We were in Berlin the day the Wall came down in 1989.

We were playing in northeast Ohio a day before the Kent State shootings. P-Funk had, if not a guardian angel, at least a connection to history.

Later that year, I reconnected with Sly Stone. He had vanished into the Bay Area, but I ran into an engineer who had worked with him, and he put me in touch with Sly, and soon enough the two of us were messing around in the studio again. We were both pretty fucked up, but we were putting down sounds that lasted. Sly had moments of real sharpness; he wasn't any less of a genius at making music, but he was less confident about it. When he let you hear what he was doing, it would knock you out. But he was just as liable to get worried that it wasn't good enough and erase it. I explained to him that someone needed to preserve the work. If it didn't turn into a song that year, it would the year after that or maybe a decade later. Slowly, he started to trust me with the files. Some of them I've held on to since then, worked with them, put new parts on top of and around them, and they're songs for 2014 or beyond.

The legal and financial malfeasance continued. In 2003, Epic Records put out an album called *Six Degrees of P-Funk*, an anthology of tracks from the P-Funk family, some of which were licensed from Uncle Jam. Despite the fact that the record went platinum, somewhere on Epic's books I'm accounted as in debt for the project. How is that possible? It used Bootsy's records, Junie's records, some other material. People got paid as producers. I wasn't contacted or consulted. I had nothing to do with it. And yet it wasn't worth fixing or even finding out the specifics of the breakage. There were messes everywhere, and most of the battle was knowing when resolution was even possible. And I wasn't clean enough to think about cleaning up the rest of it. The same thing was happening with Sly. He wasn't able to stay off drugs long enough to pursue redress in an organized fashion. And yet in some ways he was better off than I was. They have taken from him so openly—box sets of old material where not a penny finds its way back to him—that if he was to be clean for six months, he could probably make a case that he's due a significant amount. But his story isn't my story to tell, and his battle isn't my battle to fight.

I kept recording. It was all I thought to do, for the most part, though I wasn't sure what made sense in the way of releasing material. Since *T.A.P.O.A.F.O.M.*, I had seen clearly that the record industry wasn't managing its releases and sales the way it once did. Putting out music so it could just drop into a bottomless well didn't seem worth it. But around 2004 or so, I looked at the studio tapes and suddenly realized I had dozens of songs that were completely or mostly done. That became the basis of *How Late Do U Have 2BB4UR Absent?*, an album credited to George Clinton and the P-Funk All Stars that was released in 2005.

An album? Maybe that doesn't quite explain it. It's an anthology and then some, with twenty-four songs. It's a Hollywood movie and then some, with a two-and-a-half-hour running time. Some of the songs are reworks of early tracks: "I Can Dance" is built on a demo session from "Nappy Dugout," which was recorded all the way back in the early seventies. "Paradigm" was a track I had done with Prince, initially during the *Hey Man . . . Smell My Finger* sessions and then touched up over the years. There's a song on there with Bobby Womack (a cover of Jerry Lee Lewis's "Whole Lotta Shakin' Goin' On"), a song with my son Tracey ("Su Su Su"), and a song with my granddaughter Sativa ("Something Stank," which is an ode to marijuana, long before Colorado legalized it).

In many ways, the album is a showcase for the female singers who did such wonderful work for that phase of P-Funk, specifically Belita Woods and Kendra Foster. Both of them are prominently featured. Belita had been around in Detroit from the late sixties: she released a song called "Magic Corner" the same year that the Parliaments did "Testify." After that, she was the lead singer of Brainstorm, a Detroit funk and disco group that had two big hits, "Lovin' Is Really My Game" and "This Must Be Heaven." Belita joined us in the early nineties and was a big part of P-Funk for two decades. Kendra, even though she was a generation younger, was a P-Funk fanatic. She not only watched Belita, but she studied every trick on every record. The two of them were vital to the survival of P-Funk as the group evolved, as we moved away from a regular record-release schedule and became more about consistent touring and occasional recording. I wanted them to have their due on *How Late Do U Have 2BB4UR Absent?*, and one of the funny things I've found is how that record works on a kind of time delay: it's so big and sprawling that people can't absorb it all at once. But songs will surface from it. As people come up to me to talk about the record, I'll start to get the sense that they are listening to "Bounce 2 This," which is one of Kendra's songs, or "Saddest Day," which is one of Belita's.

When we put out the record, we scheduled a release party the week of the Grammy Awards. Everyone came: the old Motown royalty like Berry Gordy and Smokey Robinson, and then new talents like RZA, from the Wu-Tang Clan, and the film director Quentin Tarantino. Tarantino is a huge P-Funk fan. Years later, he invited us onto the set of *Django Unchained*, and he and Reginald Hudlin and Jamie Foxx had a kind of cutting contest to see who knew more about P-Funk. I don't remember who won. They all did pretty well. But you can't even imagine how fucking crazy that shit was, Jamie out in a cotton field with that blue Fauntleroy suit on, bopping around to "Aqua Boogie." Jamie let us use his home studio to record some new music. His mother cooked for us. A few weeks later, Samuel Jackson came to see us play in New Orleans and he took the microphone during "Maggot Brain" and did a recitation of his moment-of-clarity speech from *Pulp Fiction*.

Are there bright spots? There are some. In 2005, we saw in the trades that twenty years had elapsed and that Capitol was getting ready to approach Priority and acquire the masters of the four Funkadelic records that had been rereleased in 1993. More determined than ever to get my catalog back, I looked around for a lawyer who specialized in that kind of thing and found a man named Yale Lewis who was based in Seattle and had represented lots of music-world clients: the Jimi Hendrix estate, Buddy Holly's widow, Courtney Love. In May of that year, a forensic document expert gave his official opinion that the document showing Nene's ownership of the masters, which was the only thing that would have allowed him to sell them to Priority in the first place, was bogus. In June, Judge Real made a determination on the fate of the masters. By this point, he was starting to see the larger picture of trickery and misrepresentation: he had been the judge in the case a decade earlier, when Nene and Armen had acted like I wasn't alive. Judge Real looked at the facts of the case and decided that the masters should come right back to me. He determined that there were only three reasons they had gone away in the first place: scandalous managers, corrupt attorneys, and uninformed judges.

Getting the masters back was a huge victory, practically and morally. It gave me strength for the fight ahead. But it also exposed the degree to which I had let things get out of hand. Soon after Judge Real's decision, I was thinking about the records we had released over the past decade, and I realized that during the course of putting together *Greatest Funkin' Hits*, we had sold some of our own masters to Capitol. How could Capitol have ever needed to go to Priority for the masters when they had, years before, already acquired those masters from us? I had been so focused on the legal fight that I had overlooked an obvious solution that would have cleared things up immediately. I didn't like the effects, but—at least in part—I had produced the cause.

How Late Do U Have 2BB4UR Absent? was the last official release of that decade, though there was another Funkadelic record, *Toys*, in 2008, that was rushed out without my involvement in order to satisfy some kind of settlement agreement between Armen and Westbound and Capitol. I didn't pay it much mind, mostly because I was paying more attention to the presidential election. Like many other people, I was caught up in the excitement of finally having a black president—though maybe with a slightly different perspective on events, since I had released "Chocolate City" back in 1975 and "Paint the White House Black" in 1993. I liked Obama when he first came onto the scene, in part because he seemed comfortable moving between worlds, and that's how agreements are brokered. The strongest political decisions, like the strongest musical ones, combine black and white, tradition and innovation. Obama had the potential to be a binding force for the fabric of the country, someone slick and black who didn't seem to be full of shit. He danced without seeming like he was dancing, which is the Aqua Boogie principle: you have to have a certain rhythm to be able to appease people without appearing spineless, and you have to keep your eyes open and know for certain that there are people who are going to tear your shit down at every turn. Change is a difficult thing for people, and the more powerful they are, the more powerfully they resist change. Why would you permit any shift in a system that's disproportionately benefiting you?

It was a lesson that was equally true in politics and music. I was still in the position of seeing my catalog misused—or, rather, used in ways that didn't benefit me at all. In 2009, the indie-rock group Sleigh Bells released a song called "Rill Rill," which was built on the back of "Can You Get to That." A few years later, the song ended up being the centerpiece of a big Apple campaign for the iPhone. I didn't see a dime from that use of the song. So hearing "Rill Rill" on the television was a source of pride, but also a source of anger and disappointment. I wasn't sure what would be resolved, whether I was dealing with an *if* or a *when*. And life wouldn't go on forever, for me or for anyone else. There was a major reminder of that in the summer of 2009 when Michael Jackson died. I had followed Michael's career since it started, since Berry set up the Corporation to push the Jackson 5 into superstardom. They had done one of the first mainstream covers of one of our songs, "I'll Bet You," back in 1970; it was on their *ABC* album and also part of a promotional release with Kellogg's,

a cardboard-cutout record that came on the back of a Rice Krisp-
ies box. As he got older, Michael got better and better, a finer
singer, a more exciting dancer. But he had been something else,
too. He had been a beacon. Children loved him. People in every
country loved him. That's dangerous when you can get kids all
around the world to agree with you, when you can move across
national borders. Unity, in the hands of someone that powerful,
is a dangerous philosophy, and I came to believe about Michael
what I believed about Sam Cooke, or John Lennon: he was trying
to heal wounds that people had a vested interest in keeping open.
I never thought I'd outlive him, but I wasn't shocked when I did.

I had started working with the Parliaments, and then at Jobete, in
the late fifties. As 2008 rolled around, my time in the music business was nearing a half century, and maybe that's why I found
my mind drifting back to doo-wop and street-corner soul. Whenever we got together, Belita Woods and I would challenge each
other, sing lines from songs by all the old groups: the Capris, the
Chantels, the Elegants, the Edsels, the Shields. When I was a kid
I was in lots of Italian neighborhoods in New Jersey, and the people there were always playing shuffleboard and listening to those
songs. Over the years, I thought that maybe I should do an album
of them, just straight covers, not bring the sound into the present
but bring Parliament back into the past.

When I mentioned the doo-wop project to a friend of mine,
Bobby Eli—he had worked as a producer with the Stylistics, the
Spinners, Billy Paul, and other Philly acts—he suggested that we
do it as a tale of two cities, Philadelphia and Detroit. That grad-
ually evolved, too, into the idea of tracing the history of love in

pop music. In the fifties it was "Darling, I love you, I get down on my knees." By the nineties, she was getting down on her knees to suck something. To me, it was always the same: there were still babies that grew up to make families. Kids still danced to their music, even if it was about someone sucking a cock. When I first heard that kind of thing, it seemed jarring to me. It fucked me up. But what fucked me up worse was realizing that I had moved into the parent position. That's what people said to me in the fifties, that my music was crude and senseless, that it couldn't capture love and romance like Guy Lombardo or Harry James. Age isn't only a number: it's a way of blocking other people's numbers. Bobby picked out a set of songs for me, everything from Johnny Ace's "Pledging My Love" to Shirley and Lee's "Let the Good Times Roll" to Tommy Edwards's "It's All in the Game" to Dean Martin's "Sway" to Ruby & the Romantics' "Our Day Will Come," and we called the group George Clinton and His Gangsters of Love. There were plenty of special guests, too: I recorded "Ain't That Peculiar" with Sly Stone and El DeBarge, and Curtis Mayfield's "Gypsy Woman" with Carlos Santana.

Initially, I had imagined it as a covers-only record, but I ended up including some originals, including "Mathematics of Love," with guest vocals by Kim Burrell. Along with the songs from the past and the songs from the present, we tried to imagine the future. There's a song on that album called "Stillness in Motion" that's a kind of Zen poem surrounded by sound effects. We recorded that with Shavo Odadjian, from the band System of a Down, who was collaborating with RZA from the Wu-Tang Clan. They were making these psychedelic tracks, these dissonant spirituals that also drew on punk jazz, and Kendra Foster sang a nice little lullaby over that background:

Fly with me to the mountain
Lie under the sea
Through the stillness in motion
We can be free

When that record first came out, we promoted it heavily. We played "Ain't That Peculiar" on Jay Leno's show. We went on Letterman and played another track called "Heaven," which sampled Prince's "I Wish U Heaven." Right after Letterman, Universal, the parent label of Shanachie Records, who released the album, called and said we had to take that song off because Prince hadn't authorized the use of the sample. I had assumed that the two of us had an understanding, in part because I had gone to bat for him when Armen sued him for using "Atomic Dog" in various songs: a Nona Gaye song, a remix. I thought we were fine with "Heaven." When that came off the album, the label backed off of everything, withdrew the album. It's a shame, because there are a few songs on there that are real nice late-period funk, as abstract and strange as "Stillness in Motion." "Mathematics of Love" even got Grammy buzz when it first came out. People were calling me and telling me that it was under consideration. But when the album vanished, "Mathematics" vanished with it.

YOU GONNA GET ATE

The first time Nene brought Sly Stone around it was the late seventies, and the two of us became running buddies: getting high, making music, navigating the record business. Thirty years later we were reprising the roles. I was out in Los Angeles often during 2010 and 2011, hanging out not only with Sly but with Mark Bass, a Detroit producer I had known since the eighties. Mark, who had helped discover Eminem, was directly connected to Armen through a producer named Joel Martin, and Armen had paid Mark $6,000 to lie and say that he wrote some of the songs on *T.A.P.O.A.F.O.M.* To say that he was intimately acquainted with the crooked practices of the industry was an understatement. For months verging on years, Sly, Mark, and I spent as much time with each other as our schedules allowed. We were crackheads together, but our main thrust was getting a platform to tell our story. Dr. Drew's office even called me for *Celebrity Rehab*, and when I expressed that I wanted to have Sly and Mark on with me to discuss this circumstance, they seemed to lose interest. We were trying to make news, to get a hearing so that we could tell our story.

We also consulted with so many lawyers that I lost count. One firm represented both me and Sly. They set up a situation for him to sue BMI, which wasn't paying him properly, and his ex-managers, and they tried to get me to file a bankruptcy again. I might have done it had it not been for Jeffrey Thennisch, a lawyer in Detroit who was fighting Armen on behalf of other Detroit writers. When I was considering a second bankruptcy, Jeffrey warned me against it. Anything like that, he said, would jeopardize copyright recapture. After a certain term, he explained, copyrights revert to the original creator; any music made after 1978 was subject to a thirty-five-year term of copyright, while anything made before returned after a fifty-year term. The idea of copyright recapture went off like a grenade in my mind. It meant everything for the golden years of Parliament and Funkadelic. Specifically, it meant that starting in 2013, music would start to come back to me—everything from Parliament's *Motor Booty Affair* to Funkadelic's *One Nation Under a Groove*, not to mention records from that same year by the Brides of Funkenstein, the Horny Horns, and Bootsy's Rubber Band. The second that Jeffrey told me about that, I ran as fast as I could from the idea of bankruptcy, and from the lawyers who had recommended it.

Sly stayed with them, a little stranded. In 2010 he got booked at the Coachella festival, and decided he was going to use the spotlight to air out some of his grievances. That might have seemed like a good idea on the face of it, but I advised against it: I told him that he wasn't going to get the equipment he wanted, that the appearance wouldn't be effective. He was pissed off and stubborn, like usual, and he wouldn't listen. He went out there and launched into a big rant about how managers were stealing from him and he had effectively been kidnapped, and then he played some new music through an iPod. It wasn't that he was wrong about things. I knew how much truth there was in it. But it fell on deaf ears.

On one of my trips out West, Sly and I got some vials of drugs and smoked them. Within minutes, I knew that something was wrong. I started to feel unwell, and then worse than that. It was some nasty shit: crack hadn't been real cocaine for years. It was always partly fake, with B-12 to give you a burst of energy and who knows what else. Some of that else got to me quick. "Fuck," I said, "take me to the hospital." I ended up staying there a week.

The doctors judged that I had suffered a cardiac incident, and pointed to other factors, too: stress, exhaustion, a generally taxing lifestyle. I never like to say that something is a blessing in disguise. More trouble comes in disguise than anything else. But after that scare, I managed to kick crack. After twenty-nine years on the pipe, I got off it once and for all.

I immediately noticed the physical effects of being clean. First of all, my voice came back to me. All that fire in the pipe fucks up your throat. I regained a vocal range and quality I hadn't had in decades. I lost weight, also. In the early days of freebase, the coke was prepared using ether. But ether was in short supply in the eighties, when crack really took off, and people started using baking soda, which put a tremendous amount of sodium in the shit. I was pumping myself full of salt, which kept me full of water. I had edema in my legs. They were the size of trees. I was up close to three hundred pounds, but the minute I set the pipe down, twenty pounds just vanished. And then there was the insomnia. For decades, because of the drugs and whatever else, I wasn't sleeping well. That puts a tax on your heart, darkens your mood, does a whole lot of other nasty shit. I got an apnea mask, which helped me get real sleep for the first time in years.

It wasn't hard to kick, exactly, though there were plenty of reminders of my old life. Now and then I would find drugs in my pocket. The first few times, I couldn't see myself throwing the shit away, so I gave it to someone who wanted it. But soon I began to throw the stuff into the garbage.

The physical changes were only part of the puzzle. Sitting there in the hospital bed, I realized that I had, by luck or by providence, arrived at a point where I could focus entirely on the legal battle: on telling the story of how Armen and Nene had robbed me of my songs, taken control of my catalog and taken away the money I was due, and how they had done it systematically, over the years, in collusion with record labels, rights-management firms, lawyers, and more. I knew that if I got off the pipe, I could get to the thieves and the cheaters and catch them off guard. No one was ready to deal with a clean George Clinton. When I was high, it was too easy for people to write me off as a ranter or rambler, a paranoid—a crackpot. I had seen the way that people reacted when I talked about things at length, or noticed that I only got a hearing in the press when I popped up after a drug bust. I understood their reaction. They were listening to crackhead talk, and they behaved accordingly. But everything I was saying was true, and that's why I had to say it again, clearly, calmly, after I was through with crack. I had to set the record straight by setting the record, straight.

And so when I came out of the hospital I had the same feeling I did in 1982, when I had kept that one unsmoked crack rock for the entire length of the Atomic Dog Tour. I set off to prove everything I already knew. We collected copies of all the relevant court documents. We found contracts, compared them. We verified whatever seemed legit and tore apart what was bogus. The process took years. I gave up my coke habit but now I had a lawyer habit.

But the mountain of evidence wasn't enough. It was the equivalent of a raw track that Bootsy brought to the studio. Just like with music, I needed to produce the information, organize it, and present it the same way I had done with songs and albums. A woman named Kathryn Griffin, a human-trafficking activist in Houston, heard the stories and passed them along to one of her compatriots, Phil Cenedella, also an activist and an advocate for any victim of injustice. He got so incensed that he set up a website, Flashlight2013.com, to house all the relevant documents. While GeorgeClinton.com remains the main headquarters for the band news, Flashlight2013.com is a headquarters for broadcasting the truth about Armen, Nene, and the rest, the same way we broadcast from WE-FUNK on *Mothership Connection*. We're also planning to sell products: not only legal briefs, which are underwear with excerpts from the court documents printed on them, but also Who Stole the Soul Shoes (sneakers with the excerpts printed on the bottom) and Thinking Caps (matching hats). People say that sunlight is the best disinfectant. But in this case, it's flashlight. And soon enough, I'll take the case back to court. In my mind, the documents prove indisputably that for years there has been a consistent and conscious pattern of behavior intended to defraud, engineered by people from all levels of the industry, including those who had been entrusted with fiduciary responsibility—managers, publishers, label executives, people at the copyright office. There are clearly fabricated documents indicating a transfer of copyrights that are being used to this day. Armen is still collecting on these rights even though my opinion is that his ownership is completely illegitimate. What we've found so far, I believe, qualifies as a RICO case, as racketeering, and since there's no statute of limitations in a RICO case, there will be a filing one day. I can assure you of that.

★

What do these documents bring into the light? Armen, for starters. Back in the mid-nineties, during the court fight between Armen and Nene, Armen's former executive assistant Jane Peterer had been deposed, and she had discussed some of their crooked practices. By 2012, Jane was no longer working with Armen. She was living in Switzerland, retired, dealing with some health issues. We went to see her and asked her if she would be willing to discuss matters on the record. When she said yes, we took a statement from her in which she explained in great detail what Armen had been doing while she was in his office. Her testimony confirmed all my suspicions. Here's one sample:

> In 1990, Mr. Boladian obtained a notary stamp on the March 4, 1982 dated agreement and then refiled the document with the U.S. Copyright Office himself and thereby placed 164 separate copyright registrations for musical works related to Mr. Clinton and his groups, Parliament and Funkadelic, Brides of Funkenstein, as well as Philippé Wynne, Glen Goins, and Eddie Hazel into the name of Bridgeport Music. I only later learned that Mr. Boladian fraudulently and materially altered this March 4, 1982 document and then recorded it with the U.S. Copyright Office to create a claim of ownership in these 164 separate copyright registrations in the name of Bridgeport Music.

The passage is written in deposition language, but if you unpack it, you can see how much it weighs. The "March 4, 1982 document" that it refers to is the fraudulently backdated and altered agreement that claimed I had signed all my songs over to Armen, and that cost me my lawsuit in Florida. And the "registrations for musical works" aren't minor or marginal songs. They include "One Nation Under a Groove," "Atomic Dog," "Flash Light," "Give Up the Funk (Tear the Roof off the Sucker)," "(Not Just) Knee Deep," and more. The monies are considerable, and then some, not just because they were hits in the seventies and early eighties but because they were the root of a whole new genre in the eighties and nineties. Rap artists from Dr. Dre to Kanye West, and hundreds in between, sampled them. Not only did Armen dishonestly take over the copyrights, but he inserted himself as a songwriter. Here's Jane's account of that practice:

> Mr. Boladian falsely demanded songwriter rights and credit for musical works before the U.S. Copyright Office that he did not actually author or create by adopting false names or pseudonyms for himself and listing these false names as songwriters on musical works actually written by others, all for the purpose of gaining a financial advantage for himself. Mr. Boladian would essentially create different pseudonyms for himself so that he could derive the revenue for the musical works as an author and/or songwriter even though he was neither an actual author or songwriter.

You can read Jane's full statement in this book, too, in Appendix C. If it was a gun, it would be smoking so much that it would have a cloud around its head.

But Armen was only half of the story. Nene had falsified documents dating back years. He had claimed that as far back as the early eighties, I had assigned Uncle Jam rights over to Tercer

Mundo. The truth was that Nene knew that Armen's papers were invalid and false, so he made up invalid and false papers of his own to catch whatever copyrights fell out. They ended up fighting each other, but that may have been at least partly a smokescreen, a trumped-up conflict designed to ensure that one of them ended up with the copyrights. There's a paper trail of them interacting that stretches back decades. Separately, they were running their own games: together, it seemed to me, they were running a big game, long-term, with disastrous consequences for me. Two halves made a hole, and I fell into it.

For all the certain misdeeds of Armen and Nene, the truth is that the way P-Funk was picked clean doesn't all come down to the deceit of a few individuals. The system is crooked, too. The P-Funk catalog was published through BMI, which was supposed to administer monies fairly and efficiently. But writing credits were reassigned, or payments went to other artists with similar names. The composer George S. Clinton, and the confusion between us, came back into play, though it wasn't as funny as it had been in the seventies. Too many of my payments ended up sent out to him, and when they were returned, they went to Armen or Nene to straighten things out. At one point, my daughter Barbarella requested my book from BMI—that's the full account of all the songs and payments—and they sent her his accidentally. What it showed was that he was being incorrectly paid for many of my songs. I may have been sent a few of his checks, but he was being sent hundreds of mine. It would have only been annoying rather than alarming if it hadn't been for the fact that there seemed to be a major conflict of interest in legal representation. And Yale Lewis, the lawyer I had hired as a music-rights specialist, turned out to be more problem than solution. In my opinion, Yale did more than fall down on the job. He was put in charge of the masters to protect and collect on them. He collected one nine-thousand-dollar sample, from an Aaliyah song. As I've stated in various lawsuits, many of which are still going on, I paid him more than a million dollars and ended up owing him more than $1.6 million, and somehow he's still listed as one of the parties on the masters at the U.S. Copyright Office.

I started to speak about these matters to industry groups and even political committees. A few congresspeople, including Sheila Jackson Lee from Texas, Bobby Rush from Illinois, and John Conyers from Georgia, took a special interest in my situation. They helped me get my image together so that I could present in front of panels. I wasn't good at talking to regular audiences about these matters—I could slip into my Dr. Funkenstein persona easily enough, and I could perform all day long, but dealing with people straightforwardly was more difficult. John Conyers would put me in a church setting, or drop me off at the NAACP and let me sink or float as a normal speaker talking to normal people.

These are just the things I know for certain. The rest needs to be investigated. There are broader questions hovering nearby. Did Nene see an advantage in working with Armen, or vice versa? And who sent Nene to us in the first place? He threw money away as fast as he got it. It didn't make sense for him to even play around with us. He had ties to real-scale gangster stuff, international matters. Who wanted him in the P-Funk camp?

To this day, forces are still at work ensuring that people are keeping their distance. Recently, both ABC-TV in Detroit and the *New York Times* planned to write exposés, and both were curious enough to file motions to have documents pertaining to the bankruptcy and other trials unsealed. And we're not talking just a few documents. There were more than five hundred in all. What's in there that someone wants to keep out of sight? But after a short pursuit, both the *Times* and ABC quieted down. I want to make an issue out of that because to me it seemed like a cover-up coming from upstairs. If they thought it was important enough to unseal it, why back down? I have a theory. Jeffrey Thennisch, our Detroit lawyer, was working not only with us—and was a big part of the two exposés—but also with Barrett Strong and the estate of James Jamerson in a lawsuit against Motown. Giving Jeffrey any credence in our case would have given him momentum against Berry, who was just then staging a Motown musical that perpetuated this fiction that everything at the label was family. No one—not the *Times*, not ABC—wanted to see the underbelly of the industry, not in that way.

By now the game has been played so long, and the rules changed so often, that it's hard to imagine exactly how things will be solved. My main goal is to get everything out in the open. I want to show all that we've collected, and that it's all connected. I especially want to educate the future—my children and grandchildren—so that they can keep fighting this fight. Otherwise, the people who have been taking from me will just wait me out. I won't live forever. I have given my family a sense of history and strategy, prepared them for battle. And when I say family, I don't just mean my kids and grandkids. There's a new high school in Plainfield: the Barack Obama Green Charter High School on Watchung Avenue. Soon after it opened, I began speaking to the students there. They called the program music education, but really it was something more specific, a class in how to protect intellectual property, and what to do if others put their hands on your work. I talked to the students the same way I had talked to the kids in the barbershop a half century before, and I donated $10,000 and 25 percent of my money from the four Funkadelic masters to the school. The barbershop was a half century away, but also a minute away. Time cycles. One of those kids might be the next Billy, the next Eddie, the next Bernie. The story I'm telling has to reach them, the same way it has to reach everyone. In 2025, *Mothership Connection* moves into the copyright-recapture zone. I'll be eighty-five then, and I look forward to seeing it brought back into the fold. At some point, it's all going to blow up again—P-Funk, uncut funk, the Bomb—and when it does, I want it to explode in the right hands.

In 2010, Garry Shider was very ill with brain cancer. After some time in the hospital in Houston, he went home to Maryland. One night, after a show in New Jersey, we found out that he had taken a turn for the worse. We drove down to see him and he was still being himself—energetic, clowning a bit—but at the same time, it was over. We could tell. I lay down in his bed, on one side of him, and Ronnie Ford lay down on the other side. We stayed there all night with him, the Garry who was dying and the memory of the Garry who had lived: the one who had come to the barbershop as a kid, who had played guitar with us and written songs with us and wore a diaper onstage to help lift the crowd higher into the joy and the power of P-Funk. In the morning, the hospice nurses came to bring food, and one of them told us that it was a matter of hours. And you know what? Up until the end, with his life shrinking to nothing, Garry was preoccupied with Armen, and what Armen had done. As Garry had told me many times over the years, instead of paying out royalties, Armen instead told Garry that he was paying off Garry's house. He kept coming around to extend this unfair deal and withhold royalties, even with Garry on his deathbed. When I heard that, I knew what I had to do. I had to dedicate myself to bringing all this to light. The forces that have tried to separate all of us from our music have to be called to account. Investigate. Interrogate. Unseal. Reveal. If we don't get this right, then they win.

EPILOGUE: BROTHAS BE, YO LIKE GEORGE, AIN'T THAT FUNKIN' KINDA HARD ON YOU?

So what happens now? Am I closer to the end or just farther from the beginning? I don't know the answer to these questions. I don't even know if they are questions of theology or if they're just a paradox. The questions are too big, anyway. There are smaller questions inside of them, though, that I can more easily grasp. What's a song I can reach out and touch today? What's the music that I'm going to make tomorrow? For years, I caught hell trying to get myself back into the studio. I had to get rid of a habit. I had to change my image, not just for other people but for myself. When I started making music again, really creating, the main thing I remembered was how much fun it can be. I have a studio near my house in Tallahassee. When I'm in town, I try to go down there every day. There's a new Funkadelic record nearly finished: thirty-three tracks to commemorate the thirty-three years since the last Funkadelic record. It's called *Shake the Gate*, and I worked the way I did on *Dope Dogs* and *T.A.P.O.A.F.O.M.*, sometimes making entirely new songs, sometimes unearthing old tracks from recording sessions—

unused takes, abandoned starts—and growing new songs from them. Producers call these tracks stems, like stem cells, but I like to think of them as seeds.

Seeds, stems. Those tracks link the new work to the old work. Sometimes the link is personal rather than sonic. One afternoon, my son Tracey and I were sitting around talking about all the different aspects of poles: the word, the idea, the concept. It was like an old-fashioned Funkathon, the free-association sessions where we volleyed jokes and puns back and forth. Strippers use poles. Race-car drivers do their best to get pole position. And junkies use pipes, which are just poles with holes in them. That turned into a new song called "Pole Power." There's another song Tracey and I wrote called "Catchin' Boogie Fever" that has classic Parliament-style horn riffs, one called "Baby Like Fonkin' It Up" that revives Star Child, one called "As In" that's a beautiful piece that Jessica Cleaves recorded, and one called "Jolene" that I'm singing with Sidney Barnes, my partner from half a century ago; the guitar work on the track is by the rapper Scarface, Garry Shider, and Blackbyrd McKnight. In other places, we're looking not into the past of P-Funk but into the distant future, at the spot where time curves. Take the title song, "Shake the Gate," which is both primal and futuristic, which uses both didgeridoo (an ancient Australian wind instrument) and electronic effects. It's another dog song—"Coming up in here without shakin' the gate / Fucking bit / You gonna get ate"—that's about the gate around the planet Sirius, and the way that it protects the funk from unannounced visitors. The song is defiant, too: we've had to contend with plenty of trespassers and intruders, second-story men, larcenists. We've stationed guard dogs to protect what's ours. The song is way out of the box, like "Maggot Brain." I don't know if it's commercial, but I know that I don't care. It's not the first time.

First time, last time. In the studio, listening to songs, you lose track of time. But when you're inside music, time doesn't exactly apply. One of the songs from the new record is called "Brothas Be, Yo Like George, Ain't That Funkin' Kinda Hard on You?" It's a memoir just like this book, a song that looks at my time in the funk business and how I keep moving through it. My answer in the song is my answer now, has been my answer always: "I was hard when I started / I'll be hard when I get through." You can measure the truth of that statement by looking at the hardest world around: the prison world. Jails are full of P-Funk fans, and each one is stuck to the time when they last heard us in the free world. If they went inside in 1974, then *Cosmic Slop* might be their definitive P-Funk. If they went inside in 1983, their P-Funk of choice might be "Atomic Dog." Each of them thinks they have access to the heart of the matter. But there's a softer answer, too. When I get up there onstage, when the musicians behind me are turning the corner and heading into "Let's Take It to the Stage," when the angels of our better nature are spreading their wings and the devils are going to the lower level, I feel like the music that I'm giving is, above all, a gift. It's not a word I like to use often, but it's a word I'll use now and again.

Angels, devils. Some of my old bandmates have passed on. Catfish Collins died in 2010, the same year as Garry, Mallia Franklin, and Ron Banks. Belita Woods died in 2012, Boogie Mosson in 2013, and Jessica Cleaves in 2014. Others remain, still committed to keeping the funk alive, and still others remain committed to keeping the funk down. Armen continues to use his ill-gotten copyrights against the interest of everyone but himself. In 2013, Robin Thicke's "Blurred Lines" was everywhere, including in court: the Thicke camp sued Bridgeport Music preemptively because they knew that Armen was getting ready to sue them for copyright infringement for using the Funkadelic song "Sexy Ways," from *Standing on the Verge of Getting It On.* Armen's claim was baseless, but that didn't stop him or his lawyers from going out there and trying to grab some cash in a quick settlement. When I first heard Robin Thicke's song I loved it. I was wishing I wrote it. I can hear a little bit of the quality of my voice in the vocals, a certain urgency, but it's nothing more than that. It's certainly not plagiarism. Pharrell, who cowrote the song, is good at mimicking different characters, at imitating certain styles from the past and bringing them into the present. That's permissible. In fact, it's more than permissible. It's necessary. You've got to change up something. The rules are well known. You can't do seven notes in a row the same, so you just do six, change one, and then come back to the original model. In the early days, people bit melodies all the time and no one bothered looking into it with any degree of scrutiny. Rock and roll got no respect unless your name was, say, George Harrison—the Beatles were so big that the shit became undeniable. Anything associated with them attracted worldwide notice and mountains of cash. Plus, with "My Sweet Lord," George was putting his hand in the till of one of rock and roll's most famous songs, the Chiffons' "He's So Fine." Occasionally there are artists whose style lets them protect everything they play. Jimi Hendrix was like that: you can't even do his licks without getting sued. You have to respect the fact that he coined those phrases—not just the songs but the parts on the guitar. But those cases—the Beatles, the Hendrixes—are few and far between, and "Blurred Lines" isn't one of them. I told TMZ that I would go into court as a witness for Robin Thicke. A few months after that, there was an equally ridiculous lawsuit: the Jimmy Castor Bunch sued Ariana Grande for using the phrase "What we gotta do right here is go back, back into time," because it's similar to a line from their 1972 hit "Troglodyte." The lawyer in charge of that was Richard Busch, who was one of the architects of Armen's strategy. You can read about him in Jane Peterer's statement. But all we can do is get the word out. The word gets out. In November of 2012, Kid Rock was debuting a new song he had written about the history of Detroit music at the halftime of the Detroit Lions' Thanksgiving Day game. I went out to midfield with him, wearing a Flashlight2013.com shirt. I was proud to support the city, of course: Detroit is the most important place for American music, hands down. We have Motown, Aretha, Iggy Pop, Alice Cooper, Kid Rock, Eminem, and of course Parliament-Funkadelic. It's a Rock and Roll Hall of Fame all on its own. Last year, faced with a possibility of a highway project running through the center of Detroit, a group decided to turn United Sound studio into a museum of local music. It's beautiful now; they even restored a piano I had out at my farm and put it on display. There are framed records and photographs on the wall documenting recording sessions from Charlie Parker right up to the Chili Peppers.

Moving forward, taking back. What is past and what is present, really? You're only purely in the present once, when you're born, and then you're divided between present and past. That's why you have to reach into the future. I try to remember that we are only new once. And once you're not new, you're in that much bigger bag of old. Kids today don't know the difference between me and Snoop Dogg, or me and Stevie Wonder. Everybody

who's old is old. And because of that, being old is a growth industry. I look at other musicians my age and pay special attention
to the ones who don't stop making things. A few years ago, Paul
McCartney put out a song, "My Valentine," that was a beautiful
motherfucking piece of music. I know it was for someone special,
because it made him into someone special again. And that's after
being a Beatle, after being in a place when you're so big that you
can't even hear yourself to make music. How did Paul come back
from that point where the eeks took over, where it was all screaming girls and deafening fame? I've been on stages and heard the
crowd shriek for us. I was careful never to take audiences for
granted. The key has always been thinking of people as family,
whether it be my blood family, my family of musicians, or the extended family of fans. I think about what Sly said, gently mocking me for my sense of responsibility: "You got those little ones."
Maybe over time, those little ones make you big.

Little, big. When you don't top the chart anymore, does that
mean that everyone's over you? Or are there other ways to get
over? In the last decade, people have started to say that something popular goes "viral," that it moves around the world, usually through the Internet, on its own. That's nothing new. *Davy
Crockett: Indian Fighter* came on TV in 1954, and I sat down to
watch it in New Jersey. Davy Crockett killed a bear with his
knife. That was a time before hula hoops, before *Maggot Brain*,
before "Bop Gun." There was only Davy Crockett, or at least
that's how it seemed. I remember it so clearly: on our lunch bags,
our jackets, our hats, and toy guns. Everything was Davy Crockett. When people say "viral," it's just a new name for that same
old thing. Look at kids nine to thirteen and pay attention to where
they find their enthusiasms. These days it's on YouTube. They

spend hours looking for the silliest thing, and that's what they decide to admire. That's what they decide to imitate. And it's that world where P-Funk is resurfacing now. We have a channel there. We have videos of songs, new ones and old ones, serious performances and comedy.

Surface, submerge, surface again. The last few years have been some of the best years of my life. It's not 1970, being turned out in Boston by topless girls bearing acid. It's not 1978, with *Motor Booty Affair* rocketing up the chart and side projects bursting brightly around us like fireworks. It's not even the mid-nineties, when you could hear our songs coming out of every lowrider in Los Angeles, cut and pasted into rap anthems. I live in Tallahassee. I record. I tour. I spend as much time as possible with my family. And I'm trying new things all the time. In the last year, we've developed and sold a reality show. There's comedy and drama in it, but there's also a specific argument about the pitfalls of the record business. I want my kids and grandkids to understand what I went through. I can't lecture them from a whining stance, cry about how I was on dope and fucked up. But I can impress upon them that whether or not there's dope, you have to have each other's backs. I want to leave them with a concrete understanding of the realities of how things work, and what to do when they don't.

The other day I did a session with the rapper Kendrick Lamar. My grandkids were hyping me up on him, and I listened to his record. Even before I met him I was laughing at "Bitch, Don't Kill My Vibe," which had the same silly-serious tone we tried for in Funkadelic. He came down to Tallahassee to record with me, and it was beautiful. We did about four songs together and he took some tracks with him, and when we weren't recording, we just talked. We talked about everything. We talked about nothing. I found myself running my mouth more than I ordinarily do because he was so interested in discussing it all: the record industry, social engineering, the function of art. He acts like he's about fifty with all his theories. When I met Sly Stone, he knew of P-Funk because he heard those records himself, as they came out. When I met Rakim, he knew of P-Funk because he listened to his brother's records. With Kendrick, it was his parents' records. He didn't just know the hits. He knew the deepest of the deep cuts. When you talk about your old work with a young man with an old mind, the work feels less old. We talked about my old songs and they were renewed. When the past comes rushing into the present that way, I can see clearly that artwork is a living thing. Younger artists teach me that I taught them. That's why I'm grateful to Kendrick Lamar, and to anyone who is carrying on the P-Funk tradition, which itself carried on the tradition of Louis Jordan, the Beatles, Cream, James Brown, Smokey Robinson, Frankie Lymon. We talked about everything. We talked about nothing. We talked about my old songs and they were renewed. We talked about my old songs and we were renewed.

ACKNOWLEDGMENTS

The music has been the main thing, always, and for the musicians who have helped me make it, see the end of the discography in the appendixes. But there are nonmusical matters, too, and in that light I'd like to thank Carlon Scott, for being there for me in ways I can't fully explain. Simple gratitude isn't enough. I'd like to also thank my managers, from Cholly Bassoline to Archie Ivy, for keeping me afloat when seas got stormy. I'd like to thank politicians like Sheila Jackson Lee, John Conyers, and Bobby Rush for helping bring to light some of the dark things that have transpired in this business. I'd like to thank the writers who wrote about the funk, the artists who drew about it, the dancers who danced about it, the tour musicians who toured with it, the DJs who spun it, the photographers who captured it, and the audiences who got up out of their seats for it. And most of all, I'd like to thank my parents and my children and their children and their children's children, on into whatever infinity permits us. I love you.

APPENDIX A: SELECTED DISCOGRAPHY

The following recordings include significant contributions from George Clinton, as songwriter, producer, vocalist, bandleader, or some combination of the four. Album titles are in italics. Single titles are in quotation marks.

1959

The Parliaments, "Poor Willie/Party Boys"

1960

The Parliaments, "Lonely Island/You Make Me Wanna Cry"

1965

The Parliaments, "Heart Trouble/That Was My Girl"

1967

The Parliaments, "(I Wanna) Testify/I Can Feel the Ice Melting"

The Parliaments, "All Your Goodies Are Gone/Don't Be Sore at Me"

The Parliaments, "Little Man/The Goose (That Laid the Golden Egg)"

1968

The Parliaments, "Look at What I Almost Missed/What You Been Growing"

The Parliaments, "A New Day Begins/I'll Wait"

The Parliaments, "Good Old Music/Time"

1969

Funkadelic, "Music for My Mother/Music for My Mother (Instrumental)"
Funkadelic, "I'll Bet You/Open Our Eyes"

1970

Funkadelic, *Funkadelic*
Mommy, What's a Funkadelic? / I'll Bet You / Music for My Mother /
I Got a Thing, You Got a Thing, Everybody's Got a Thing / Good Old Music /
Qualify and Satisfy / What Is Soul / Can't Shake It Loose

Funkadelic, *Free Your Mind . . . and Your Ass Will Follow*
Free Your Mind and Your Ass Will Follow / Friday Night, August 14th /
Funky Dollar Bill / I Wanna Know If It's Good to You /
Some More / Eulogy and Light

Funkadelic, "Fish, Chips and Sweat"

Parliament, *Osmium*
I Call My Baby Pussycat / Put Love in Your Life / Little Ole Country Boy /
Moonshine Heather / Oh Lord, Why Lord / Prayer / My Automobile /
Nothing Before Me but Thang / Funky Woman / Livin' the Life /
The Silent Boatman [Later editions, titled *Rhenium*, add singles like
"Come in Out of the Rain," "Fantasy Is Reality," and more.]

1971

Funkadelic, *Maggot Brain*
Maggot Brain / Can You Get to That / Hit It and Quit It / You and Your Folks,
Me and My Folks / Super Stupid / Back in Our Minds / Wars of Armageddon

1972

Funkadelic, *America Eats Its Young*
You Hit the Nail on the Head / If You Don't Like the Effects, Don't Produce
the Cause / Everybody Is Going to Make It This Time / A Joyful Process /
We Hurt Too / Loose Booty / Philmore / I Call My Baby Pussycat / America
Eats Its Young / Biological Speculation / That Was My Girl / Wake Up

1973

Funkadelic, *Cosmic Slop*
Nappy Dugout / You Can't Miss What You Can't Measure / March to the Witch's Castle / Let's Make It Last / Cosmic Slop / No Compute / This Broken Heart / Trash A-Go-Go / Can't Stand the Strain

1974

Funkadelic, *Standing on the Verge of Getting It On*
Red Hot Mama / Alice in My Fantasies / I'll Stay / Sexy Ways / Standing on the Verge of Getting It On / Jimmy's Got a Little Bit of Bitch in Him / Good Thoughts, Bad Thoughts

Parliament, *Up for the Down Stroke*
Up for the Down Stroke / Testify / The Goose / I Can Move You (If You Let Me) / I Just Got Back / All Your Goodies Are Gone / Whatever Makes Baby Feel Good / Presence of a Brain

1975

Funkadelic, *Let's Take It to the Stage*
Good to Your Earhole / Better by the Pound / Be My Beach / No Head, No Backstage Pass / Let's Take It to the Stage / Get Off Your Ass and Jam / Baby I Owe You Something Good / Stuffs & Things / The Song Is Familiar / Atmosphere

Parliament, *Chocolate City*
Chocolate City / Ride On / Together / Side Effects / What Comes Funky / Let Me Be / If It Don't Fit (Don't Force It) / I Misjudged You / Big Footin'

Parliament, *Mothership Connection*
P-Funk (Wants to Get Funked Up) / Mothership Connection (Star Child) / Unfunky UFO / Supergroovalisticprosifunkstication / Handcuffs / Give Up the Funk (Tear the Roof off the Sucker) / Night of the Thumpasaurus Peoples

1976

Funkadelic, *Tales of Kidd Funkadelic*
Butt-to-Butt Resuscitation / Let's Take It to the People / Undisco Kidd /
Take Your Dead Ass Home! (Say Som'n Nasty) / I'm Never Gonna Tell It /
Tales of Kidd Funkadelic (Opusdelite Years) / How Do Yeaw View You?

Funkadelic, *Hardcore Jollies*
Comin' Round the Mountain / Smokey / If You Got Funk, You
Got Style / Hardcore Jollies / Soul Mate / Cosmic Slop [live] /
You Scared the Lovin' Outta Me / Adolescent Funk

Parliament, *Clones of Dr. Funkenstein*
Prelude / Gamin' on Ya! / Dr. Funkenstein / Children of Production /
Gettin' to Know You / Do That Stuff / Everything Is on the One /
I've Been Watching You (Move Your Sexy Body) / Funkin' for Fun

Bootsy's Rubber Band, *Stretchin' Out in Bootsy's Rubber Band*
Stretchin' Out (in a Rubber Band) / Psychoticbumpschool /
Another Point of View / I'd Rather Be with You / Love
Vibes / Physical Love / Vanish in Our Sleep

1977

Parliament, *Live: P-Funk Earth Tour*
P Funk (Wants to Get Funked Up) / Supergroovalisticprosifunkstication
Medley / Do That Stuff / The Landing (of the Holy Mothership) /
Undisco Kidd (The Girl Is Bad!) / Children of Production / Mothership
Connection (Star Child) / Swing Down, Sweet Chariot / This Is the
Way We Funk with You / Dr. Funkenstein / Gamin' on Ya! / Tear the
Roof off the Sucker Medley / Night of the Thumpasaurus Peoples

Parliament, *Funkentelechy vs. the Placebo Syndrome*
Bop Gun (Endangered Species) / Sir Nose D'Voidoffunk
(Pay Attention—B3M) / Wizard of Finance /
Funkentelechy / Placebo Syndrome / Flash Light

Bootsy's Rubber Band, *Ahh . . . The Name Is Bootsy, Baby!*
Ahh . . . The Name Is Bootsy, Baby! / The Pinocchio Theory / Rubber
Duckie / Preview Side Too / What's a Telephone Bill? / Munchies
for Your Love / Can't Stay Away / Reprise: We Want Bootsy

Eddie Hazel, *Game, Dames and Guitar Thangs*
California Dreamin' / Frantic Moment / So Goes the Story / I Want You (She's
So Heavy) / Physical Love / What about It? / California Dreamin' (Reprise)

Horny Horns, *A Blow for Me, A Toot to You*
Up for the Down Stroke / A Blow for Me, a Toot to You / When in
Doubt: Vamp / Between Two Sheets / Four Play / Peace Fugue

1978

Funkadelic, *One Nation Under a Groove*
One Nation Under a Groove / Groovallegiance / Who Says a Funk Band
Can't Play Rock?! / Promentalshitbackwashpsychosis Enema Squad (The
Doo-Doo Chasers) / Into You / Cholly (Funk Get Ready to Roll!) /
Lunchmeataphobia (Think, It Ain't Illegal Yet!) / P.E. Squad / Doo-Doo
Chasers ["Going All-the-Way-Off" Instrumental Version] / Maggot Brain [Live]

Parliament, *Motor Booty Affair*
Mr. Wiggles / Rumpofsteelskin / (You're a Fish and I'm a) Water Sign /
Aqua Boogie (A Psychoalphadiscobetabioaquadoloop) / One of Those
Funky Thangs / Liquid Sunshine / The Motor-Booty Affair / Deep

Bootsy's Rubber Band, *Bootsy? Player of the Year*
Bootsy? (What's the Name of This Town) / May the Force Be with You / Very
Yes / Bootzilla / Hollywood Squares / Roto-Rooter / As In (I Love You)

Brides of Funkenstein, *Funk or Walk*
Disco to Go / War Ship Touchante / Nappy / Birdie /
Just Like You / When You're Gone / Amorous

Parlet, *Pleasure Principle*
Pleasure Principle / Love Amnesia / Cookie Jar /
Misunderstanding / Are You Dreaming? / Mr. Melody Man

Bernie Worrell, *All the Woo in the World*
Woo Together / I'll Be with You / Hold On / Much Thrust / Happy
to Have / Insurance Man for the Funk / Reprise: Much Thrust

1979

Funkadelic, *Uncle Jam Wants You*
Freak of the Week / (Not Just) Knee Deep / Uncle Jam / Holly Wants to
Go to California / Field Maneuvers / Foot Soldiers (Star Spangled Funky)

Parliament, *Gloryhallastoopid (Or Pin the Tale on the Funky)*
Prologue / (Gloryhallastoopid) Pin the Tail on the Funky / Party
People / The Big Bang Theory / The Freeze (Sizzaleenmean) / Colour
Me Funky / Theme from the Black Hole / May We Bang You?

Bootsy's Rubber Band, *This Boot Is Made for Fonk-N*
Under the Influence of a Groove / Bootsy (Get Live) / Oh Boy Gorl /
Jam Fan (Hot) / Chug-a-Lug (The Bun Patrol) / Shejam
(Almost Bootsy Show) / Reprise (Get Live)

Brides of Funkenstein, *Never Buy Texas from a Cowboy*
Never Buy Texas from a Cowboy / I'm Holding You Responsible / Smoke
Signals / Mother May I? / Party Up in Here / Didn't Mean to Fall in Love

Horny Horns, *Say Blow by Blow Backwards*
We Came to Funk Ya / Half a Man / Say Blow by Blow Backwards /
Mr. Melody Man / Just Like You / Circular Motion

Parlet, *Invasion of the Booty Snatchers*
Ridin' High / No Rump to Bump / Don't Ever Stop /
Booty Snatchers / You're Leaving / Huff-N-Puff

1980

Parliament, *Trombipulation*
Crush It / Trombipulation / Long Way Around / Agony of Defeet / New
Doo Review / Let's Play House / Body Language / Peek-a-Groove

Bootsy Collins, *Ultra Wave*
Mug Push / F-Encounter / Is That My Song? / It's a Musical /
Fat Cat / Sacred Flower / Sound Crack

Parlet, *Play Me or Trade Me*
Help from My Friends / Watch Me Do My Thang / Wolf Tickets / Play Me or
Trade Me / I'm Mo Be Hittin' It / Funk Until the Edge of Time / Wonderful One

Sweat Band, *Sweat Band*
Hyper Space / Freak to Freak / Love Munch / We Do It All Day
Long / Jamaica / Body Shop / We Do It All Day Long (reprise)

Philippé Wynne, *Wynne Jammin'*
Never Gonna Tell It / Put Your Own Puzzle Together /
You Make Me Happy (You Got the Love I Need) / We Dance So Good
Together / Hotel Eternity / Breakout / You Gotta Take Chances

1981

Funkadelic, *Electric Spanking of War Babies*
The Electric Spanking of War Babies / Electro-Cuties / Funk Gets Stronger
(Part 1) / Brettino's Bounce / Funk Gets Stronger (Killer Millimeter
Longer Version) / She Loves You / Shockwaves / Oh, I / Icka Prick

Xavier, "Work That Sucker to Death"

1982

George Clinton, *Computer Games*
Get Dressed / Man's Best Friend / Loopzilla / Pot Sharing Tots / Computer
Games / Atomic Dog / Free Alterations / One Fun at a Time

"Shine-O-Myte (Rag Poppin')," on William "Bootsy" Collins, *The One Giveth,
The Count Taketh Away*

1983

George Clinton, *You Shouldn't-Nuf Bit Fish*
Nubian Nut / Quickie / Silly Millameter / Last Dance /
Stingy / You Shouldn't-Nuf Bit Fish

P-Funk All Stars, *Urban Dancefloor Guerillas*
Generator Pop / Acupuncture / One of Those Summers / Catch a Keeper /
Pumpin' It Up / Copy Cat / Hydraulic Pump / Pumpin' It Up

1985

George Clinton, *Some of My Best Jokes Are Friends*
Double Oh-Oh / Bullet Proof / Pleasures of Exhaustion (Do It Till I Drop) /
Bodyguard / Bangladesh / Thrashin' / Some of My Best Jokes Are Friends

Red Hot Chili Peppers, *Freaky Styley*
Jungle Man / Hollywood / American Ghost Dance / If You Want
Me to Stay / Nevermind / Freaky Styley / Blackeyed Blond / The
Brothers Cup / Battle Ship / Lovin' and Touchin' / Catholic School
Girls Rule / Sex Rap / Thirty Dirty Birds / Yertle the Turtle

Jimmy G. and the Tackheads, *Federation of Tackheads*
Break My Heart / Clockwork / All or Nothin' / Lies /
Slingshot / I Want Yo Daughter

"May the Cube Be with You," on Thomas Dolby, *Aliens Ate My Buick*

1986

George Clinton, *R&B Skeletons in the Closet*
Hey Good Lookin' / Do Fries Go with That Shake? / Mix-Master Suite:
a) Startin' from Scratch, b) Counter-Irritant, c) Nothin' Left to Burn /
Electric Pygmies / Intense / Cool Joe / R&B Skeletons (in the Closet)

1988

INCorporated Thang Band, *Lifestyles of the Roach and Famous*
Body Jackin' / Storyteller / Still Tight / Androgynous View / Jack of All
Trades / I'd Do Anything for You / What if the Girl Says Yes? / 44–22–38

1989

George Clinton, *The Cinderella Theory*
Kredit Kard / Rita Bewitched / Airbound / Tweakin' / The Cinderella Theory /
Why Should I Dog You Out? / Serious Slammin' / There I Go Again / (She
Got It) Goin' On / The Banana Boat Song / French Kiss / Airbound (reprise)

Various Artists, *George Clinton Presents Our Gang Funky*
Beautiful / Nice / Manopener / Hooray / He Dance Funny / I Want Your Car

Otis Day and the Knights, *Shout!*
Something Dumb / I Knock the Bottom Outta Mine / Ice Melting /
You and Your Folks / Shout / Function at the Junction / (I Wanna)
Testify / Who's Making Love? / Shama Lama Ding Dong

1990

"We Can Funk," on Prince, *Graffiti Bridge*

1991

"Sons of the P," on Digital Underground, *Sons of the P*

1992

Trey Lewd, *Drop the Line*
I'll Be Good to You / Hoodlums Who Ride / Duck and Cover /
Yank My Doodle / Rooster / Nothing Comes to a Sleeper but a
Dream / Wipe of the Week / Drop the Line / Man of All Seasons /
The Next Thing You Know (We'll Be) / Squeeze Toy

1993

George Clinton, *Hey Man . . . Smell My Finger*
Martial Law / Paint the White House Black / Way Up / Dis Beat Disrupts / Get
Satisfied / Hollywood / Rhythm and Rhyme / The Big Pump / If True Love /
High in My Hello / Maximumisness / Kickback / The Flag Was Still There

"Fox Hunt," "Love Deeper," and "Pizzazz," on Andre Foxxe, *I'm Funk and I'm*
  Proud

"Flex," "Time Was (Events in the Elsewhere)," and "Dissinfordollars" on Bernie
  Worrell, *Blacktronic Science*

"Bop Gun" on Ice Cube, *Lethal Injection*

1994

"Stomp" and "Erotic City" on *PCU: Original Motion Picture Soundtrack*

"Give Out but Don't Give Up," "Funky Jam," and "Free" on Primal Scream, *Give*
  Out but Don't Give Up

1995

Parliament-Funkadelic/P-Funk All Stars, *Dope Dogs*
Dog Star (Fly On) / U.S. Custom Coast Guard Dope Dog / Some Next
Shit / Just Say Ding (Databoy) / Help Scottie, Help (I'm Tweaking
and I Can't Beam Up) / Pepe / Back Up Against the Wall / FiFi / All
Sons of Bitches / Sick 'Em / I Ain't the Lady (He Ain't the Tramp) /
Pack of Wild Dogs / Tales That Wag the Dog / My Dog

1996

George Clinton and the P-Funk All Stars, *T.A.P.O.A.F.O.M.*
If Anybody Gets Funked Up (It's Gonna Be You) / Summer Swim / Funky
Kind / Mathematics / Hard as Steel / New Spaceship / Underground
Angel / Let's Get Funky / Flatman & Bobbin / Sloppy Seconds / Rock
the Party / Get Your Funk Up / T.A.P.O.A.F.O.M. (Fly Away)

2005

George Clinton and the P-Funk All Stars, *How Late Do U Have 2BB4UR Absent?*

Bounce 2 This / Su, Su, Su / Paradigm / U Can Depend on Me / U Ain't Runnin' Shit / Inhale Slow / Because / Last Time Zone / Neverending Love / Sexy Side of You / Saddest Day / I Can Dance / I'll Be Sittin' Here / Don't Dance Too Close / More Than Words Can Say (Live) / Butt-a-Butt / Something Stank / Our Secret / Viagra / Gypsy Woman / Whole Lotta Shakin' / Goodnight Sweetheart, Goodnight / Whatchamacallit / Trust in Yourself / Booty

2008

George Clinton, *George Clinton and His Gangsters of Love*

Ain't That Peculiar / Never Gonna Give You Up / Mathematics of Love / Let the Good Times Roll / Pledging My Love / Gypsy Woman / It's All in the Game / Heart Trouble / Our Day Will Come / Sway / You're a Thousand Miles Away / As in / Stillness in Motion / Fever

2014

Funkadelic, *Shake the Gate*

Baby Like Fonkin' It Up / Get Low / If I Didn't Love You / Fucked Up / Brothas Be, Yo Like George, Ain't That Funkin' Kinda Hard on You? / I Mo B Yodog Fo Eva / In Da Kar / Radio Friendly / Mathematics of Love / Creases / Not Your Average Rapper / Shake the Gate / Roller Rink / Jolene / Nuclear Sports / Open Your Eyes / You Can't Unring the Bell / Old Fool / Pole Power / Boom There We Go Again / As In / Burnadette / Meow Meow / Catchin' Boogie Fever / The Naz / Talking to the Wall / Where Would I Go? / Homicide / Zip It / The Wall / Snot n' Booger / Yellow Light / Dipety Dipety Doo Stop the Violence

Mr. Clinton would like to remind readers that these albums would not have been possible without the contributions of the following musicians, producers, singers, and artists, and to apologize if he has accidentally omitted anyone: Jimmy Ali, Jerome Ali, Sa'D "The Houchild" Ali, Mickey Atkins, Darrell Banks, Ron Banks, J. J. Barnes, Sidney Barnes, Harold Beane, Danny Bedrosian, Pedro Bell, Big Chris, Taka Boom, Steve Boyd, Greg Boyer, Rev. Uriah Boyington, Jerome Brailey, Michael Brecker, Randy Brecker, Diane Brooks, Jeff "Cherokee" Bunn, Kim Burrell, Ron Bykowski, Gordon Carlton, Jimmy Calhoun, Dennis Chambers, Jessica Cleaves, Darryl Clinton, George Clinton III, Lashonda "Sativa" Clinton, LuShawn Clinton, Tracy "Tra'zea" Clinton, Phelps "Catfish" Collins, William "Bootsy" Collins, Gary "Mudbone" Cooper, Ruth Copeland, Benjamin Cowan, Monte Cristo, Star Cullars, Lige Curry, Rodney "Skeet" Curtis, Charles Davis, Raymond Davis, Hunter Daws, El Debarge, Del tha Funkee Homosapien, Darryl Dixon, Doug Duffy, Ron Dunbar, Dewayne Dungey, Barrence Dupree, Ronald "Stozo" Edwards, Joe Farrell, Joseph "Amp" Fiddler, Eli Fontaine, Ron Ford, Kendra Foster, Mallia Franklin, Larry Fratangelo, Zachary Frazier, John Frusciante, Ramon "Tiki" Fulwood, Rick Gardner, Gentry, Jimmy Giles, Glen Goins, Gabe Gonzalez, Larry Grams, Lonnie Greene, Richard "Kush" Griffith, Kathy Griffin, Mary Griffin, Clayton "Chicken" Gunnels, Michael Hampton, Roy Handy, Ernie Harris, Joe "Pep" Harris, Clarence "Fuzzy" Haskins, Lily Haydn, Eddie Hazel, Paul Hill, Sheila Horne, Ebony Bonn'e Houston, Gary Hudgins, Brad Innis, James Wesley Jackson, Kennedy "Kenny Keys" Jacobs, Cheryl James, Prakash John, Joel "Razor Sharp" Johnson, Robert "P-Nut" Johnson, Brad "Scarface" Jordan, Rey Joven, Louis Kabbabie, Rodney Krutcher, Tony Lafoot, Robert Lambert, Tyrone Lampkin, Patavian Lewis, Tracey "Trey Lewd" Lewis, Vivian Lewis, Theresa Lindsey, Overton Loyd, Lynn Mabry, Rob "G Koop" Mandell, Howard Mann, Kim Manning, Joseph "Foley" McCreary, Janette MacGruden, DeWayne "Blackbyrd" McKnight, Walter "Junie" Morrison, Cordell "Boogie" Mosson, Nestor Mumm-Altuve, Johnny

Murray, Bruce Nazarian, Billy "Billy Bass" Nelson, Tonysha Nelson, Shavo Odadjian, Michael "Clip" Payne, William Tyler Pelt, Red Hot Chili Peppers, Bouvier "Payso Paid" Richardson, Jerome Rogers, Dayonne Rollins, Lucius Tunia "Tawl" Ross, Ricardo "Ricky" Rouse, RZA, Carlos Santana, Manon Saulsby, Brandi Scott, Garrett Shider, Garry Shider, Linda Shider, Calvin Simon, Dawn Silva, Carl "Butch" Small, David Spradley, Donnie Sterling, Babs Stewart, Sly Stone, Ricky Tan, Mike Terry, Grady Thomas, Greg Thomas, Tony Thomas, William Thoren, Thurteen, Ivan Toni, Jim Vitti, Frankie "Kash" Waddy, Jeanette Washington, Steve Washington, Fred Wesley, Andre Foxxe Williams, Rose Williams, Clyde Wilson, Ernesto Wilson, Belita Woods, Bernie Worrell, Debbie Wright, Ron Wright, Philippé Wynne.

APPENDIX B: SELECTED SAMPLEOGRAPHY

P-Funk's music has been sampled in thousands of songs in the hip-hop and modern pop era. Here are a few examples.

Above the Law, "Black Triangle" samples "Eulogy and Light"

Ant Banks, "Pimp Style Gangastas" samples "No Rump to Bump"

Beastie Boys, "Car Thief" samples "I Bet You"

Beastie Boys, "Hey Ladies" samples "Pumpin' It Up"

Bell Biv DeVoe, "Ghetto Booty" samples "I Got a Thing, You Got a Thing"

Big Daddy Kane, "Get Down" samples "Atomic Dog"

Black Sheep, "Butt in the Meantime" samples "Four Play"

Bone Thugs-N-Harmony, "Mo Murda" samples "I'd Rather Be with You"

Common, "Cold Blooded" samples "Funkin' for Fun"

The Coup, "Busterismology" samples "Mommy, What's a Funkadelic?"

The Coup, "Me and Jesus the Pimp in a '79 Grenada Last Night" samples "Swing Down, Sweet Chariot"

Cypress Hill, "Psychobetabuckdown" samples "Aqua Boogie (A Psychoalphadiscobetabioaquadoloop)"

Da Lench Mob, "Guerillas in tha Mist" samples "Flash Light"

Da Lench Mob, "Mellow Madness" samples "Hollywood Squares"

De La Soul, "Millie Pulled a Pistol on Santa" samples "Mommy, What's a Funkadelic?" and "I'll Stay"

De La Soul, "Me Myself and I" samples "(Not Just) Knee Deep"

De La Soul, "Potholes in My Lawn" samples "Little Ole Country Boy"

Del tha Funkee Homosapien, "Dr. Bombay" samples "Rumpofsteelskin"

Del tha Funkee Homosapien, "Mistadobalina" samples "(Gloryhallastoopid) Pin the Tale on the Funky"

Dell tha Funkee Homosapien, "What Is a Booty" samples "Pumpin' It Up"

Digable Planets, "Black Ego" samples "Generator Pop"

Digable Planets, "Escapism (Gettin' Free)" samples "Mothership Connection (Star Child)"

Digital Underground, "Doowutchyalike" samples "Flash Light"

Digital Underground, "Heartbeat Props" samples "Freak of the Week"

Digital Underground, "Hip Hop Doll" samples "Funkin' for Fun" and "Funkentelechy"

Digital Underground, "Humpty Dance" samples "Let's Play House"

Digital Underground, "Kiss You Back" samples "(Not Just) Knee Deep"

Digital Underground, "Rhymin' on the Funk" samples "Bootzilla" and "Flash Light"

Digital Underground, "Same Song" samples "Theme from the Black Hole"

Digital Underground, "Sex Packets" samples "The Motor-Booty Affair"

Digital Underground, "Underwater Rhymes" samples "Aqua Boogie (A Psychoalphadiscobetabioaquadoloop)"

DJ Jazzy Jeff and the Fresh Prince, "A Dog Is a Dog" samples "Man's Best Friend"

The D.O.C., "Beautiful but Deadly" samples "Cosmic Slop"

Dr. Dre, "Bitches Ain't Shit" samples "Adolescent Funk"

Dr. Dre, "The Chronic" samples "Colour Me Funky"

Dr. Dre, "Dre Day" samples "Aqua Boogie (A Psychoalphadiscobetabioaquadoloop)," "The Big Bang Theory," and "(Not Just) Knee Deep"

Dr. Dre, "Let Me Ride" samples "Mothership Connection"

Dr. Dre, "The Roach" samples "P-Funk (Wants to Get Funked Up)"

Easy-E, "Eazy-Duz-It" samples "Bootzilla" and "A Joyful Process"

EPMD, "I'm Mad" samples "Let's Take It to the Stage"

EPMD, "Play the Next Man" samples "Sir Nose D'Voidoffunk"

EPMD, "Whose Booty" samples "Loose Booty"

EPMD, "You Gots to Chill" samples "More Bounce to the Ounce"

Eric B. & Rakim, "Lyrics of Fury" samples "No Head, No Backstage Pass"

Erick Sermon, "Hittin' Switches" samples "Last Dance"

Everlast, "Never Missin' a Beat" samples "(Not Just) Knee Deep"

Fat Joe, "Say Word" samples "Munchies for Your Love"

Fu-Schnickens, "Back Off" samples "Atomic Dog"

Gang Starr, "Step in the Arena" samples "A Blow for Me, a Toot for You"

Gerardo, "We Want the Funk" samples "Give Up the Funk (Tear the Roof off the Sucker)"

Geto Boys, "Homie Don't Play That" samples "Pumpin' It Up"

Ice Cube, "Dirty Mack" samples "Unfunky UFO"

Ice Cube, "Ghetto Bird" samples "Aqua Boogie (A Psychoalphadiscobetabioaquadoloop)"

Ice Cube, "I Wanna Kill Sam" samples "Chocolate City" and "One of Those Funky Things"

Ice Cube, "Man's Best Friend" samples "Atomic Dog"

Ice Cube, "Say Hi to the Bad Guy" samples "P-Funk (Wants to Get Funked Up)"

Ice Cube, "The Wrong Nigga to Fuck Wit" samples "Flash Light"

Ice Cube, "Who Got the Camera?" samples "I Got a Thing, You Got a Thing"

Ice-T, "Mind over Matter" samples "I Bet You"

Jungle Brothers, "Tribe Vibe" samples "Big Footin'"

Jungle Brothers, "What U Waiting 4?" samples "Give Up the Funk (Tear the Roof off the Sucker)"

Kriss Kross, "Freak da Funk" samples "Free Your Mind"

LL Cool J, "Nitro" samples "(Not Just) Knee Deep"

Madvillain, "Raid" samples "Computer Games"

MC Hammer, "Pumps and a Bump" samples "Atomic Dog"

MC Hammer, "Turn This Mutha Out" samples "Give Up the Funk (Tear the Roof off the Sucker)"

Mystikal, "Unpredictable" samples "Sir Nose D'Voidoffunk"

Nas, "One Love" samples "Come in Out of the Rain"

N.W.A, "100 Miles and Runnin'" samples "Get Off Your Ass and Jam"

Outkast, "Elevators" samples "Come in Out of the Rain"

Outkast, "Pink & Blue" samples "The Goose"

Paris, "Bush Killa" samples "Atomic Dog"

Pete Rock and C. L. Smooth, "If It Ain't Rough, It Ain't Right" samples "Come in Out of the Rain"

Pete Rock and C. L. Smooth, "The Basement" samples "Atomic Dog"

PM Dawn, "Comatose" samples "Atomic Dog"

Public Enemy, "Bring the Noise" samples "Get Off Your Ass and Jam"

Public Enemy, "Nighttrain" samples "Flash Light"

Public Enemy, "911 Is a Joke" samples "Flash Light"

Public Enemy, "Party for Your Right to Fight" samples "Butt-to-Butt Resuscitation" and "Do That Stuff"

Public Enemy, "Revolutionary Generation" samples "Deep"

Redman, "Blow Your Mind" samples "The Big Bang Theory" and "Theme from the Black Hole"

Redman, "So Ruff" samples "Bop Gun"

Ruff Ryders, "Ryde or Die Boyz" samples "I'm Holding You Responsible"

Run-D.M.C., "Bob Your Head" samples "Good Old Music"

Salt-N-Pepa, "He's Gamin' on Ya" samples "Chocolate City"

Scarface, "Good Girl Gone Bad" samples "Good Old Music"

Schoolly D, "Godfather of Funk" samples "Give Up the Funk (Tear the Roof off the Sucker)"

Sir Mix-A-Lot, "Sleepin' Wit My Fonk" samples "The Pinocchio Theory"

Snoop Doggy Dogg, "The Shiznit" samples "Flash Light"

Snoop Doggy Dogg, "Who Am I (What's My Name)?" samples "(Not Just) Knee Deep" and "Give Up the Funk (Tear the Roof off the Sucker)"

Stetsasonic, "Speaking of a Girl Named Suzy" samples "Atomic Dog"

Tone-Lōc, "Funky Cold Medina" samples "Get Off Your Ass and Jam"

Too $hort, "Hoes" samples "Take Your Dead Ass Home!"

Too $hort, "Gettin' It" samples "I'd Rather Be with You"

Too $hort, "It's Your Life" samples "Dr. Funkenstein"

A Tribe Called Quest, "Ham 'N' Eggs" samples "Nappy Dugout"

Tupac, "Holler if You Hear Me" samples "Atomic Dog"

Tupac, "Young Black Male" samples "Good Old Music"

UGK, "Diamonds and Wood" samples "Munchies for Your Love"

Warren G, "Regulate" samples "Mothership Connection (Star Child)"

X-Clan, "Earth Bound" samples "Free Your Mind" and "One Nation Under a Groove"

Yo-Yo, "Make Way for the Motherlode" samples "Mothership Connection (Star Child)"

APPENDIX C: STATEMENT OF JANE PETERER THOMPSON

I, Jeanne "Jane" Peterer Thompson, formerly d/b/s Jane Peterer Music Corporation (collectively, JPMC) do hereby declare, state, and affirm as follows.

1. I have personal knowledge of the matters discussed herein and am able to testify as to the matters set forth herein, as called as a witness.

2. I formerly maintained a working relationship with Mr. Armen Boladian ("Mr. Boladian") and Bridgeport Music, Inc. et al of Southfield, Michigan, and at times other companies under Mr. Boladian's control, ownership and/ or affiliation including Southfield Music, Inc., Bloomfield Music Inc., and Rosuki Music (collectively referred to as "Bridgeport Music") for approximately 24 years beginning in 1984 and ending in January 2008.

3. During that period of time I worked as an administrator where my primary task was to administer the copyrights of Bridgeport Music.

4. Those duties included, among others:

(i) Filing documents before the U.S. Copyright Office at the request, instructions, and direction of Bridgeport Music and Mr. Boladian.

(ii) Performing administrative duties; and

(iii) Compiling, tracking, and recording royalty account data which included mechanical royalties, synchronization fees, and other income (collectively, "the Royalties") by song titles on a software program maintained by me for songwriters that Bridgeport music led me to believe were under its contractual control or authority.

I would prepare royalty reports on a semiannual or "semester" basis utilizing a proprietary software product created for this purpose which was purchased and maintained by JPMC and commonly known in the music industry as "Music Maestro."

5. Specifically, in August 1990, under the direction of Mr. Boladian, I personally filed an assignment agreement with the U.S. Copyright Office in Washington, DC, which transferred and assigned ownership of certain musical works from Malbiz Music, a publishing company owned by George Clinton (Mr. Clinton) to Bridgeport Music. The assignment which Mr. Boladian directed me to file with the U.S. Copyright Office in August 1990 was actually dated March 4, 1982 and contained an addendum document.

6. This August 1990 filing was rejected by the U.S. Copyright Office and returned to me on the basis that the submitted agreement was not original, nor was it notarized. I then forwarded this document, together with the U.S. Copyright Office's basis for rejecting the filing to Mr. Boladian.

7. In 1990, Mr. Boladian obtained a notary stamp on the March 4, 1982 dated agreement and then refiled the document with the U.S. Copyright Office himself and thereby placed 164 separate copyright registrations for musical works related to Mr. Clinton and his groups, Parliament and Funkadelic, Brides of Funkenstein, as well as Philippé Wynne, Glen Goins, and Eddie Hazel into the name of Bridgeport Music.

8. I only later learned that Mr. Boladian fraudulently and materially altered this March 4, 1982 document and then recorded it with the U.S. Copyright Office to create a claim of ownership in these 164 separate copyright registrations in the name of Bridgeport Music.

9. On April 30, 1992, again under the direction of Mr. Boladian, I personally filed and registered a copyright registration in the name of Westbound Records with the U.S. Copyright Office as a work for hire known as the Funkadelic Sound Recordings SR 142111 titled: "Funkadelic: Let's Take It To The Stage" asserting a June 15, 1975 date of first publication, unaware of the fact that no actual work for hire agreement existed for this sound recording.

10. On February 8, 2002, again under the direction of Mr. Boladian, I personally filed and registered:

(i) a copyright registration in the name of Westbound Records with the Copyright Office as a work for hire known as the Funkadelic Sound Recording SR 318917 titled: "Cosmic Slop" asserting a June 17, 1973 date of first publication; and

(ii) a copyright registration in the name of Westbound Records with the Copyright Office as a work for hire known as the Funkadelic Sound Recording SR 318918 titled: "Standing on the Verge of Getting It On" asserting a September 15, 1974 date of first publication, unaware of the fact that no actual work for hire agreement existed for either of these sound recordings.

11. In addition, under the direction of Bridgeport Music and its various legal counsel over the years, including at least Attorney Richard Busch, Attorney Edward Wallace, Attorney Barry Richard, and Attorney Joseph Della Maria, I participated in numerous legal proceedings involving Bridgeport Music as both a plaintiff or defendant in legal actions to:

(i) obtain money damages and a percentage of copyright ownership from third parties relating to the alleged unauthorized use of the Bridgeport Music copyrights

(ii) defend various claims that songwriters may have brought against Bridgeport Music seeking to get their Royalties paid, and/or return the copyrights to the original authors or their estates; and/or

(iii) to receive proper accounting and payment

12. JPMC's participation in these legal proceedings would include research and pinpointing unauthorized sample uses, contacting third parties, including publishing companies, record companies, and artists to address the claims without litigation, and supporting the legal counsel of Bridgeport Music in the event of litigation, including declarations, depositions, and testimony for Bridgeport Music.

13. Specifically, in 1996–1997, there was a special master proceeding before the U.S. District Court for the Central District of California in Los Angeles, California for the purpose of providing an accounting to the songwriters of the Malbiz/Bridgeport catalog. The Special Master, Theodore Friedman, hired me to issue the statements and amounts relating to the copyrighted musical works in the Malbiz catalog for the various named songwriters for the Malbiz musical works.

14. As part of my involvement in the Special Master proceeding before the U.S. District Court for the Central District of California, Mr. Boladian and Bridgeport Music took the position that they did not owe funds to the applicable Malbiz songwriters because of certain unspecified financial costs or expenses that were allegedly incurred by Bridgeport Music. In the case of George Clinton, Mr. Boladian asserted that he was, in fact, owed money

from Mr. Clinton based upon Mr. Boladian's payments to maintain a certain parcel of real property owned by Mr. Clinton located in Brooklyn, Michigan. However, I am not personally aware that any such payments were actually made by Mr. Boladian for the benefit of Mr. Clinton or any of the other Malbiz songwriters. I do have specific knowledge that the Malbiz songwriters were not paid any royalties. This specific conduct was done to the detriment of all the Malbiz songwriters, including Mr. Clinton, in the Special Master proceeding in Los Angeles, California.

15. In January 2001, there was a trial involving Mr. Boladian, Bridgeport Music and Mr. Clinton before the U.S. District Court for the Northern District of Florida over the Malbiz catalog of musical works. Mr. Boladian and his attorneys at the time, Attorney Barry Richard, Attorney Joseph Della Marie, and Attorney Richard Busch intentionally concealed and withheld the fact that Mr. Boladian had materially altered the March 4, 1982 assignment agreement.

16. As part of these cases, including a 2001 action filed by Bridgeport Music in Nashville, Tennessee against hundreds of defendants, I was also deposed in numerous occasions in cases where Bridgeport Music sued various record companies and musical artists for copyright infringement and alleged unauthorized music "sampling." Many of these cases included claims by Bridgeport Music that it was the copyright owner of various musical works of many artists, including Mr. Clinton and others, which were alleged to have been sampled and interpolated by artists in new musical works without authorization. I have now learned that Bridgeport Music was not, in fact, the legal owner of these works, knew that it was not the legal owner, but pursued these claims anyway.

17. More recently, in 2002, as part of a Michigan state court action, Mr. Clinton's auditor, Arthur Erl, was granted access to the Bridgeport Music files and records that were in my possession. However, I did not actually possess the true income and financial amounts that were generated by the Bridgeport Music works, including the musical works in the Malbiz catalog since Mr. Boladian never provided or accounted to me monies and revenues owed to any writers for the releases on Westbound records, including any mechanical license amounts or payments flowing from these works disseminated by Bridgeport Music as well as the sound recording works and copyrights filed by me and discussed above.

18. Regrettably, based upon my dealings with Mr. Boladian from 1984 through 2008, this was his continued and collective modus operandi for most of the songwriters affiliated with the Bridgeport Music, which were also under contract with Mr. Boladian's affiliated record labels known as Westbound Records, Eastbound Records and Sound of Gospel.

19. Sadly, these unethical acts also extend to Bridgeport Music's lawyers as well. For example, during the course of the Bridgeport Music case involving Mr. Clinton and the Malbiz catalog of musical works before the U.S. District Court for the Northern District of Florida and also in cases in federal courts in New York and California, the Bridgeport Music counsel, Howard Hertz, testified on behalf of Bridgeport Music before these Courts. Nevertheless, months later and to the best of my knowledge, Attorney Hertz always submitted an invoice for his testimony on behalf of Bridgeport music and was later paid for the time and testimony even though he never informed the court personnel that he was, in fact, being paid for his testimony.

20. Likewise, I also have express knowledge that Mr. Boladian, as the owner of Westbound Records, Inc., never accounted for any mechanical royalties resulting from sold and paid sales of records, artist royalties, and/or other uses from at least my involvement with Bridgeport Music in 1984 through January 2008 which were all issued or paid to Mr. Boladian and/or where Mr. Boladian made direct license agreements with third parties, such as for internet downloads, ringtones, and digital downloads. These additional amounts, which include mechanical rights due to the songwriters and any artist royalties generated by sales from either Westbound Records and licensees, such as Ace Records and others, for artist royalties, as well as any internet or digital downloads. I requested Mr. Boladian to provide me with statements for the internet downloads so that they could be included in the Royalty Reports which were generated by JPMC, but he never complied with these requests.

21. In addition, based upon my personal interaction with Mr. Boladian, it was my strong impression that Mr. Boladian was racially motivated against African-Americans and looked upon this process as some type of "game" where he believed that African-Americans, such as Mr. Clinton, lacked the education and intelligence to understand issues such as copyright infringement and legal proceedings. I found such remarks to be

highly racially offensive, not only because my late husband at the time was African-American, but as a European national was also surprised that such racist views continued to exist in the United States.

22. In addition, from 1999 through the end of my involvement with Bridgeport Music in 2008, I also discovered that Mr. Boladian falsely demanded songwriter rights and credit for musical works before the U.S. Copyright Office that he did not actually author or created by adopting false names or pseudonyms for himself and listing those false names as songwriters on musical works actually written by others, all for the purpose of gaining a financial advantage for himself.

23. Mr. Boladian would essentially create different pseudonyms for himself so that he could derive the revenue for the musical works as an author and/ or songwriter even though he was neither an actual author or songwriter. Specific examples of such false names are B. Baine, Beida Baine, L. Crane and Louis Crane and is best exemplified in a musical work named SET IT OUT, which was actually written by a Bridgeport Music songwriter named Abrim Tilmon, Jr. However, when SET IT OUT was originally registered by Southfield Music, Inc. on September 30, 1974 it claimed and recited a total of three (3) authors as follows: A Tilmon, B. Baine, and L. Crane. Under this filing and ownership, each of the three (3) named authors receive a % right and interest in, and to, the musical work.

24. Under the belief that this was the correct authorship for the work, I prepared and filed a copyright renewal application for SET IT OUT, which was issued by the U.S. Copyright Office in Washington D.C. on February 18, 2004 where I properly recited the Tilmon Estate as the claimant since Mr. Tilmon was deceased as of July 6, 1982.

25. However, after I filed the renewal document for SET IT OUT on February 18, 2004, I personally asked Mr. Boladian who each of "B. Baine" and "L. Crane" were and where they could be located under the naïve belief that they were each actual human beings and songwriters for the work that should be receiving their applicable ⅓ right and interest in this musical work.

26. To my shock and surprise, Mr. Boladian informed me that he was both B. Baine and L. Crane and that those names, among others, were pseudonyms used by Mr. Boladian to falsely assert joint authorship/ownership over certain musical works and thereby receive ongoing royalties directly to

him under the pseudonyms. After some additional investigation, I discovered further musical works in the name of B. Baine, Beida Baine, L. Crane, and Louis Crane—all pseudonyms of Mr. Boladian.

27. I found this conduct to be beyond despicable since it dilutes the proper and true authorship/ownership of the underlying musical works, attempts to rewrite history by stating that a non-existent person wrote a song before the U.S. Copyright Office, and is a clear form of identity theft using the U.S. Copyright Office as the tool and instrument of fraud. I do not know if any income tax has ever been paid under these pseudonyms for any of the income derived from these false "songwriter" credits.

28. I declare under penalty of perjury under the laws of Switzerland and the United States of America that the foregoing is true and correct.

Executed on July 6, 2012. United States Consulate in Zurich, Switzerland

SWISS CONFEDERATION CANTON AND CITY OF ZURICH
CONSULAR AGENCY OF THE UNITED STATES OF AMERICA

PHOTO CREDITS

Frontispiece: Photo courtesy of Isaac Turner

Insert 1

1: Photo courtesy of George Clinton
2: Photo courtesy of Elizabeth Bishop
3: Photo courtesy of Isaac Turner
4: Photo courtesy of George Clinton
5: Photo courtesy of Elizabeth Bishop
6: Photo courtesy of Isaac Turner
7: Photo courtesy of Isaac Turner
8: Photo courtesy of George Clinton
9: Photo courtesy of George Clinton
10: Photo courtesy of George Clinton
11: Photo courtesy of George Clinton
12: Photo courtesy of George Clinton
13: Photo courtesy of Elizabeth Bishop

14: Photo courtesy of Isaac Turner
15: Photo courtesy of George Clinton
16: Photo courtesy of Elizabeth Bishop
17: Photo courtesy of Elizabeth Bishop
18: Photo courtesy of George Clinton
19: Photo courtesy of Isaac Turner
20: Photo courtesy of Elizabeth Bishop
21: Photo courtesy of George Clinton
22: Photo courtesy of Elizabeth Bishop
23: Photo courtesy of George Clinton
24: Photo courtesy of George Clinton
25: Photo courtesy of George Clinton

Insert 2

26: Photo courtesy of Isaac Turner
27: Photo courtesy of Isaac Turner
28: Photo courtesy of Tim Kinley
29: Photo courtesy of Isaac Turner
30: Photo courtesy of Isaac Turner
31: Photo courtesy of George Clinton
32: Photo courtesy of Isaac Turner
33: Photo courtesy of George Clinton
34: Photo courtesy of Elizabeth Bishop
35: Photo courtesy of George Clinton
36: Photo courtesy of Elizabeth Bishop
37: Photo courtesy of Elizabeth Bishop

38: Photo courtesy of Isaac Turner
39: Photo courtesy of Isaac Turner
40: Photo courtesy of Isaac Turner
41: Photo by Will Thoren
42: Photo by Will Thoren
43: Photo by Will Thoren
44: Photo by Will Thoren
45: Photo by Will Thoren
46: Photo by Will Thoren
47: Photo by Will Thoren
48: Photo courtesy of George Clinton
49: Photo by Carlon Thompson

INDEX